D1688152

A Flutter of Banknotes

Detail of 20 mark-note, Reichsbank, 1915, obverse, 140 x 90 mm (5.51 x 3.54 in.). DBB.

René Brion and Jean-Louis Moreau

A Flutter of Banknotes

From the First European Paper Money to the Euro

MERCATORFONDS

Preface

The honour I feel in being asked to introduce this book is matched only by the pleasure I experienced in reading it. Indeed, Mercatorfonds is offering the public a veritable work of art. What impresses me most is its enormous wealth of illustrations – and the quantity of facts with which it is packed, often entertaining, always indispensable. The two authors deserve every praise for producing a valuable and highly readable history.

For instance, did you know that in the second half of the nineteenth century, two Belgians suggested the idea of a universal banknote, soon abandoned in the face of scepticism by the authorities of the time? Or that some states were inundated with notes forged by hostile neighbours plotting to undermine their economies?

Throughout its history, the banknote has indisputably fulfilled the role of symbol: for the sum it represented, of course, but also for the economic and political states of the nations. 'Every design has a motive', as the authors succinctly put it. For example, it is hardly coincidental that a picture of a locomotive appears on a Belgian note during the Industrial Revolution. Or notes representing Victory and Peace after 1945. Or emergency issues during time of war.

The story of the banknote is, in itself, symbolic – of Europe. Since the earliest 'papers' issued by the Bank of Amsterdam in the 1600s, through the notes of the Bank of England or the Stockholms Banco and the troubled *assignats* of the French Revolution, banknotes have clearly had a European destiny. Their history is part of that of our continent, mimicking its twists and turns. On the eve of the introduction of coins and notes of the single currency to more than three hundred million Europeans, one question acquires real pertinence: is a single currency the prelude to a political union of the Old Continent?

Here is a challenge which we are all bound to take up.

Didier Reynders
Belgian Minister of Finance

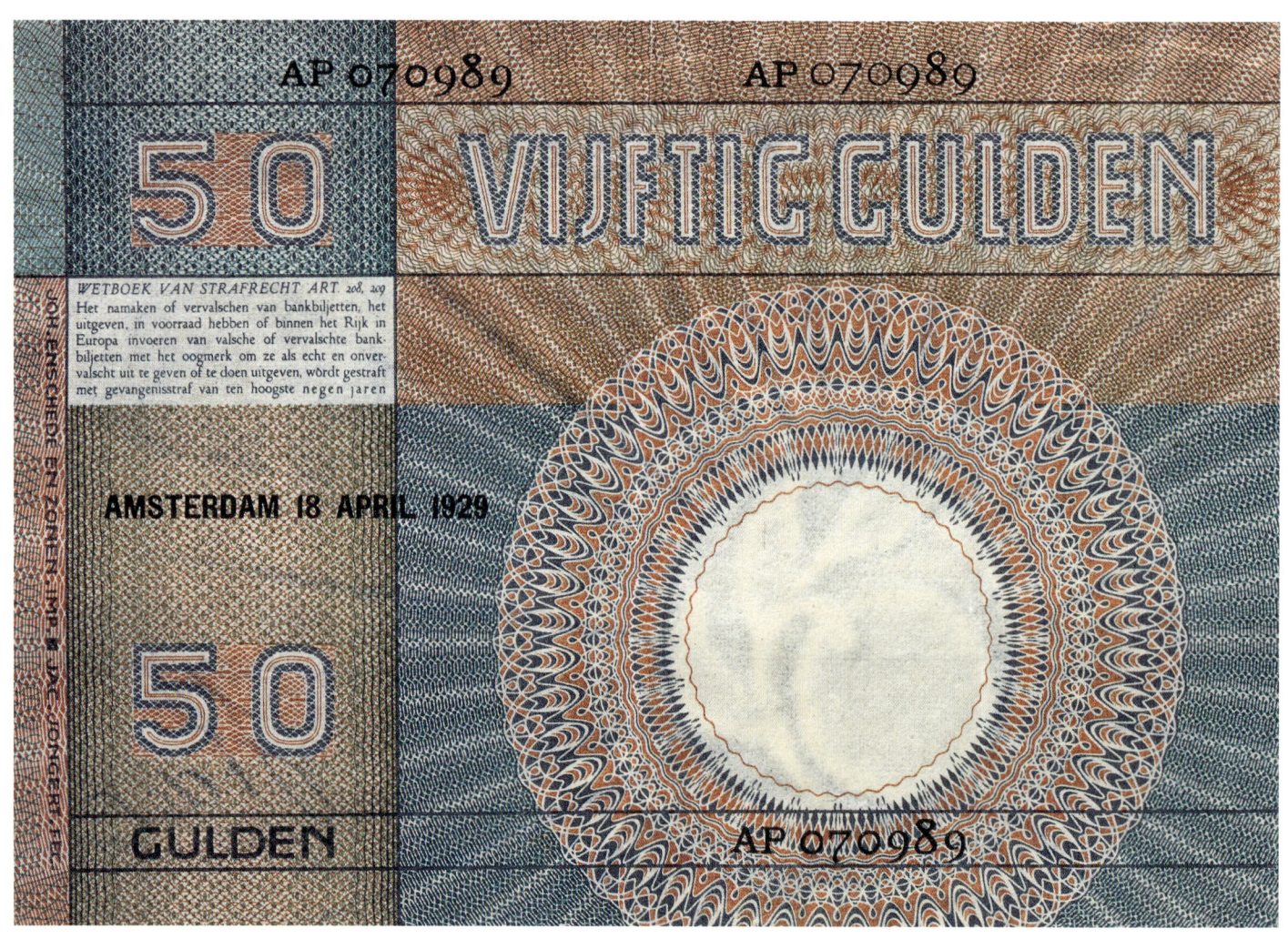

50-florin note, Nederlandsche Bank, 1930,
reverse, 135 x 95 mm (5.31 x 3.74 in.). DNB.

Foreword

The imminent introduction of a new European currency was on its own sufficient justification for the publication of a book of this type. But the present volume by René Brion and Jean-Louis Moreau derives especial interest from their view that banknotes represent far more than a convenient means of payment. During the course of the last two centuries, paper money has, along with the institutions issuing it, become one of the principal means by which citizens identify with the state in which they live. This phenomenon can be ascribed as much to the monetarisation of modern economies and the fact that the banknote has become part of our daily lives as to historical processes that have often linked the destinies of nations with those of their currencies. Both governments and central banks have recognised the implications and banknotes, through their iconography and symbolic content, have developed into vehicles of national identity.

In the course of their research, René Brion and Jean-Louis Moreau retrace the threads which, during the nineteenth century, gradually came to link issuing banks and the circulation of notes with statements of national identity. For an example, we have only to glance at the creation of the Reichsbank in 1875, symbolising the unification of Germany in the wake of the Franco-Prussian War. Within the historical framework of individual states, the centralisation of banknote issue in the hands of a single institution was one of the defining features of the age. The management of currencies was subjected still further to state control during the century just ended, due either to altering concepts of the role of money in the economy or to historical events: the Banque de France, for instance, nationalised in 1945, became, in fact as well as name, the 'bank of France', whilst successive deaths and resurrections of the mark were synonymous with the ongoing development of Germany.

The use of banknote designs to proclaim national identity and the permanence of states is based on very old iconographic traditions. Thus the armorials of German cities or states were succeeded from 1876 by the imperial eagle, while notes issued by Belgium, Spain, Greece and Italy displayed the arms of the kingdom. In 1900, the Austro-Hungarian bank introduced the two-headed Austrian eagle and the Hungarian crown. Others preferred an allegorical representation of the mother country, like the Bank of England, which has featured a likeness of Britannia since 1697. Several states followed suit, experimenting with depictions of Belgica, Hispania, Finlandia or Italia. Yet it was during the conflicts of the twentieth century that the destinies of nations and banknote designs were most closely associated; France introduced a helmeted Marianne and the Chevalier Bayard, Portugal turned to Alfonso de Albuquerque, while the English St George once more set about the dragon.

Nowadays the question is whether the notes of the new Central European Bank will help strengthen the concept of European identity, or at least foster a greater sense of belonging amongst the member nations. Agreed, the advantages of monetary unification, considered for decades as the inevitable corollary of establishing a common market, now meet with little ideological opposition. All the same, the reasoning behind the process can seem, to the vast majority of people, a matter of abstraction, in a way similar to the perceptions nationals may entertain of the actions of 'their' centralised banks. The ability to cross national frontiers without the need to change currency, just as one can visit another country without Customs formalities, sends out a much more tangible signal about the reality of European unification.

Europeans, however, will rapidly grow used to a universal currency, in the same way as they now take for granted unrestricted travel. So it is in the daily use they make of the new notes, in their physical relationship with them, that people will relate to this new symbol of membership. Indeed, MM Brion and Moreau make a point of showing us how the feel of a note alone is sufficient to identify it.

And it will be a more or less permanent relationship. But once people have seen the new designs, will they simply get used to them and cease to give them any thought? There is no doubt that these designs reflect the fundamental political processes responsible for the development of European integration during the twentieth century. From this point of view, they go beyond the far too limited historical framework which might have resulted from basing the series on the 'founding fathers' of Europe or symbols of member nations. The new notes are thus designed to underline unity rather than diversity.

But they also symbolise dynamic processes at work – the unity of an age-old civilisation is pictured through successive styles of architectural fashion. They open up new vistas of enlightenment – where, in some sort, the universal outweighs the particular – encapsulating, as banknotes always have done, the way Europeans see the rest of humanity. They also represent the broadening of an institutionalised Europe, which, since its first conception between the wars, has ever been destined to extend its boundaries. Finally they are a bridge towards the future. Europe does not seek to set itself up in opposition to other continents but to dwell in harmony with them, within the framework of a universal architecture to whose development its members are eager to contribute. The new Euro-pean notes, then, contain an inbuilt programme: to educate and inform. As such, they perpetuate a tradition which the following pages will endeavour to explain.

ERIC BUSSIÈRE

Jean Monnet Professor of the History of the European Unification at the Université de Paris-Sorbonne

MICHEL DUMOULIN

Professor at the Université catholique de Louvain, President of the Institut d'études européennes (UCL),

pôle européen Jean Monnet

Contents

1 – PAPER INTO MONEY   2

     The first European banknotes   3
     An experiment in disaster: the story of John Law   5
     A bank of issue in every town   6
     From free-for-all to monopoly:
     the long road   10
     The banknote's 'democratisation'   17
     Utopia: the universal banknote   19
     The triumph of the banknote   22

2 – MIRROR OF THE NATIONS   26

     The bankers' pantheon   27
     Showers of gold   30
     The Industrial Revolution and Mother Earth   31
     The Russian eagle vs. the Finnish lion   33
     A political agenda   34
     In search of a cultural identity   43
     Life expectancy of banknotes   44
     Portraits of the ancestors   47
     A parable: the banknote that preached charity   49
     The colonial era   52

3 – EMERGENCY ISSUES   56

     The fragile Europe of the Vienna Congress   57
     Necessity knows no law:
     the horrors of the Great War   60
     Making a virtue of necessity   64
     Inflation runs amok   65
     The political problems
     of the inter-war years   68
     War, yet again   70
     Strike notes   70
     Notgeld – a closer look   74

4 – SECURITY MEASURES AND THE WAR AGAINST FORGERY   76

     Forgery and counterfeit notes   77
     Marks of authenticity   79
     Scraps of paper   84
     The watermark   87
     The evolution of printing techniques   87
     The play of light   88
     Security hanging on a thread   93
     The choice of printer   94
     The colour of money   96

5 – THE BANKNOTE AS ART   100

     Portrait of the artists   101
     The sources of inspiration   108
     Constraints and criticisms   110

6 – THE FUTURE IS IN THE EURO   116

     Enter the €   117
     The mirror of Europe   119
     Electronic money: the death knell
     for the banknote?   120
     Relics of the past   121

A FLUTTER OF BANKNOTES: CATALOGUE   122

     Belgium   124
     Denmark   126
     Germany   128
     Greece   131
     Espagne   133
     France   135
     Eire   137
     Italy   139
     Luxembourg   142
     The Netherlands   143
     Austria   146
     Portugal   148
     Finland   150
     Sweden   152
     United Kingdom: England   154
     The Euro Zone   156

     Bibliography   160
     Index   162
     Photographic credits   166
     Acknowledgements   167

Paper into Money

1

The Amsterdam Stock Exchange in the eighteenth century was a melting-pot for innovative financial procedures. BNB.

The first European banknotes

The origin of banknotes can be traced to the sixteenth century when goldsmiths and merchants issued receipts or certificates of deposit to members of the bourgeoisie or the upper classes who left their gold and silver for safekeeping. The goldsmiths were the more attractive choice, as their workshops were so constructed as to guarantee the best available security. Originally, each sum deposited with these private businessmen would be kept totally separate, contained in a bag sealed with the depositor's seal. The 'depositary' returned the original coins on the owner's demand, and received a fee for his trouble. Sometimes the receipts that he issued would change hands, as the circulation of these pieces of paper now permitted the heavy metallic coinage to come under new ownership without leaving the depositary's vaults.

At the start of the seventeenth century, papers issued by the Bank of Amsterdam allowed traders – who were accepting payment in gold and silver coinage of widely varying weights and metallic content – to deal with each other in notes of a standardised exchange value; these were obtained from the Bank on the deposit of a certain quantity of pure metal. The effect was to drive a coach and horses through the rights of the moneychangers' corporation. Two decrees (1608 and 1609) handed a kind of local monopoly to the Bank, and further legislation made the use of notes mandatory for major transactions.

But neither the receipts issued by goldsmiths against deposits of specie nor the documents of the Bank of Amsterdam were banknotes in the strict sense; they simply replaced specie with paper, and in no way increased monetary circulation. A banknote proper does not only engage to pay the bearer a certain sum; the engagement is also made within the framework of a credit transaction. However, when a depositary receiving sums in specie – the goldsmith or the bank – deems that the sums entrusted him are remaining more or less stable, he is inclined to issue notes bearing promises of repayment for amounts greater than his specie reserve. These promises of repayment will be supplied to investors needing loans: merchants, industrialists, the self-employed, government departments. As long as the public has confidence in the issuer, the notes will circulate from one individual to another without anyone feeling it worthwhile to exchange them i.e. convert them into specie.

In short, the genuine banknote arrived when the total of 'promises to pay' in circulation exceeded the amount of specie held by the issuing bank. This situation arose for the first time in mid-seventeenth-century Sweden. In 1652, a certain Johan Palmstruch, born at Riga in 1611 and a citizen of Amsterdam, drew up a project for the establishment of a bank in Stockholm. Four years later, a second project was approved by Sweden's ruler, Charles X. The bank thus created was a private law organisation, but in actual practice it displayed all the attributes of a department of state; subject to surveillance by the Treasury, it enjoyed the receipt of customs duties and surrendered half its profits to the Crown. There were two departments: one for currency exchange (specie against notes) and another for short-term loans and advances. The two departments were, moreover, mutually dependent, since the sums deposited acted as security for moneys lent. Like the Bank of Amsterdam, Palmstruch's institution issued depositors with receipts which allowed the heavy copper Swedish coinage – bars weighing 20 kg (44 lb) in some cases – to be 'exchanged' without physical handling.

These receipts carried interest; each time they changed hands, the bank had to pay out. In 1661, the

Kreditivsedlar for 100 silver dalers issued in January 1666 by the Stockholms Banco and probably the earliest European banknote, signed by, among others, Johan Palmstruch (1611–71), 198 x 154 mm (7.80 x 6.06 in.). BNB. The dry seal or stamp is a very old means of authentication: it continued in use until the early 1800s, when banks abandoned it because the raised surface abraded too quickly.

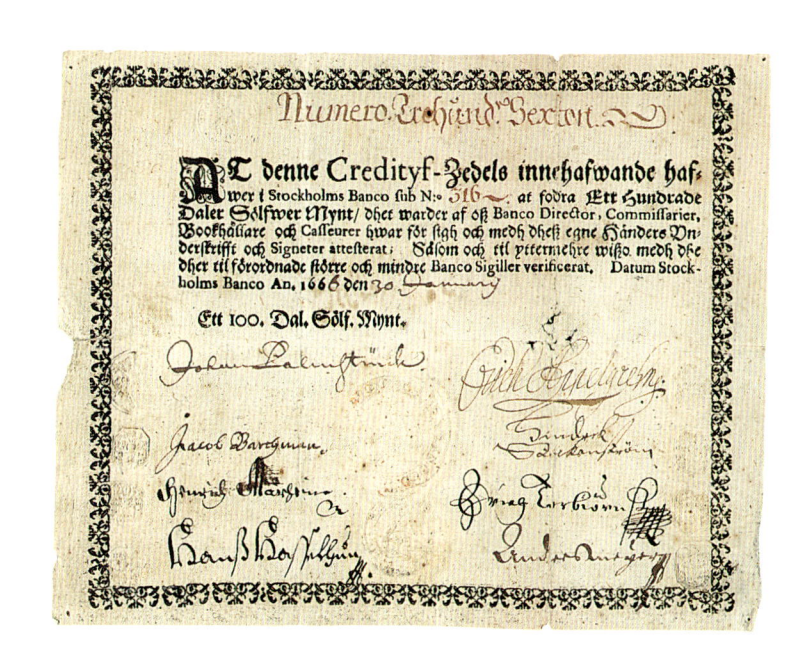

'Promissory note' for £50 sterling, partially printed, Bank of England, 1771. BE. As time went by, all countries adopted the idea of numbering their notes mechanically, the Bank of England leading the way in 1809. Face values, also handwritten at first, were eventually printed when it became clear that counterfeiters were erasing or falsifying them.

Stockholms Banco began to issue a new kind of credit note (*kreditivsedlar*) payable to the bearer, this time carrying no interest, which simplified the system and accelerated the circulation of paper. Moreover, the bank issued notes for amounts exceeding its metal reserves, while continuing to guarantee repayment in cash to those demanding it. Palmstruch no doubt considered it improbable that all the holders would request repayment at the same time.

These were true banknotes: they represented a sum payable on demand by the issuer to the bearer, and in metallic coinage but not totally secured by it. To facilitate their circulation, the bank issued notes in rounded values, but also made freely available bills of small denomination, i.e. fractional currency. Nobody was forced to accept them but, in practice, they were well received. Unfortunately, the Stockholms Banco soon succumbed to the temptation to issue these credits indiscriminately and, from the autumn of 1663, it found itself in severe difficulties. The ensuing inquiry held Palmstruch responsible for the Bank's losses, with the state having to come to the aid of the stricken institution. In 1668, the Swedish parliament founded a new institution, the Riksens Ständers Bank (Bank of the States of the Kingdom) to operate under its direct supervision. The country produced no further examples of banknotes payable to the bearer before the early nineteenth century.

What Palmstruch had done in Sweden, English goldsmiths were also doing at roughly the same time, issuing bills that were not completely guaranteed by specie deposits. But the establishment of the Bank of England in 1694 institutionalised the use of banknotes in this country. Created to finance the war with Louis XIV of France, it immediately began to issue notes. These original 'promissory notes', with their inscription 'We promise to pay to Mr X or bearer the sum of Y pounds on demand', yielded interest. The fact that the note could be cashed not only by the person who had received it in exchange for a deposit, but also by anyone presenting it, allowed it to circulate from hand to hand before redemption. The Bank did not enjoy any monopoly of issue – in fact, the issue of banknotes was not even mentioned in the royal charter its founders received from the king – but it rapidly acquired an appreciable share of all the notes put into circulation. In 1708, legislation was enacted outlawing the creation in England of banks with more than six partners. This measure assured the Bank of England of a *de facto* monopoly on the London exchange and restrained the rush to create new banks. Around 1750, there were still only a dozen or so in England; it was not until the second half of the eighteenth century that their numbers would expand more dramatically, a phenomenon closely linked to the Industrial Revolution.

In Scotland, banking legislation had remained more flexible than south of the border. A Bank of Scotland was founded in 1695. Whilst the majority of institutions still only carried on credit activities as a sideline, being prima-

An experiment in disaster: the story of John Law

The politics of Louis XIV had brought France to the verge of bankruptcy. When he died in 1715, there was general agreement on the urgent need to consolidate the debt and devise a system of paying it off. In May of the following year, John Law was authorised to create a Banque générale, subject to oversight by the state, but more than a mere appendage of government, which would allow the Crown to monetise its debt. The capital was subscribed as 25 per cent cash and the rest in treasury bonds. The Bank was authorised to issue notes payable on demand to the bearer in écus. Taxpayers could settle their bills using the new notes. In 1717, Law launched the Compagnie d'Occident, later to become the Compagnie française des Indes, which won the right to trade with Louisiana and Canada, the Indies and Africa. The capital for this company was subscribed in state bonds, accepted at par, but traded at a third of this nominal value! As the Compagnie amassed capital, Law convinced large numbers of holders of government bonds to exchange them against his company's shares. With speculation rife, the value of its bonds rocketed.

Meanwhile, the Banque générale had become a state bank; in December 1718, the Crown became its sole shareholder, buying back the founders' shares. Thenceforth, the Bank's activities were dependent solely upon the needs of the Treasury. Law began to print money to buy back the shares of the Compagnie des Indes. This whimsical issue of paper money was based on the fragile confidence of the public, a confidence he shattered by imposing a fixed exchange rate and withdrawing silver and gold coins from circulation. In May 1720 panic broke out and it proved impossible to reimburse many of the note-holders.

Jean-François Huguet (1679–1749), *Exchanging Notes at the Hôtel des Monnaies, Rennes*, 1735. Musée de Bretagne, Rennes.
The painting was executed from memory, fifteen or so years after the panic which saw the downfall of John Law (1671–1729) and his bank.

rily commercial or industrial enterprises, the Bank of Scotland was perhaps the first institution in the world created with private capital for the express and exclusive purpose of banking operations unconnected with the authorities. Immediately, it issued its first banknotes. In contrast, the Bank of Ireland was only born in 1783, though it was as an exclusive bank of issue, with the monopoly for the region around Dublin.

The Bank of England and the Bank of Scotland were issuing true banknotes backed by specie reserves and the public's confidence. From the time of the *Ancien régime*, states had also issued paper money, that is to say, paper destined to cover part of the national debt and enjoying the same status of legal tender as metallic coinage. In France, the first public experiment with paper money took place as early as 1716; the ill-fated venture of banker John Law ended in total disaster, leaving a lingering legacy of distrust for paper money not only amongst the French but throughout Europe. Notwithstanding, other paper moneys began to circulate elsewhere during the 1700s. In Italy, the first appeared in 1746, when the Kingdom of Piedmont and Sardinia issued its *Biglietti della Regia Cassa*. In 1785 the Monte di Pietà in Rome began to issue notes with various values of between 3 and 1,500 écus. The Banco di Santo Spirito di Roma followed suit a year later. In Austria, the first paper money was issued in 1762 by the Wiener-Stadt-Banco; in Germany three years later by the Giro-und-Lehn-Banco, Berlin; and in Spain, in 1780, by King Charles III.

A Bank of Issue in Every Town

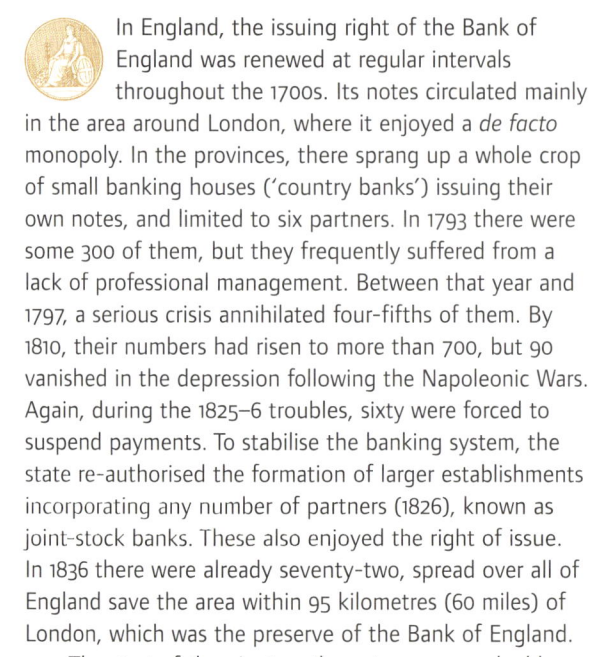

In England, the issuing right of the Bank of England was renewed at regular intervals throughout the 1700s. Its notes circulated mainly in the area around London, where it enjoyed a *de facto* monopoly. In the provinces, there sprang up a whole crop of small banking houses ('country banks') issuing their own notes, and limited to six partners. In 1793 there were some 300 of them, but they frequently suffered from a lack of professional management. Between that year and 1797, a serious crisis annihilated four-fifths of them. By 1810, their numbers had risen to more than 700, but 90 vanished in the depression following the Napoleonic Wars. Again, during the 1825–6 troubles, sixty were forced to suspend payments. To stabilise the banking system, the state re-authorised the formation of larger establishments incorporating any number of partners (1826), known as joint-stock banks. These also enjoyed the right of issue. In 1836 there were already seventy-two, spread over all of England save the area within 95 kilometres (60 miles) of London, which was the preserve of the Bank of England.

The start of the nineteenth century was marked by an explosion in the numbers of small Irish banks but, as one financial downturn succeeded another, the majority collapsed. Towards 1820, virtually the only remaining examples were in Dublin, Cork and Belfast. In 1821 the Government backed an increase in the Bank of Ireland's capital. In return, the Bank was obliged to accept the creation of new banking companies within its 'perimeter'.

Seventy years after the unhappy demise of Law's bank, another disaster occurred in France, this time involving the *assignats* or Revolutionary banknotes. Like the notes issued by Law's Banque générale, this was a tender imposed by the state. It was backed by the nation's wealth, confiscated from the clergy and nobles fleeing the Revolution. But to finance the war, the government did not hesitate to print money. The total of *assignats* in circulation rose from 400 million in 1789 to 20 billion in 1793! The debacle that followed once more threw all forms of fiat money into disrepute, not merely in France, but in all the areas occupied by French troops. Close on the heels of this, in 1811, a third calamity struck, when the Wiener-Stadt-Banco went bankrupt; this was the Austrian state bank, whose paper money, produced on a conveyor-belt scale to finance the war, proved completely worthless.

The hour of the private bank and its notes of issue had now arrived, confirming the significance of the English example. Some issuing banks were created from the ruins of state institutions. In Austria, following the collapse of the state bank, the Privilegirte Österreichische Nationalbank was set up in 1816, with a monopoly throughout the Empire. In France, several new private banks of issue appeared in the last years of the eighteenth century. In January 1800, Napoleon Bonaparte approved the statutes of the Banque de France, a private establishment, but subject to a certain degree of state control. In 1803, he granted it the monopoly of issue for the Paris region. From 1836 to 1848, the Banque de France set up a dozen branches in the provinces, also exercising a limited monopoly in their localities. Other issuing banks, known as *départementales*, received a similar privilege in a number of French towns: Rouen (1815), Nantes and Bordeaux (1818), Lyons and Marseilles (1835), then Lille, Le Havre, Orléans and Toulouse. But the development of these departmental banks was handicapped by the reluctance of the population to accept banknotes, more so in the provinces than in Paris, and by the wild variations in the banks' reserves. Paris, destination of a ceaseless stream of taxes and investments, was draining the specie resources of the provinces. Hence the local banks were forced to limit the volume of the notes they issued.

On the other hand, in Sweden, the regional banks stole a march on the official institutions. The Riksens Ständers Bank, later the Sveriges Riksbank (1866) was, in 1800, the country's sole bank. Between 1817 and 1824, it opened two new 'lending branches' at Gothenburg and Lamo. Elsewhere in the country, there was a dire shortage of credit institutions. Between 1830 and 1893, thirty-one private banks of issue were opened, though their notes were never recognised as legal tender. Nor were they offi-

In 1793, the devaluation of *assignats* was so severe that people used them to ornament everyday objects like snuffboxes, or the fan seen here. '*Assignats? So much hot air!*' Musée de la Révolution française, Vizille.

500-franc note of the Banque départementale de Bordeaux, 1838, by Cornouailles, 230 x 125 mm (9.06 x 4.92 in.). BF.
Until 1848, regional banks competed in the provinces with the Banque de France. The façade of the Bordeaux bank is shown in the cartouche below.

cially accepted in payment by the authorities, although, in actual practice, this is what progressively happened. In 1869, the Riksbank was forced to accept notes issued by private banks. From then on, these almost completely supplanted the Riksbank's own notes in general circulation.

Banks of issue began to multiply throughout Europe. In Spain, following the granting of excess credits to the state, the Banco Nacional de San Carlos, Spain's first issuing bank (1783) was reorganised in 1829 under the name of Banco Español de San Fernando. The latter enjoyed a monopoly in Madrid, and sought to extend this to the whole of Spain. In fact, legislation enacted in 1856, designed to encourage local initiatives, established a system of multiple issuing banks, each with a limited monopoly; the Banco Español de San Fernando, though now renamed the Banco de España, remained no more than a Madrid institution. The 1856 law resulted in an explosion in the numbers of provincial issuing banks; in 1864, Spain possessed twenty-one operative establishments. They enjoyed varying fortunes, but all contributed to the popularisation of the banknote as a means of transaction.

In Portugal, the monopoly conceded in 1821 to the Banco de Lisboa extended, in theory, to the entire national territory. Despite this privilege, the Banco Comercial do Porto, founded in 1853, obtained rights of issue 'by special dispensation'. In 1846, following a serious economic and political crisis, the activities of the Banco de Lisboa were taken over by a new establishment, the Banco de Portugal, which found itself with a monopoly on issue for the whole kingdom. Unfortunately, as in Spain, the authorities decided (1850) to encourage the economic development of the country by re-establishing the principle of multiple banks of issue. Between 1856 and 1873, seven new banks in the north of the country were accorded issuing rights. Nonetheless, only the Banco de Portugal's notes could legally be accepted as payment by the Treasury.

Around 1840, then, we can distinguish in Europe various categories of issuing banks. Some were institutions more or less controlled by the politicians (the Sveriges Riksbank is the best example); others were partnerships from whose management the state kept its distance, as with the English 'country banks'. Yet others possessed exclusive rights of issue for a particular region: the Banque de France had a monopoly in Paris from 1803, the Banco de Lisboa for all Portuguese territory (1821), and the Banco Español de San Fernando for Madrid (1829). Or else they enjoyed a monopoly – *de facto* if not *de iure* – within a certain area, as was the case with the Bank of England in the London region from the end of the seventeenth century. There were even some in direct competition with one another in the same towns or cities: the Société générale de Belgique and the Banque de Belgique were in this situation in Brussels between 1835 and 1848.

Three remarks on the fragility of the issuing banks. First and foremost, they did not limit their activities to the issuing of notes: they were also credit houses; they provided mortgages and property loans; they were invest-

20,000-real note, Banco Comercial do Porto, by J.B. Ribeiro, c. 1836; and 1,200-real note, Banco de Lisboa, c. 1846. BP. Though enjoying a theoretical monopoly over all Portuguese territory, the Banco de Lisboa was in fact in competition with the Banco Comercial do Porto in the north of the country. The subject matter of the 1,200-real note is an allegory of the Four Ages of Man.

1,000-real note issue, Banco Español de San Fernando, 1847, 138 x 130 mm (5.43 x 5.12 in.). BESp. In the nineteenth century, many Spanish, French, Finnish, Belgian and Portuguese notes featured two clasped hands, recalling that commercial transactions are based on mutual confidence. No one at the time was obliged to accept a banknote; it was a matter of trust.

ment companies; they handled deposits and guarantee funds, business banking and savings. This plurality of activities was to render them hostages to fortune, in that when a crisis occurred, they frequently found their funds tied up in long-term investments despite the need for immediate means to reimburse their notes. Second, most of them were not subject to any control over the volume of notes they circulated: even if their statutes provided for strict limits, they all too easily became involved in speculation. In boom times they would print huge amounts of paper – without any proper guarantee – to finance often hazardous ventures. We have already witnessed the devastating effects of this on the English 'country banks'; Italian, Portuguese and Belgian banks were later to fall into the same trap. Finally, the so-called 'privileged' banks, the ancestors of most of today's national banks of issue, remained under the thumb of the authorities, who pressured them to print paper money on the scale of commercial papers. A flagrant case was that of William Pitt, who set the presses of the Bank of England rolling to finance the war with France. Some banks were moreover created for the purposes of writing off the state's debt – Madrid's Banco Nacional de San Carlos (1783) and the Banco de Lisboa (December 1821). Again, there were constant disputes in a number of countries between the authorities and the issuing banks over the power of the former to issue commercial papers in parallel with the banknotes being circulated by the latter.

From free-for-all to monopoly: the long road

The nineteenth century is commonly associated with the emergence of the nation state. A kind of centripetal force was in action in all domains: political, economical and cultural. The abolition of local customs barriers, the reduction of travel time with the advent of the railway, the gradual replacement of dialects by national languages, all struck a serious blow at regional isolationism. The more or less rapid evolution of centralised states impacted, quite naturally, on the issue of banknotes. In effect, there was a progressive realisation that standardisation of fiduciary money would promote its acceptance as well as a rational development of the credit system.

We should note in passing that the tendency towards a monopoly of issue was encouraged by the management of the banks themselves. In 1802, the board of the Banque de France regarded the rivalry between issuing banks, whether in Paris or in the provinces, as prejudicial to the regular development of commerce and industry: ' Rivalry between traders may not be a problem; the resulting competition may even stimulate trade, to the benefit of the consumer and the public. The same cannot be said of banks. Their influence upon each other and on commerce in general can never be anything but decisive, so that any bank which suffers damage from a rival will in turn inflict a deadly wound on public confidence and the reputation of our institutions.' The lament was taken up by other 'privileged' banks during the first half of the nineteenth century. But we are justified in casting a certain amount of doubt on the objectivity of this argument. Were not these establishments merely seeking totally exclusive rights in the discount market and, by implication, an enhancement of their power over the economy? Be this as it may, from the 1840s onwards, we can discern an ever more obvious tendency to grant extended monopolies to banks of issue.

In England, this movement towards monopoly of issue on a national scale was set in train by the crisis of 1842–3, during which twenty-nine issuing banks had to suspend payments, and the Bank of England was constrained to borrow gold from the Banque de France. It was against this background that the Peel Act was passed in 1844, forbidding the granting of new issuing rights and limiting those previously empowered to the volumes of notes already issued. In theory, 208 'country banks' existed, with an issuing power of £5.2 million, together with seventy-two joint-stock banks (£3.4 million). But already, the notes issued by the Bank of England represented 76 per cent of the total in national circulation. Further, a ceiling was now imposed on issues by rival institutions, and, in the case of a merger, these issuing rights were cancelled. All in all, then, the Bank of England enjoyed a monopoly, even if, for a long time to come, private issuing banks continued to cling to life. The last, Fox, Fowler and Co., only disappeared in 1921. In Ireland, in the wake of the Peel Act, the number of issuing banks was limited to six, and only notes of the Bank of Ireland were acceptable for the payment of taxes. The Currency Act of 1927 set up the Currency Commission of Ireland, which, in the following year, issued a series of notes with the status of legal tender. All the same, it authorised eight private banks to continue their issues, in parallel with its own notes. It was only in 1943 that a new organisation, the Central Bank of Ireland, was granted exclusive rights of issue in the Irish Republic. In Scotland, on the other hand, the multiplicity of issuing banks has continued to the present day.

In France, it was the crisis of 1848 that led to the centralisation of note issue. The monopoly of the Banque de France was extended to the entire national territory. The nine departmental banks were transformed into branches of the national institution. For Gilles Jacoud, a French specialist in the history of credit, it cannot be claimed that the coexistence of several French banks automatically unleashed a process of elimination at the end of which one establishment would be left with a national monopoly of issue. For a nineteenth-century businessman, control of monetary issue by a central bank was far from a simple matter of common sense: 'Similarly, in a generation's time,

Would paper money replace gold until the latter was found lying around the pavements with the rubbish? The mid-nineteenth-century Parisian caricaturist 'Cham' (1819–79), whose work appeared in *Le Charivari*, would have none of it. For him, no sane person should accept banknotes except at the price of the paper: four sous per pound!

100-florin note, Privilegirte Österreichische Nationalbank, 1825, 157 x 107 mm (6.18 x 4.21 in.). ONB. As its name indicates, this establishment enjoyed a monopoly on issue throughout the Austrian Empire.

we might perhaps consider that the creation of a central European bank was inevitable, but for the decision-makers of today, there are still several choices. Such *ex post facto* reasoning is therefore highly questionable.' Jacoud concludes that, in the final analysis, the attribution of an exclusive monopoly on issue for the entire national territory resulted from the ambitions of the Banque de France's management and the eagerness of the authorities to reinforce their control over monetary circulation.

In Belgium, the 1848 crisis also instigated a radical overhaul in the way notes were issued, a reform that was enshrined in the establishment of the Banque nationale de Belgique two years later. The bank did not, properly speaking, enjoy exclusive rights of issue, but the issuing of notes by other banks required special legislation. The rights granted to various banks in the past were not rescinded, but bought out by the Banque nationale.

In Italy and Germany, the move towards exclusive issuing rights went hand in hand with progress towards national unification. In 1815, the Congress of Vienna had divided the Italian peninsula into eight distinct states: the Kingdom of Piedmont and Sardinia, comprising Nice, Savoy, Piedmont, Genoa and the Island of Sardinia; Lombardy–Venetia, subject to Austria; Parma, Modena and Tuscany; the Papal States; and the Kingdom of the

Detail of a 1 pound note, Currency Commission Irish Free State, 1928, reverse, 151 x 84 mm (5.9 x 3.3 in.) CBI. Allegorical representation of an Irish river.

Two Sicilies (i.e. Sicily and Naples). In 1849, the two issuing banks of the Kingdom of Piedmont and Sardinia merged to form the Banca Nazionale negli Stati Sardi. In Tuscany, the banks of Florence and Livorno (Leghorn) amalgamated in 1857 under the title of Banca Nazionale Toscana, which absorbed four other issuing banks in 1860. Following the unification of Italy in 1861, only six issuing banks remained in the peninsula, i.e. three in the north (Banca Nazionale Toscana, Banca Nazionale negli Stati Sardi, Banca Toscana di Credito), one in the Papal States (Banca dello Stato Pontifico, the future Banca Romana) and two in the south (Banco di Sicilia, Banco di Napoli). With political unification evolving around Piedmont, the Banca Nazionale negli Stati Sardi was chosen by the government to fulfil the role of central bank and extend the usage of banknotes, at a time when they counted for less than 5 per cent of the money in circulation. In 1866, its name was modified to the Banca Nazionale nel Regno d'Italia.

But the Banca Nazionale was at this period only *prima inter pares*: despite the efforts of the government to persuade them to merge, the other banks maintained their issuing rights. In 1866, an attempt to link the Banca Nazionale nel Regno d'Italia with the Banca Nazionale Toscana proved fruitless: both in Tuscany and in the Mezzogiorno (South), the ruling classes feared that amalgamating banks would deprive their regions of vital resources. In the 1880s, rivalry between banks intensified, and some took additional risks by financing long-term investments. After these years of folly, several establishments found themselves in dire straits, having issued too much paper money. In 1892, a Deputy publicly denounced the scandal, and a parliamentary inquiry revealed a whole gamut of fraudulent practices involving excess issues and

Carlo Bossoli (1815–84), *The Arrival of C.L. Farini on the Piazza San Carlo, Turin, 18 March 1860*. Museo Nazionale del Risorgimento Italiano, Turin.
The amalgamation of Parma, Modena and the Romagna with Piedmont (March 1860) preceded that of the southern states by a few months.

100-lire note, Banco di Napoli, 1911, obverse, 175 x 95 mm (6.89 x 3.74 in.). BNB. This fine issue with its art nouveau portrait of the poet Torquato Tasso was produced by one of two southern Italian banks who continued to enjoy issuing rights up to 1926.

Anton von Werner (1843–1915), *Proclamation of the Reich in the Hall of Mirrors at Versailles, 18 January 1871.* Bismarckmuseum, Friedriechsruh. The birth of the Second Reich was based on, among other things, the principle of monetary union. But it was only progressively that the Reichsbank succeeded in imposing a monopoly on issue.

illegal printing. The Banca Romana, for instance, had deliberately exceeded its ceiling, reissuing entire series of notes with identical serial marks and numbers. In August 1893, in a climate of suspicion and personal vendettas, the existing banks were combined to form the Banca d'Italia. Only the two southern institutions, the Banco di Napoli and the Banco di Sicilia, were allowed to retain a certain independence to pacify regional opposition. They continued to exercise this right until 1926, but lost all importance in this respect in comparison with the Banca Nazionale.

Why did it take the Italian state thirty years to provide itself with a central bank, when voices were already raised in favour of such a body back in 1863, and monetary unification became a reality in 1862? Among the reasons advanced by Italian historians we may quote the lack of political will, in a state brought to birth too rapidly; an economy which lagged behind that of other European countries; and the hostility of regional pressure groups.

In 1847, the Giro- und Lehn-Banco of Berlin, the state bank of issue, was reorganised into a joint-stock company under the name of the Preussische Bank (Bank of Prussia). The state retained a mere one-sixth of the capital. The management was in the hands of civil servants, but the bank did not enjoy exclusive issuing rights. The example of Prussia set a trend for the German Confederation, which then numbered forty-one states; on the creation of the German Empire in 1871, there existed thirty-four private issuing banks throughout its territory. More than two-thirds of notes in circulation had been issued by the Preussische Bank. In December 1871, a new gold standard was adopted: the mark, which replaced the five standards currently in use in the Empire. All new issues of notes were subject to authorisation by the central government, and a ban was placed on the circulation of paper denominations under 100 marks, which were considered dangerous to the financial stability of the Reich. Württemberg and the Duchy of Baden, however, retained the right to establish banks of issue, none existing there at the time. Finally, there were plans to set up a national issuing institution, considered by the partisans of a centralised state as the keystone of Germany's financial unification. However, several states in southern Germany violently opposed the creation of a single federal-type bank. Fearing the political and economic hegemony of Prussia, they protested that a regional bank would be better placed to understand and defend local economic interests. There followed a long series of disputes until the banking act of 14 March 1875 settled the constitution of the Reichsbank, which arose, in effect, from the ashes of the Preussische Bank

The organic legislation voted on its foundation envisaged the Reichsbank's pre-eminence over other issuing banks, to the extent that it was to control the global volume of notes issued by all establishments. In theory, the issuing rights of the other banks were retained; the practical obstacles, however, which henceforth dogged the existence of small banks of issue were such that by 1876 sixteen of them renounced their rights. The share of regional issuing banks in the overall issue of German notes was already reduced to 19 per cent. Despite the persistence of the southern states – Bavaria, Saxony, Baden and Württemberg – in opposing a federal-type centralisation of issuing rights, this share had further fallen to a mere 3.7 per cent on the eve of the First World War. Notwithstanding, it took the Great Depression of the 1930s before Minister Schacht could compel the four remaining issuing banks to renounce their privileges in ex-

500,000-mark 'inflation note', Badische Bank, 1923, reverse. DBB.
In Germany, several regional banks were permitted to issue notes up to 1935.

Laying of the first stone of the new Reichsbank building in Berlin, 5 May 1934. DBB.
In the front row the main figures are Chancellor Adolf Hitler, and, to his left, the minister Hjalmar Schacht, who ended the issuing privileges enjoyed by the southern states of the old Empire.

Counters in the Banque national de Belgiue at the beginning of the twentieth century. BNB

change for a state guarantee. This policy was also in step with the aims of National Socialism, which sought the elimination of all private sources of opposition. Another reason was the desire to concentrate gold reserves in the hands of the Reichsbank. In 1935, whilst the gold reserves of the Reichsbank were only 2.3 per cent, those of the Bayerische Notenbank still totalled 44.2 per cent!

What are we to make of all this? Maybe that in Germany, as in Italy, a single currency and the emergence of a single issuing bank were the essential ingredients for consolidating a variety of heterogeneous bodies, amongst whom an anti-centralist force was at work in the political domain. It is hardly necessary to remind ourselves that in the first quarter of the nineteenth century, the presence of large minorities (Poles, Lithuanians and Danes), the exclusion of German Austrians and the attraction of the southern states to the Austrian Empire all remained sources of tension within a unified Germany. We also need to take into account the difficulties experienced by the authorities in providing the Reich with national symbols acceptable to all its citizens. In 1871, the Germans were agreed on neither a common flag nor a national anthem nor the date of a national holiday, but they recognised the mark as the sole form of currency, and the Reichsbank was already issuing more than three-quarters of all the notes in circulation. The debate remains open as to whether the existence of regional banks of issue still retained any sense at this period, and if they still had a role to play in regional economic development.

Sole banks of issue were imposed successively in Spain (1874), Portugal (1891), Sweden (1904) and Greece (1920). These 'central' banks were born, often in a climate of crisis, from the need to standardise the issue of notes and control the total amount of available credit. Before these exclusive rights were granted, the circulation of notes was a heterogeneous affair, involving issues by commercial banks whose solvency, and especially liquidity were liable to fluctuate. Furthermore, the dispersal of reserves amongst a more or less large number of commercial banks prevented their effective mobilisation when it came to assisting a bank in difficulties.

Around 1900, a 'central' issuing bank enjoyed a prominent position or a monopoly in the majority of European countries, even if frequently this *de facto* monopoly required time to transfer itself onto the statute books: the Nederlandsche Bank, with issuing rights since 1814, and exercising such a right from 1830, only saw this privilege officially confirmed in 1943! Where regional and private issuing banks lingered on, their activities were steamrollered by the rising power of the central establishments. Finally, only Scotland (and Ireland up to 1928) retained a system where fiat money was circulated by multiple private banks.

The centralisation of note issue was accompanied by specialisation, with the issuing banks having to agree to abandon most of the traditional commercial activities of a bank. This was the case with the Bank of England in 1844, the Banque nationale de Belgique (1850), the Banca d'Italia (1893), the Sveriges Riksbank from 1897 and the Bank of Greece (Τραπεζα τησ Ελλαδοσ) as late as 1928. But they were to take on one new and vital function – that of 'banks of last resort', on which other credit establishments would call for aid in case of trouble, with the aim of halting a crisis before it ran out of control. Henceforth, the banking system in the various countries of Europe consisted of a two-level structure. Locally, there were the commercial banks, with deposits convertible into the banknotes of the central institution. At the central level, notes were convertible into metallic currency. The reserves of commercial banks no longer consisted of such currency, but of either banknotes belonging to the central bank or deposits placed with it. All the same, centralisation could sometimes prove risky. Enjoying an exclusive or quasi-exclusive right perceived to be fit for a sovereign, the banks of issue frequently came under pressure from impecunious governments to finance wars or large-scale construction projects.

Bank messenger's satchel, Banque nationale de Belgique, probably from early twentieth century. BNB. At the turn of the century, national banks became authorities in financial matters and began to settle into their role as bankers of last resort.

Leather wallet by the firm Delvaux, probably from early twentieth century. It contains compartments for bills of different denominations.

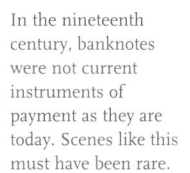

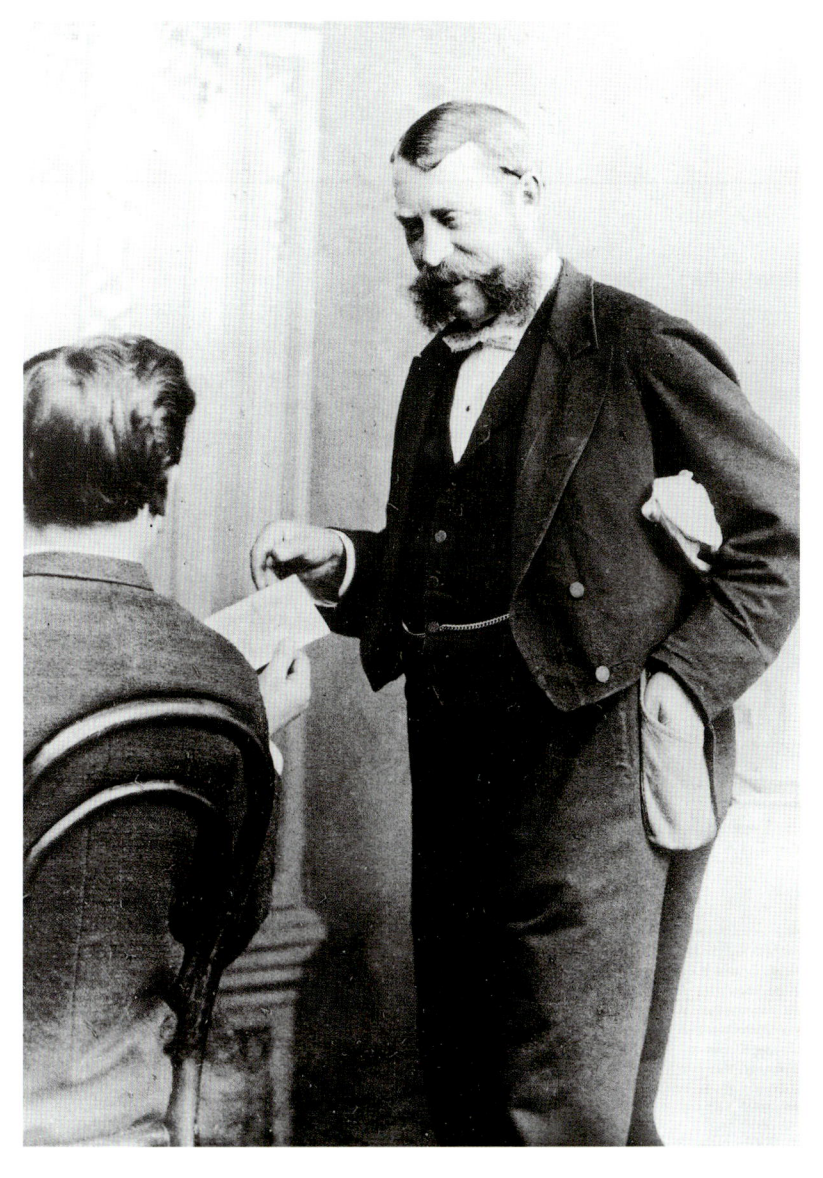

In the nineteenth century, banknotes were not current instruments of payment as they are today. Scenes like this must have been rare.

The banknote's 'democratisation'

25 The banknote took time to acquire popularity. Many potential users had no confidence in this form of payment. In their defence, it has to be said that numerous experimental issues in the 1600s and 1700s had ended in tears. Whether in France, Belgium, the Nether-lands, Germany or Italy, the unfortunate affair of the *assignats* lingered long in the popular memory. In France, in 1801, a Rouen banker noted that the paper money of the Banque de France was avoided, despite all the propaganda: 'It is returned almost as soon as it is issued.' Issues of notes in Germany were rare and on a small scale in the first fifty years of the nineteenth century. In his *Faust*, Goethe displayed the typical German's contempt for paper money by making it an invention of the Devil. And it was to no avail that in Spain a general meeting of the shareholders of the Banco Nacional de San Carlos, disappointed with the failure of its *cédulas*, decided (1825) to offer a reward of 6,000 *reals* to the author who could produce the most cogent justification for the use of paper money. Finally, in southern Italy, the first notes payable to the bearer only began to circulate in the 1870s.

Other factors militated against the popularisation of banknotes, one being their limited geographical distribution. Traders and businessmen used only the notes of their regular banks; they would not trust those issued in a neighbouring town, and whenever they travelled away from their bases, they would settle their affairs in specie. In 1802, the economist Nicolas François Mollien wrote: 'The Bank of London is not a universal bank, but a local one; it is the Bank of London, not the Bank of England.' According to him, it was quite impossible to extend the activities of a single bank throughout an entire country like France. It presented too many practical problems, such as where to keep the specie reserves so customers could cash notes on demand at any branch. In Tuscany, the notes issued by the six banks of Florence, Livorno, Siena, Pisa, Lucca and Arezzo circulated only in their allotted areas, which made transactions more awkward than in Piedmont, where one bank controlled the whole circulation. If notes circulated with difficulty from region to region, state frontiers proved even more of an obstacle. In 1848, a Belgian publicist remarked: 'Many people find no use for banknotes. If they have some small payment to make, if they have to travel or make a transaction abroad, it means going to the *bureau de change* and losing a more or less considerable sum in the exchange.' In Germany, however, it frequently proved easier to pay with banknotes than specie; there were six different monetary systems in use in the Confederation's territory, and a payment in specie often involved complicated calculations. In contrast, the banknotes of the different states, often in denominations of the Prussian *thaler*, offered the advantage of being a standardised method of payment. This explains the sudden rise in the popularity of banknotes in Germany from the 1850s. Moreover, paper money was recognised for the first time as an international means of payment in the Treaty of Frankfurt (1871), which stipulated that the indemnity imposed on France could be paid in notes of, amongst other institutions, the Bank of England, the Preussische Bank, the Nederlandsche Bank and the Banque nationale de Belgique.

The spread of notes had also been hampered by excessive face values, which prevented them from becoming a routine method of payment and limited their use to large businesses. This was deliberate, since small denominations of paper money came in for harsh criticism from the economists, who denounced the ease with which notes could be forged and accused them of helping to fuel inflation. Especially, they charged them with being the cause of panics that forced banks to suspend payment in times of crisis. In 1802, the Banque de France, which issued only notes of 1,000 and 500 francs – the equivalent of a whole year's wages for a labourer – vigorously criticised the Banque Territoriale for issuing denominations of 50 francs: 'The fools who have created all this paper money have not stopped to think that they are handing out a massive number of demands on their tills. All these customers will soon be queuing at their doors, spreading alarm and panic about every note issued by every bank.' Boards were fearful of the 'democratisation' of the banknote, envisaging that a public little used to handling paper would try and get rid of it as soon as possible. Should the use of banknotes be confined to the chosen few? Adam Smith thought so, and in his *Wealth of Nations* had argued that the authorities responsible for monetary circulation should devise one means of transaction between traders and another for use between traders and consumers. In Germany, between 1870 and 1880, the minimum denomination was fixed at 100 marks to protect the 'little man' should an establishment go bankrupt. For all the issuing banks of that era, notes were only a substitute for gold, and the staff needed to be able to exchange them for gold or silver coinage at any given moment.

But confidence in the banknote suffered above all from political tensions or economic crises. Each time the future was thrown into doubt, holders of notes formed jostling queues at the banks of issue to redeem the value of their paper. Such panics occasionally compelled governments to take the action dreaded by note-holders – suspending convertibility. This happened in England in 1797 on the announcement that French forces had landed on British soil; in Belgium, during the revolution of September 1830 (the circulation of notes, which had reached 4 million in July 1830, bottomed out at around 1 million); and in Portugal in 1846, against the background of a home affairs crisis. In 1848, political events caused depositors to besiege banks and savings offices all over Europe. In France, a fixed rate of exchange was imposed on 15 March 1848 and remained in force until 1850. The same measure was introduced five days later in Belgium, then, in turn, the storm hit banks in Germany, Austria, Italy and Greece.

Other crises were more localised. In the mid 1850s, a serious depression engulfed the Russian Empire as a result of the cost of the Crimean War; in Finland, the National Bank suspended the repayment of its own and Russian notes. The Banque de France took similar measures during the Franco-Prussian War, and convertibility was not restored until 1878. The fixed rate periods lasted particularly long in Italy and Greece. In the former, the political upheavals linked to the *Risorgimento* gave rise in turn to economic difficulties, and there were runs on the issuing banks. From 1866, the state had to impose a fixed rate on notes of the various regional banks within their specific areas. Those of the Banca Nazionale had to be accepted as payment throughout Italy. In April 1874, the banking system was reformed: the law now authorised the group of six banks to issue *biglietti consorziali* in return for placing funds at the state's disposal. These notes, whose denominations ranged from 0.5 to 1,000 lire, had a set rate of exchange, and were guaranteed by the issuing banks' own notes. In 1881, the situation improved; the state was able to consolidate its debt thanks to loans from abroad; the consortium was dissolved, the *biglietti consorziali* exchanged for specie or commercial papers, and in 1883 the fixed rate was ended.

In Greece, there was a run on the banks in December 1868 when the revolt of the Greek population of Crete against Turkish rule degenerated into open conflict. The government imposed a fixed rate, though it lasted only fourteen months. On the other hand, the imposition of June 1877, in the context of the crisis in the East (1876–8), continued until 1885. And it was immediately reintroduced, with the country making new preparations for war and its finances in chaos as a result of speculation linked to the demonetisation of gold coinage. In fact, the fixed rate was not rescinded until 1928!

Wars, revolutions, crises and periods of fixed exchange rates produced a variety of apparently contradictory side effects. There was a loss of confidence in the banknote, but, paradoxically, their circulation – and even their use – increased. In fact, as soon as a fixed rate was declared, people hoarded specie. When that ran out, banks were forced to issue notes at a reduced face value to keep the wheels of the economy turning. And in these exceptional circumstances, new strata of the population became accustomed to handling paper. This had already been the case in England in 1797: when the fixed rate was announced, the Bank of England was authorised to issue denominations of £1 and £2 as long as convertibilty was suspended. In 1848, in the middle of another fixed-rate period, the Banque de France circulated 100-franc notes and, during the 1870 war, it issued the first 25-franc denomination.

There is general agreement that, globally, it was in the last quarter of the nineteenth century that the bank-

100-mark Reichsbank note, 1883, reverse, by Paul Thurmann (1834–1908), 160 x 102 mm (6.30 x 4.02 in.). DBB.
This issue was nicknamed 'the blue' to distinguish it from the 1,000-mark denomination, 'the brown'. Until 1906, the Reichsbank was forbidden to issue notes with a value of less than 100 marks.

Utopia: the universal banknote

In the nineteenth century, Utopians were already dreaming of a universally acceptable form of paper money. In 1876, two Belgian businessmen, Van Geetruyen and Jourdain, set up a study group with the aim of establishing a bank in Brussels that would issue notes for international circulation. The standard for this bank money of account would be a kilogram of pure gold or silver. The promoters of what they called the 'Banque internationale' hoped that such notes would limit the transfer of specie and even level out exchange and bank rates. The project received support from a few financiers, but aroused the distrust of the Banque nationale de Belgique, which considered that it flew in the face of its exclusive rights. Further, were these really banknotes, or merely warrants backed by silver or gold? The idea was buried rapidly and without ceremony by the Belgian finance minister Jules Malou.

note really took off. The total of notes in circulation in the German Reich tripled between 1876 and 1913. Over the identical period, it multiplied by a factor of 2.2 in France and two in the Netherlands. In Spain, the substantial increase in circulation coincided with a national monopoly on issue granted to the Banco de España in 1874: in fifteen years, banknote circulation increased tenfold, rising from 80 to 700 million pesetas by 1888, to 1,500 million in 1900 and 4,000 million in 1920. Belgium was remarkable for a relatively high circulation of notes from the end of the nineteenth century: the establishment of the note as legal tender in 1873, the issuing of small-denomination bills and the rarity of counterfeiting encouraged the use of paper. From 1870 to 1914, the share of notes in the gross domestic product rose from 4 to 12 per cent. In Germany, even if paper money only played a secondary role as a method of payment, and although metallic coinage still represented some 60 per cent of the global monetary circulation in 1914, the adoption of 20- and 50-mark denominations from 1906 did much to popularise notes. Until then, private individuals still employed gold coinage, but afterwards the note became the most popular monetary instrument, being employed for the majority of important payments not better settled through clearing operations. The hoarding of gold and silver became more pronounced, though in France gold coinage continued to circulate until the eve of the First World War.

The outbreak of hostilities in 1914 was the decisive factor in the undeniable triumph of the banknote. Everywhere, people hoarded their specie. Issuing banks had to produce very small denominations: notes of 1, 2 or 5 francs in Belgium; 10 shillings and £1 in England; short-term notes of 1 or 2 lire in Italy; 1- or 2-crown notes in Austria. The war also sparked off an enormous rise in the amount of fiduciary money in use. In France, for instance, the number of notes in circulation rose from 50 million in 1914 to 653 million in 1919. In Italy, the Banca d'Italia's issue ceiling had been fixed at 660 million lire in 1910, but by 1919 the total of notes in circulation amounted to 12,700 million lire! In Germany, the circulation of bills and notes had multiplied tenfold. And in Belgium, notes in circulation doubled their share of the gross domestic product. With gold and silver too rare to continue in use, states ceased to mint coinage in precious metals.

20-franc note, Banque de France, 1873, obverse, by Camille Chazal (1826–75), 151 x 99 mm (5.94 x 3.90 in.). BF. This, the first two-colour French note, was to have replaced a monochrome bill of the same denomination issued in 1871; in the end, the Bank abandoned it in favour of a coin.

Gold, by Pierre Falké (1884–1947), published in *La Charette*. BNB. 'Banknotes are for those who can read'. Even in the 1930s, many private individuals had little faith in banknotes and preferred to hoard specie.

21
PAPER INTO MONEY

— Les billets, c'est bon pour ceux qui savent lire...

This late eighteenth-century caricature shows Prime Minister William Pitt as Midas, transforming everything he touches into paper (money). BE.
Here we have a denunciation of the fixed rate of exchange imposed by the British government on Bank of England notes as a means of financing the war against France.

THE TRIUMPH OF THE BANKNOTE

Was the banknote a form of currency? The answer may be obvious today, but this was not the case in the nineteenth century. Originally, the banknote was, so to speak, a matter of private law: an acknowledgement of debt made by the bank to the bearer of a bill guaranteed genuine by various authentication marks. A gradual evolution saw the notes issued by certain privileged banks become a recognised and legal means of payment, and finally a form of currency proper, non-convertible, save into other forms of fiat currency.

In the statutes of numerous privileged banks founded in the first half of the nineteenth century with government aid or support, it was stipulated that their banknotes would be accepted in payment by the treasury to pay income tax, for instance. This measure was designed to popularise their circulation, giving them a kind of official guarantee. The Nederlandsche Bank, the Banco de Lisboa, the Société générale des Pays-Bas, for example, were granted this privilege on their foundation in 1814, 1821 and 1822 respectively. In addition, attempts to imitate their notes were frequently treated as forgery and punished as such. Such legal dispositions caused banknotes to fall within the scope of public law. In Luxembourg, the government was at first hesitant to guarantee banknotes issued by the Internationale Bank in Luxemburg by accepting them in payment. The administration realised that this would be equivalent to somehow associating the state with the Bank, since the coffers of the state, in times of crisis, would be inundated with notes which could not be refused, and the state would thus risk being compromised. However, the notes were accepted for income tax payments in 1859.

The recognition of banknotes as legal tender popularised them in comparison with specie. The effect was to oblige individuals to accept the notes in payment, whatever their prejudices on the subject. In Sweden, from 1745, every citizen was compelled to accept notes. The notes of the privileged banks received the status of legal tender in England in 1833; Belgium followed in 1873, France in 1875, Portugal in 1891 and the Netherlands in 1904. In several cases, the measure was adopted to prevent panic. The explanatory clauses of the 1873 Belgian legislation cite the interests of both the state and individuals: 'When, sometimes without a serious reason, panic breaks out amongst note-holders, a large number of people are anxious to exchange their notes for specie in order to make sure they can meet payments that are due and through fear that notes will be refused. Imposing legal tender is thus a means of forestalling these crises, or at least of reducing their gravity'. In 1906, the Reichsbank was authorised to issue 20- and 50-mark notes with the force of legal tender. This was in line with the Reichsbank's policy of hoarding gold – a policy pursued since the Moroccan crisis of the year before, when the international situation was steadily deteriorating and there were preparations for war.

MUTUAL ACCOMMODATION.

MADAME LA BANQUE AND THE OLD LADY OF THREADNEEDLE STREET.

*The Bank of England, by relieving the Bank of France of its surplus silver, afforded great relief to the latter establishment.—December, 1860.

In the 1800s, England had adopted the gold standard, while France opted for bimetallism (silver and gold). In this cartoon, English and French issuing banks are exchanging stocks of precious metals to balance their respective reserves. BNB.

The status of legal tender was extended to all Reichsbank notes in 1909.

But the most fundamental and crucial debate surrounding the banknote concerned its convertibility. Despite the numerous periods of fixed rates described above, it is safe to say that globally, until 1914, unrestricted convertibility of notes was a doctrine accepted almost universally. The bitter experiences of Europeans had, in the main, left them allergic to paper money. However, it soon became clear that notes issued by private banks were no less vulnerable to the results of bankruptcies, as institutions printed money all too freely. From this arose the idea of limiting issues. In England, with the Peel Act of 1844, the principle emerged that the banknote was more or less a form of coinage and that henceforth every issue should be covered by a corresponding reserve of gold. By its nature, this legislation set a limit on the circulation of notes, even if, in cases of emergency, the government could authorise extra issues. In France, by contrast, the issuing rights of the Banque de France were limited not by its specie reserves but by a legally imposed ceiling, fixed originally at 12 million francs, but gradually raised in accordance with economic activity. In practical terms, however, its metal reserves covered only a proportion of banknote issues, with this ratio slipping throughout the nineteenth century from three-quarters to roughly one-third. Similarly, on the creation of other European issuing banks, a straightforward ceiling was imposed. Often, account was taken of the bank's own funds. Repeatedly, in various states, banking crises forced the authorities to either raise or lower the limit.

In 1847, the Preussische Bank adopted the innovative measure of imposing a legally enforceable ratio between metallic reserves and the circulation of paper money, with the former to be immediately available for reimbursement on demand. The Bank was obliged to hold 33 per cent cover for its notes in precious metals or metallic coinage. This principle of a proportional reserve was adopted from 1850 by the Banque nationale de Belgique and copied afterwards by other European nations. Yet it was not until 1928 and 1946 respectively that French and Portuguese legislation abandoned the concept of a flat limit on fiduciary circulation in favour of proportionality.

At the end of the nineteenth century, a clique of radical economists, supporters of increased state control,

Handling gold stocks at the Banque nationale de Belgique between the wars. BNB.
The convertibility of banknotes was suspended everywhere in the 1930s: it was never to be reintroduced.

100-pesetas note, Banco de España, 1946, obverse, 130 x 78 mm (5.12 x 3.07 in.). BEsp.
The inscription 'payable to the bearer' which appeared on certain notes after the Second World War implied that they were still convertible into gold. The reality was quite different.

Visit of the Federal German Chancellor Helmut Kohl to the Deutsche Bundesbank, July 1988. DBB. Nowadays, the reserves of central banks no longer consist entirely of gold, but also of foreign currencies.

suggested that convertibility should be either abandoned or reduced. They argued that as a 'bond issued by the state with the backing of the nation's wealth', currency had no need of another guarantee and could be deprived of any intrinsic value. The First World War and the proclamation of a fixed rate would partially justify their reasoning. Convertibility was suspended on 31 July 1914 in Germany, 3 August in Belgium, 4 August in Luxembourg and 5 August in France. Only a temporary suspension was envisaged, but, in actual fact, internal convertibility was never re-established despite the Herculean efforts of the authorities to bring about a return to normality in the 1920s.

After the First World War, the foremost problem was inflation, and most countries were forced to introduce savage devaluations in the mid 1920s. Having sacrificed part of their currency's value, European states began to think about re-establishing convertibility. It was a laborious task. From 1922, it was agreed that the reserves of issuing banks could consist of either gold or convertible coinage: a system known as the Gold Exchange Standard. In 1924, the gold value of the mark was laid down. The following year, Great Britain announced a return to gold convertibility. But this was convertibility on a relative scale: the Bank of England was no longer obliged to exchange its notes for coins; it promised only to sell gold at the fixed price of £3.17 shillings per ounce, and by ingots of 400 ounces. It goes without saying that many banks were unable to offer convertibility. In the same year, the Italian lira was tied to the pound sterling. In December 1926, the Banque de France declared itself ready to exchange its notes against foreign currencies which were themselves convertible into gold: American dollars and pounds sterling. A fixed relationship was thus re-established with gold. Then, in June 1928, direct convertibility of French notes into gold was reintroduced, but only at the head office of the Banque de France and if the notes presented amounted to the equivalent of 12 kilos of gold. In Greece, the gold value of the drachma was fixed in 1928. These rather theoretical attempts at re-establishing gold convertibility had at least the advantage of making one currency convertible against another at fixed rates.

The Depression of the 1930s wiped out all the effort lavished on maintaining convertibility. Already highly compromised, it was 'provisionally' suspended in Great Britain, Finland and Greece in 1931 and in 1936 in France; it was never reintroduced. The 1930s were, as a result, a time of great interest in the banknote, especially during the banking crisis at the start of the era, then again in 1938 when the imminence of a new global conflict encouraged people to empty their current and savings accounts and keep their moneys to hand. After the Second World War, each European country instigated vast operations of demonetisation and exchange of notes in circulation. There was hardly any question of returning to convertibility. In 1958, on the dissolution of the European Payments Union, external convertibility of currency was re-established. One of the major obstacles to free trade had now disappeared. But it was becoming ever more clear that gold was of little further use as a standard in the way it had been in the previous century. Henceforth, the benchmark would be the dollar. Granted, the Bretton Woods Agreements (1944) had suggested a fixed relationship between gold and the various national currencies. But following strident alarms over inflation, this system of stable parities at first had to be re-engineered, and then, in the seventies, fell apart after the Americans themselves renounced it. Little by little, all references to gold were removed from legal definitions of currencies. The glittering mirage had finally faded.

Mirrors of the Nations

THE BANKERS' PANTHEON

In every country, the design of banknotes was at first sober – not to say severe. In the eighteenth century, most banks of issue contented themselves with elements necessary to authenticate the note, showing little interest in decorative features except perhaps a frame composed of palms and cable-twist.

From 1697, however, the Bank of England included a medallion featuring Britannia, its emblem. The use of figurative designs was adopted during the 1700s by other English banks to distinguish their issues from those of rivals. Several created a monogram from the interlaced initials of their partners. The Southampton Commercial Bank chose a boat as its emblem, the Great Yarmouth Bank a coat of arms, while the Shepton Mallet and Somersetshire opted for a sheep. The engravings were simple enough, with a few exceptions like the panorama of the city of Nottingham which appeared on a 1746 note belonging to the bank of Abel Smith & Co. In Spain before 1847 and Belgium before 1851, in the Netherlands until 1860 and in Finland up to 1863, decoration was limited to a framework with the occasional degree of sophistication and a few little *culs de lampe* or cornucopias. Banks paid little attention to format, focusing their attention on the wording and authentication marks. But soon it became evident that the paucity of illustration was a gift to counterfeiters. At the end of the eighteenth century, more complex decoration was introduced on France's *assignats* and early banknotes, as well as on notes issued in Piedmont. It is on these that we first glimpse the principle of incorporating figurative elements into an overall design, as opposed to a mere juxtaposition of features fulfilling legal requirements. The notes of the Banque de France released in 1800 and 1806 were indisputably aesthetic successes, and the decoration was enriched with identifiable elements such as mythological personages or symbolic animals. The following issues not only set the banknote on the road to becoming a work of art, but also turned it into a national symbol. Gradually, in France and elsewhere, banknotes became more eloquent; no longer mere monetary ciphers, they were mirrors of the nations that issued them.

Where more complex designs developed, the note frequently featured deities from the Greco-Roman pantheon. Most often pressed into service were Mercury and the goddesses Ceres, Minerva and Fortune. The presence of Mercury (Hermes) god of commerce (and thieves!), recognisable by his winged sandals (*talaria*), *petasus* or travelling-hat (often also with wings), and wand (*caduceus*), reminds us that in the nineteenth century banknotes were primarily targeted at the commercial classes. Mercury figures on countless issues, from Spain to Sweden, and, above all, his caduceus is ubiquitous. Is there a link between the banknote and alchemy? Hermes, the god of trade, had also been the alchemists' guide to spiritual research. His Roman equivalent, Mercury, was identified with the element fundamental to all transformations. One of the major themes of alchemy is the changing of base metals into gold. What could be baser than paper? By including Hermes on the note, the designer was reminding users how, by a subtle form of alchemy, paper money

1,000-franc note, Banque de France, Germinal (1806), by Charles Percier (1764–1838), 250 x 130 mm (9.84 x 5.12 in.). BF.
In the Latin countries, many nineteenth-century notes were printed with counterfoils or stubs. The counterfoil was detached and remained with the issuing bank, thus allowing eventual authentication of the note by a comparison of the dates of issue and serial numbers on the two parts. The halves were separated along a marked and more or less regular pattern; users could then tell by the shapes of the edges whether they had two halves of the same note. Some Italian issues, even after the First World War, perpetuated a system that owed its origins to the medieval 'charter-party'.

could be transformed – on demand – into gold.

Numerous notes bore likenesses of Ceres (Demeter), the mother goddess, guardian of the harvest and agriculture, understandable at a time when the European economy was, to a vital extent, based on farming. Ceres is found on German, Belgian, Finnish, French and Italian issues. Athene (Minerva), patroness of the arts, sciences and industry – and, paradoxically, of war – was also the personification of wisdom. She is one of the most frequently encountered figures on European notes of the nineteenth century, recognisable by her helmet, her shield with its owl-emblem, and the Aegis (with its Gorgon's head) on her breast. We find her on the notes of France (1806), Prussia (1835), Austria (1848), Spain (1866) and Belgium (1869). Greece, quite naturally, had an interest in Athene, who recurs ceaselessly on various denominations of the country's paper money after 1841. Here, the 'grey-eyed goddess' has become, so to speak, the personification of the state, just as she was for Athens in the age of Pericles.

Fortune appears on some nineteenth-century notes. Her attributes are, according to circumstances, the rudder or prow of a ship, ears of corn, a caduceus or a wheel. And her eyes are covered; we all know Fortune is blind! The cornucopia, an attribute she shares with Ceres, deserves particular mention, being probably the most hackneyed of symbols, the last resort of issuers lost for inspiration. For the Ancients, the cornucopia possessed a very precise meaning: it symbolised the inexhaustible riches on offer to Man without him even earning them. The 1,000-franc notes issued in 1806 by the Banque de France portrayed Minerva helmeted and bearing a shield in company with Fortune. This was the pictorial translation of the bank's motto: *La Sagesse fixe la Fortune*, or 'Wisdom establisheth Fortune'. The founders had in mind all the excesses which had disfigured the financial policies of the infant Republic. Eager to distance themselves from these and reassure users of notes, they appealed to the wisest of divinities. The French 100-franc note of 1888 shows a fickle-looking Fortune and a helmeted Minerva attempting to hold her back. This interpretation is based on the classical etymology of the word *fortune*: hazard, luck, chance. Fortune, for the Ancients, was the incarnation of ephemeral happiness. Because of the arbitrary manner in which she dealt with men, she could hardly be considered as a virtue.

Other deities were invoked to sustain faith in banknotes, though less frequently. Vulcan, for example, the god of fire and craftsmanship, patron of minters, appeared on a few examples, like the 1799 issue of France's Caisse des comptes courants, or on a Finnish note of 1882. For Sylvie Peiret, 'the probable intention was to recall the powerful link still existing at the time between the banknote and precious metals'. Hercules, the civilising hero and symbol of strength and duty done, figures on denominations of the Banco de Cadiz from 1840–50; he is forcing apart two columns, the mountainous capes bordering the Straits of Gibraltar (where the city of Cádiz was built), from ancient times nicknamed the Pillars of Hercules. Apollo, god of the sun and harmony, patron of the arts, makes a notable appearance on a Belgian note of 1869: the personification of progress, he rides a chariot drawn by two winged horses towards the rising sun. Neptune (Poseidon), god of the sea, features occasionally, and his presence takes on a special significance in relation to notes of maritime cities or states, like Portugal (1840s), Le Havre (1840), Sundvall (Sweden, 1865) or the Hanseatic city of Königsberg (1866).

Apart from the gods of classical antiquity, many notes pre-dating the First World War bore not only allegorical figures, frequently female, representing various aspects of human activity (Industry, Commerce, Agriculture, Navigation, the Arts and Sciences), but also virtues to be cultivated by mankind (such as Work), the state he strives to attain (Well-being, Knowledge), or again, the fundamental qualities of a nation based on right (Law, Justice). It is perhaps astonishing to find Science and Art on an

Pediment of the Banque de France, sculpted in 1870 by Albert Ernest Carrier-Belleuse (1824–87), featuring Minerva (personifying Wisdom), and the goddess Fortune, with her eyes blindfolded. BF.
The same divinities also appear on the 1,000-franc notes released in 1806 by the Bank, whose motto was 'Wisdom establisheth Fortune'.

Preliminary design for a 50-franc note of the Banque nationale de Belgique, 1909, by Constant Montald (1862–1944). Watercolour and Indian ink on paper, 350 x 230 mm (13.78 x 9.06 in.). BNB. Allegory was a common feature in the design of pre-First World War notes; here the themes are the arts, sciences and commerce.

equal footing with Commerce, Industry and Agriculture; however, all share in the same basic myth of Western society: progress. The allegorical personages, wearing classical costume, can be identified by their attributes, the objects that they carry or which accompany them. Ships' profiles, barrels, roped bundles or the caduceus signify Commerce. Agriculture is surrounded by sheaves of corn, fruits, hoes and carts. Cogwheels and anvils represent Industry. Science holds a mirror, a torch and a book.

The primary task of banknote design was to inspire confidence, so that we frequently come across symbols of permanence and durability. Among such is the anchor, an explicit reference to the maritime activities and commercial vocation of certain towns or countries, but also to the stability of the issuing banks. The hive which is found on notes of almost all European countries is the symbol of order – bees operate a strict hierarchical system – and zeal for work. Quite a number of notes, even recently, have featured towers or lighthouses, associated with confidence and strength: towers withstand sieges, the lighthouse pierces the darkness and beats back the attacking waves just as banks must resist economic storms. The open eye symbol (Portugal, 1830; Spain, 1847) denotes vigilance – that of the bank of issue on the lookout for possible counterfeiters, a theme already found on certain French *assignats* in proximity to warnings to anyone contemplating forgery. Doubtless the same explanation applies to occasional depictions of lamps, and, more frequently, cockerels. A cock also figures in an 1808 bas-relief on the façade of the Banque de France.

Preliminary sketch for a 500-franc note, Banque nationale de Belgique, 1887, by Henri Hendrickx (1817–94), watercolour and Indian ink on cardboard, 730 x 510 mm (28.74 x 20.08 in.). BNB. Left: allegory of science and industry with different attributes – including a telegraph pole, alluding to a recent invention.

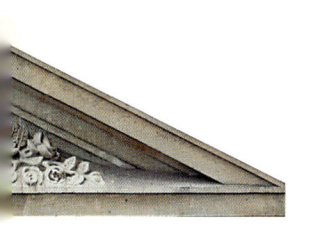

Showers of Gold

In the nineteenth century, the notes of many issuing banks depicted coins implied to be of gold or silver. The seal of the Bank of England, designed in 1694 and afterwards reproduced on its notes, showed Britannia contemplating a heap of gold. The 1759 watermark of the Sveriges Riksens Ständers Bank featured cornucopias filled with gold coins. German, Austrian, Belgian, Spanish and Portuguese banks all opted for similar images: putti minting coins, for instance, or emptying horns brimming with gold. These cascades of gold certainly exude an aura of wealth. The design was supposed to reassure the users, reminding them that, at any moment, they could exchange their notes for good, hard cash. There is also a 500-peseta Spanish note of 1903 where Mercury is scattering handfuls of gold and bundles of banknotes.
A rare case of banknotes illustrated by banknotes!

100-florin note, Privilegirte Österreichische Nationalbank, 1841, by Peter Franz Fendi (1796–1842), 222 x 122 mm (8.74 x 4.08 in.). ONB.
The depiction of coins on notes reminded users that they were convertible into specie.

50-mark issue of the Internationale Bank in Luxembourg, 1900, obverse. BIL.
The Bank opted to emphasise the duality of the Luxembourg economy, in future to be based on industry as much as agriculture.

The Industrial Revolution and Mother Earth

The nineteenth century was one of revolutions, both political and economic. Banks of issue can scarcely have appreciated the former, but a number were passionately interested in the Industrial Revolution. In Great Britain, the cradle of the movement, many banks in the first half of the century produced designs showing factories with smoking chimneys. In Belgium, a heavily industrialised nation, issues of the nineteenth century frequently featured 'panoplies' honouring progress, modernity and the cult of the machine. The 1,000-franc note of 1853 is a particularly fine example. Against a background of smoking chimneys we can make out, in a kind of studied disorder, the profile of a locomotive, cogwheels, a technical blueprint, blacksmith's tools and even a gas lamp. Such designs were intended to remind the population that the future of the country did not depend upon agriculture alone, but on a competitive industry exporting abroad. On an 1869 issue, the Banque nationale de Belgique presented a typical miner and smith standing side by side, wearing the dress of antiquity – doubtless in reference to the gods Hades and Vulcan – but provided with nineteenth-century equipment: pick, helmet with lamp and a small wagon for carting mineral ore. These two seminal industries of the nineteenth century – iron and coal – were again evoked in two Luxembourg notes of 1900. On the Iberian peninsula, little homage was paid to industry, despite the large number of notes released during the century. Two or three designs stand out, however. One, produced in the 1860s by the Banco de Bilbao, included two vignettes showing a blast furnace and a landscape bristling with chimneys. Biscay was, at the time, one of the most industrialised areas of Spain. A private bank in the Minho, a similarly advanced region in Portugal, made use of the same theme from 1870 to 1880. Some regional issues explicitly referred to local industries: the Geraer Bank (Germany) and the Norrköpings Enskilda Bank (Sweden), both in major textile centres, chose a girl working a spindle (1856 and 1877 respectively). Later, in 1903, the Banco de España issued a 100-peseta note featuring Pegasus, the winged horse of legend, in curious juxtaposition with an industrial landscape: factory chimneys and the Atocha station, Madrid. A comparison, perhaps, between the speed of the mythical horse and the power of the 'iron steed'?

The image which leaps most immediately to mind whenever the Industrial Revolution is mentioned is probably the railway: 80,000 km (50,000 miles) of track were laid in Europe between 1850 and 1870. It was logical that this key element of progress should weigh heavily with the issuing banks, especially since the railroads were often, like currency, a factor in national unity. Trains or locomotives figure on German notes of 1847 (Dessau) and 1855 (Saxony), on Belgian issues of 1853 and 1887, on the first note produced by the Reichsbank in 1876, on Portuguese notes of 1879 and

10-florin note, Nederlandsche Bank, 1904, obverse, by Nicolaas van der Waay (1855–1936), 168 x 99 mm (6.61 x 3.90 in.); and cartoon inspired by this, by Albert Hahn (1877–1918), published in *De Ware Jacob* in October 1904. DNB.

The Russian eagle vs. the Finnish lion

In 1809, after a centuries-long struggle, Finland had been swallowed up in the Russian Empire. As a Grand Duchy under the direct control of the tsar, the region still enjoyed a certain autonomy, and was allowed to print its own banknotes. From 1851 to 1887, these bore the Russian double-headed eagle, and, in much smaller format, the arms of Finland: a heraldic lion brandishing a sword and trampling the hilt and guard of a Russian sabre. In 1887, the Suomen Pankki (Bank of Finland) decided on a design where, for the first time, the national arms would appear alone, and writ large. Nonetheless, to avoid antagonising the Russians, the overtly aggressive pose of the Finnish lion was modified; its two hind feet were placed only on the blade of the Russian sabre, leaving the hilt accessible. It was not until a few years later, in 1897, that the Bank ventured to issue a series reproducing the Finnish arms in precise detail.

Details of 10-mark (1886) and 20-mark (1897) issues of the Suomen Pankki (Bank of Finland). SP.
The lion's pose, modified in 1886 to appease the Russian government, was restored to the original in 1897.

1890, on five notes of the Banco de España between 1872 and 1884 and in a Greek design of 1903.

The manufacturing revolution was accompanied by the emergence of a new figure, the industrial worker, leading to what was called the 'social question'. A Dutch note of 1904 proposed a somewhat simplistic answer to the problem. It shows Work, in the form of a powerfully built smith, and Well-being, a young girl draped in a classical tunic, stretching out their hands to each other. Between these two figures is a winged hourglass, allegory of fleeting time. Such a concept of the workers' future was evidently too idealistic for some. It was laughed to scorn by the caricaturist Albert Hahn, who published a pastiche of it in the periodical *De ware Jacob*: Work, a poor starving wretch, is begging bread from a fat and sour-tempered matron. Well-being is wagging a disdainful fan – doubtless to protect herself from the smell of this ragged worker. A Spanish note of the same year quite possibly aroused identical sentiments. It reproduced a painting by José Villegas showing a half-naked workman carrying out one of the most demanding tasks of the first Industrial Revolution – stoking a boiler.

Industrial workers and peasants were clearly perceived as belonging to two distinct social classes, but often featured side by side. This duality in society is reflected on notes issued by Austria (1863 and 1902), Italy (1878), Spain (1876 and 1884) and Luxembourg (1900). Curiously, while nineteenth-century agriculture underwent changes as fundamental as those in industry, it was portrayed on banknotes as archaic and static. The myth of Nature in all her pastoral and peaceful innocence, born in the century before, survived into the nineteenth, even the twentieth century. It was a vision that acted as a counterweight to progress and symbolised the durability of certain values. It was this myth which fostered the scenes of ploughing, sowing or threshing found, for instance, on designs in France (1817), Spain (1872) Italy (1897) and Denmark (1910), or in Portugal as late as 1928–32. Agricultural scenes also had a part to play in the logic of productivity dear to bankers: in order to harvest, it is necessary to sow (i.e. invest). And 'bread' is slang for 'cash'.

Commerce is the third pillar of the economy, along with agriculture and industry. It is sometimes represented very explicitly, as on an Italian note of 1898 that details the country's wine trade, sometimes indirectly, with pictures of ships at sea or in port. The sea is a theme found again and again on notes released by banks based in seaports like Santander, Bilbao, Danzig, Le Havre, Glasgow or Oporto.

A Political Agenda

From the beginning, paper money produced by the issuing banks, whether these enjoyed exclusive rights or not, made explicit references to their native country or city. The presence of coats of arms and heraldic beasts made this clear. In Greece, Belgium and Spain, the arms of the kingdom figured on designs from 1841, 1851 and 1856 respectively. The devices of numerous German states and cities appeared between 1870 and 1875, and the German eagle was readopted for all issues by the Reichsbank after 1876. The issue of the first notes of the Banca d'Italia was approved by ministerial decree in 1896, at the same time as the details of the arms of the Italian state which would feature compulsorily on all notes of this bank and those of southern Italy. In the Netherlands, the national arms form the principal element of a design issued from 1860 and which continued to circulate until after the First World War. They were flanked by a flag and a lion with curiously human-like features; the story is that the artist gave it the appearance of the bank's Secretary of the time, Willem Cornelis Mees!

Changes of political regime sometimes had a knock-on effect on patriotic symbolism. In 1867, the Austro-Hungarian Empire had adopted a dual structure; in recognition of this, notes released in 1900 by the Österreichisch-Ungarische Bank (formerly the Privilegirte Österreichische National bank) featured the Hungarian crown as well as the two-headed Austrian eagle. In 1910, on the installation of a republican government in Portugal, the authorities were at first content to change the crown into a REPUBLICA on the bills of what was now emphatically no longer a monarchy; on later issues, however, the royal arms were also erased and several series even bore an allegory of the Republic (a young girl wearing a Phrygian bonnet). And when Germany became a republic in 1919, the crown worn by the imperial eagle was similarly sacrificed.

Heraldic animals and coats of arms are not by any means the only references to the state and its authority to appear on banknotes. Other examples are allegorical representations of Law and Justice, traditionally portrayed with sword and scales and often with eyes blindfolded, and the *fasces*. In ancient Rome, the *fasces* borne by the lictors were the ultimate symbol of the state's power; they consisted of an executioner's axe around which a bundle of rods was bound with a red strap, symbolising the classes in society, held together by the state. This symbol was revived in modern Europe long before the Fascists took it over: it appears on certain French *assignats*, on Austrian notes of 1848 and 1858, on an issue of the Hannoversche Bank (1857) and on the 1,000-florin bills issued by the Nederlandsche Bank in 1921.

In the nineteenth century, it was rare for portraits of monarchs to appear on banknotes. This was probably because, unlike the minting of coins, banknote issue was then a private affair. There were few exceptions. In 1876, the Banco de Portugal used the portrait of the reigning king (Luis I) on a bill that remained in circulation for only a few months. In Germany, Emperor Wilhelm II was the model for the watermark of the Reichsbank's 1908 100-mark issues. For much of the century, some private banks in England portrayed Queen Victoria. And in 1881, the Banco di Napoli brought out a 100-lire note showing Victor Emmanuel II – but posthumously, since he had died a few years before. Several sovereigns did, though, appear on notes issued by states, as in Saxony (1855), Austria-Hungary (1880s) or Italy (1878–1944).

In place of the sovereign's portrait, all the European issuing banks used designs featuring a personification of the mother country – a motif which, like coats of arms and heraldic beasts, was borrowed from coinage. From 1864, English notes carried a picture of Britannia. She had already appeared on coins, armed with a trident – alluding to the importance of the sea in the nation's development. The Britannia selected for the Bank of England was, however, armed with a lance and an olive branch, emblem of probity. Redesigned on several occasions, she would remain the sole figurative element on Bank of England notes until 1957. In 1729, the Sveriges Riksens Ständers Bank stamped its issues with a seal, the principal figure, in a medallion, being Svea, the mother country, in the form normally found on coinage. Hibernia was featured on the first notes of the Bank of Ireland in 1783. She is seen seated with a Celtic harp, the traditional emblem of the green land of Erin. On several notes produced by private British establishments in the nineteenth century we find Hibernia side by side with Scotia and Britannia: an obvious political and economic message. In Portugal, the seal of the Banco de Lisboa – the emblem designed for the Bank in 1822 by Domingos Antonio de Sequeira

25-florin note, Nederlandsche Bank, 1860, by Johannes Hendericus Morriën (1819–78), 220 x 105 mm (8.66 x 4.13 in.). DNB. One of a series known as *reliëfrand*, this issue gave pride of place to the arms of the Netherlands.

20,000-real note, Banco de Portugal, 1876, obverse, 189 x 189 mm (7.44 x 7.44 in.). BP. This was the first time a bank portrayed a living person on a note: the sovereign, Dom Luis I.

1,000-franc note, Banque nationale de Belgique, 1919, obverse, by Jean-François Freund and Guillaume Minguet, 223 x 135 mm (8.78 x 5.31 in.). BNB.
Following the First World War, an upsurge of patriotic sentiment in Belgium resulted in the issue of the so-called 'nationalist' series bearing profiles of the reigning monarchs.

and printed on every note issued – featured a female allegory of the country, her arm extended, with the sea in the background and a boat set against a rising sun.

The way the mother country was presented received a radical shake-up when, on the initiative of Franz von Salzmann, Chief Accountant at the Privilegirte Österreichische Nationalbank, Austria introduced the 'spirit of the nation' on a note of 1841. The Bank chose to show Austria as a smiling young woman, her head profiled in a medallion. Returning to a more bellicose style, the Nederlandsche Bank issued notes in 1860 with a helmeted personification of the country: a *Nederlandsche maagd* or Dutch maiden, whom the designer of the medallion, the German Heinrich Nüsser, described as 'a woman with blond hair and Nordic features'. Here too, the Nederlandsche Bank was merely harking back to the sixteenth- and seventeenth-century custom of decorating coins with an armed woman symbolic of the Republic's independence. Sixty years later, on the circulation of a note by artist Nicolaas van der Waay showing the Netherlands as a young dreamy-looking female, some people were so put out that they referred to her as 'a trollop in a nightgown'.

Further, we find representations of Hispania (notes of the Banco de España between 1856 and 1876), Belgica (1856 and 1869) and Finlandia (1863). In Italy, Italia appears on the first notes of the Banca Nazionale nel Regno d'Italia, in 1866, as the head of a woman wearing a mural crown. From 1893, a seal was added to all notes by the authorities; it showed Italy in profile, facing towards the left and crowned with a diadem. In France, it was as the Prussian forces were marching on Paris (1870) that a designer first personified the country in the form of a young woman.

In Germany, even before the unification of the Reich, it was customary to personify towns and states with allegorical figures on commercial papers or notes issued by the authorities and private banks. Between 1849, when a commercial paper was released with a portrait of Badenia, emblem of the Grand Duchy of Baden, and 1875, the year of the creation of the Reichsbank, female allegories appeared in turn in the Grand Duchy of Saxe-Weimar (1854), the city of Frankfurt (1855), Danzig (1857), the Grand Duchy of Posen (1857), the Grand Duchy of Hesse (1865), Bavaria (1866), Darmstadt and Bremen (both 1870). The Reichsbank followed suit: by 1891, Germania was already in evidence on the 100-mark issue. On the so-called deposit certificates issued in the 1870s by the Banco Italo-Germanica, an institution with German funding which aimed to shift capital from the Reich to Italy, Germania and Italia are shown shaking hands.

Central banks exercising nationwide monopolies on issue rarely include local or regional material on their notes. In Belgium, tension rose during the nineteenth century as a result of demands for recognition of the Dutch language of Flanders in the administration, political life, the judiciary and higher education. For a long while the French-speaking

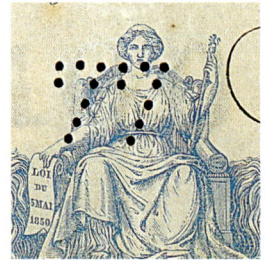

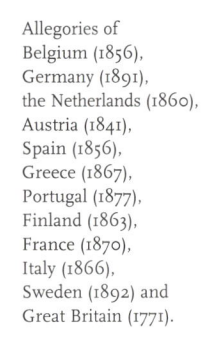

Allegories of Belgium (1856), Germany (1891), the Netherlands (1860), Austria (1841), Spain (1856), Greece (1867), Portugal (1877), Finland (1863), France (1870), Italy (1866), Sweden (1892) and Great Britain (1771).

intelligentsia ignored the problem. It was only in 1887 that a note was printed for the first time in both French and Dutch. Two Belgian notes (1852 and 1887) displayed the arms of the nine provinces, and a third (1894) the armorials of thirty-nine Belgian towns on the reverse; no one, however, dared to tackle the split between Flanders and Wallonia. When, at the beginning of the 1930s, the Fleming Étienne Vloors produced a preliminary sketch for a banknote showing the Walloon cockerel squaring up to the lion of Flanders, he was forced to alter his design and remove these over-explicit allusions to what was becoming a serious problem. The producers of the so-called 'national' notes issued from 1921 to 1922 succeeded in finding a fair compromise between the various areas of the kingdom; they devoted the 100-franc note to the arms manufactories in Liège, the 20-franc issue to Brussels' Grand-Place and the 100-franc denomination to the Flemish lace industry.

But it was undeniably in the Austro-Hungarian Empire that regional tensions were felt most strongly during the nineteenth century. In 1850, the Empire included populations speaking Polish, German, Serbian, Czechoslovakian, Ukrainian, Italian, Slovenian, Croatian, Hungarian and Romanian. The Austrian defeat at Sadowa (1866) destabilised the Empire and allowed the Hungarian population to press its claims for increased autonomy. In February 1867, the *Ausgleich* (compromise) between Austria and Hungary granted the Hungarians control over internal affairs in the eastern half of the Empire. Austria and Hungary retained nothing in common except their diplomats, their army – and their banknotes. The union of the two crowns was enshrined in the person of the emperor, Franz Joseph I. The Empire's dual structure was

20-mark denomination of the Suomen Pankki, 1897, obverse, 144 x 89 mm (5.67 x 3.50 in.). SP; and photograph by Daniel Nyblin of the Helsinki Monument to Tsar Alexander II (1894), sculpted by Walter Runeberg (1838–1920). National Museum of Finland, Helsinki.
Finnish issues of 1897 reproduced details of the monument – here, the allegory of Knowledge. By insisting on the role of Alexander as protector of Finland, the Suomen Pankki was sending out a discreet but clear signal to his descendant Nicholas II to respect the autonomy granted to Finland in 1809.

Preliminary design for a 100-franc or 20-belga note of the Banque nationale de Belgique, 1933, by Emile Vloors (1871–1952), 380 x 230 mm (14.96 x 9.06 in.). BNB. The allegorical treatment of the rivers Escaut and Meuse and the Albert Canal appeared in the final version, but not the Walloon cockerel or the Flemish lion in the medallion.

translated into pictorial form on the notes of the Österreichisch-Ungarische Bank, formerly the Privilegirte Österreichische Nationalbank. From 1881 to 1918, they virtually all included two young women symbolising the dual Austro-Hungarian monarchy. In fact, the designs of the two nations' notes were identical, save that one was printed in German and the other in Hungarian. At the time of the first printing, in 1881, no thought had been given to the other ethnic minorities, with the result that the new 10-florin notes had to be overwritten by hand with extra wording in Czechoslovakian. From 1900, the value of notes was expressed in ten different languages!

Curiously enough, the appearance of rivers on banknotes often conceals a political motive. It is a frequent theme: allegorical representations of the Danube are found on an Austrian note of 1841, of the rivers Tagus and Douro on issues of the Banco de Lisboa (1840s) and in Belgium of the Meuse and the Escaut (1851, 1869, 1887 and 1933). The Danube symbolised the unity of the Austro-Hungarian Empire. The Meuse and the Escaut were instances of political correctness, being euphemistic references to Belgium's two linguistic regions. And in Portugal, it was important to emphasise that the Banco de Lisboa was the bank of all Portugal, as it had a rival based at Oporto on the mouth of the Douro.

The First World War caused an abrupt transition in the story of the banknote. During the conflict, a number of banks of issue produced new types of low-value notes whose designs related to the harsh realities of the moment. Several countries, including France and Italy, circulated notes with Minerva no longer figuring as goddess of wisdom but of war. In France, one issue used a helmeted Marianne (the female personification of the country), another the Chevalier Bayard; the latter was no accidental choice, for this knight *sans peur et sans reproche* had fought at the beginning of the sixteenth century during the war between France and the House of Austria. Portugal, drawn into the struggle through its alliance with Great Britain, brought out a note with a portrait of Alfonso de Albuquerque, a fifteenth-century warrior nicknamed the 'Portuguese Mars'. In Germany, a commercial paper of February 1918 offered a Teutonic knight in full armour; in Britain it was St George slaying the dragon. The reverses of these various notes honoured men and women at work on the home front and contributing to the war effort: in France, a docker, a peasant woman and a reaper; in Italy, a ploughman guiding his team; in Germany, a worker rolling up his sleeves, symbolising his readiness to 'do his bit'.

After the war, there was a heightened expression of national sentiment all over Europe, though with different degrees of intensity. In several kingdoms, the population united in solidarity around the monarch. In Belgium, the portrait of the royal couple figured on a series of notes released in 1921–22. Innovative it was, and by design. At the time, Belgium was renouncing its neutrality, clamouring to increase its territory and sharing with France in the military occupation of the Ruhr basin. The Belgian banknotes presented the sovereigns in a rigid pose; this was in no way considered a problem. Josse Allard wrote on the subject to the governor of the Banque nationale: 'The sovereign's por-

50-crown note, Österreichisch-Ungarische Bank, 1902, by Rudolf Rüssler (1864–1954), 150 x 100 mm (5.91 x 3.94 in.). ONB.
Reflecting the dual Austro-Hungarian monarchy, the note shows two women. One face shows the Austrian eagle, the other St Stephen's Crown. The denomination is expressed in the Empire's eight languages. Since the technicalities of printing both sides in intaglio had not yet been mastered, the Bank used a process known as heliogravure, which allowed both kingdoms to be treated equally, even as regards the printing.

100-mark note, Reichsbank, 1908, reverse, by Friedrich Wanderer (1840–1910), 207 x 102 mm (8.15 x 4.02 in.). DBB.
The eye is drawn to the impressive flotilla of battlecruisers steaming across the horizon – Admiral von Tirpitz's legacy to the German Reich, making it the second largest naval power in the world.

20-franc note, Banque de France, 1916, obverse, by Georges Duval. 160 x 95 mm (6.29 x 3.74 in.). BF.
It bears the portrait of the Chevalier Bayard, champion of France in the struggle against the House of Austria in the sixteenth century.

Detail of 20-mark Reichsbank note, 1915, reverse, by Arthur Kampf (1846–1950), 140 x 90 mm (5.51 x 3.54 in.). DBB. Banknotes issued in wartime often emphasise the virtue of work.

Detail from £1-note issued by the Currency Commission of the Irish Free State, 1928, obverse, by John Harrison. 151 x 84 mm (5.94 x 3.31 in.). CBI.
Head of Lady Hazel Lavery, in traditional Irish costume. The higher values in the series featured a young woman leaning against a harp.

trait must be given a hieratic quality. Little by little, it becomes a sacred image. Sometimes it can depart from nature to a noticeable extent: this does not matter, for it only needs to fulfil the public's expectation of what, conventionally, it should look like.' In Spain, another first – a note was issued in 1927 showing King Alfonso XIII. Finally, in the Netherlands, under pressure from a section of public opinion, the board of the Nederlandsche Bank drew up plans in 1935 for a note featuring the late queen mother Emma (1858–1934). The project finally came to fruition in 1940.

The inter-war period was one of rapid political change. Two countries, Finland and Eire, obtained their independence, the former in 1918 after a few months of civil war, the latter in 1921 following an open struggle lasting years. In Finland, a new series of notes was rapidly put into circulation, minus the two-headed imperial Russian eagle. Eire brought out its first series of notes in 1928 through the Currency Commission of the Irish Free State. Printed in English and Gaelic, they were a tangible celebration of recently won independence. The design included a girl in traditional costume, the archetypal Irish maiden, her elbow resting on a harp, with a hillside for background. On the reverse were a series of heads symbolising native rivers. The Bank of Ireland continued with the design until the 1980s. Note that the words 'Republic of Ireland' did not appear on the note, as this would have been a tacit admission of the island's partition between the State of Eire and the North.

There now sprang up a succession of authoritarian and ultra-nationalist regimes: Fascism in Italy (1922), National Socialism in Germany (1933), while Franco was seizing power in Spain from 1936 to 1939. In Italy, the party emblem – the *fasces* – featured on all notes after 1926, but in Germany the first swastika is not found until ten years later. These details aside, the designs of notes were not modified: in financial matters, the German and Italian dictators displayed liberal and orthodox views in perfect harmony – at least in peacetime – with those of the issuing banks. The management of the Reichsbank, in particular, unwilling to countenance a return to the inflationist policies of 1914–24, successfully maintained the impression of a perfect continuity in monetary politics.

In France, the government was apparently preoccupied with restoring the old order of things, that is, the pre-war situation. After the wartime interruption with its 'realist' designs, there was a mass return to allegorical and mythological figures. Indeed, some notes released in the 1920s and 1930s had been designed before the 1914 conflict. Among the issues with political content, two are noteworthy: one dedicated to 'Victory' (1934), and the other to 'Peace' (1939). There was, it is true, still reason to believe in peace when the designs were being drawn up. During the Second World War, the theme of France at work resurfaced: notes focused on miners, fishermen, farmers and shepherds, with women in traditional costumes on the reverse. The policy of the Vichy regime, as we know, was rooted immovably in conservatism.

100-franc note, Banque de France, 1945, reverse, by Robert Poughéon, 130 x 85 mm (5.12 x 3.35 in.). BF. This note, issued in 1947, features the sort of realist design predominant during the war and celebrates conservative virtues: work and the family.

5-Reichsmark note, Reichsbank, 1942, obverse, by J. Seger. 140 x 70 mm (5.51 x 2.76 in.). DBB. Features the head of a young man with a haughty and somewhat hypnotic gaze – supposedly the archetypal Aryan.

In Search of a Cultural Identity

From the nineteenth century, figures typifying the national character began to appear on notes. In Finland, for instance, two issues of 1863 featured the heads and shoulders of young people: a student, a boy taking off his hat, a teenage girl with a handkerchief – an evident homage to the youthful vitality of the Finns. Other countries set out to discover the faces of their peoples. Spanish notes of the 1870s showing sailors or farmers obviously had an economic message, but there were also genre scenes which added up to a social panorama of the age.

Exploiting a country's folklore is a backdoor form of nationalism. In 1888 and 1939, the National Bank of Greece produced notes illustrated with young Greeks in traditional costume. The reverse of a 1933 Austrian issue also has a girl in national dress. The Nederlandsche Bank's 10-florin note of 1926 carried the portrait of a peasant woman from Zeeland; the picture was posed by a clerk in the Bank's Middelburg branch who donned a costume unearthed in a folklore museum. A section of the press criticised the note on the grounds that it would reinforce the popular misconception abroad of a country still living in clogs. The public did not react to its use of folklore, but they were shocked by its lack of artistic value and its trivial symbolism. It became landed with the nickname *kop en schotel*, or 'head on a plate', because of the peasant's imposing headgear.

If folklore can be considered a romantic evocation of the mother country, then the same applies to landscape studies. A Finnish note of 1877, for example, has a fine picture of the Great North: in the four corners are animals typical of the region (bear, elk, swan, fish eagle), whilst the central medallion frames a northern landscape. The Finns also liked to adorn their notes with trees, considered as genuine national symbols: birch, pine and spruce appear from the 1870s. The notes designed by Eliel Saarinen in 1909 belong to this romantic tradition. If Finnish notes featured economic themes with images of fishing, stock-rearing, navigation, agriculture and industry, the sentimental style with which these were treated lent them a timeless and symbolic quality: pines or waterfalls ceased to be mere references to forest management or hydroelectric energy and became symbols of life and love of country.

For their part, the private Swedish banks exploited pagan mythology. Originally, they had followed the example of other nations and called upon the classical gods of the Mediterranean region, like Mercury and Ceres. From the 1870s, certain banks, in keeping with a renewal of interest in Scandinavian legends, unhesitatingly featured not only the gods of pre-Christian mythology, such as Odin and Thor, but also a cult centre of Swedish paganism, Gamla Uppsala, the ancient capital. In Finland, the Suomen Yhdyspankki Bank also developed designs

500-mark note, Suomen Pankki (Bank of Finland), 1877, reverse, by Ferdinand Klimsch (1812–90), 125 x 199 (7.83 x 4.92 in.). SP. A romanticised view of the Great North.

inspired by mythology (1882): one shows the forest god Tapio, with an animal skin thrown over his head, another 'the daughter of Pohjola, god of the North, spinning the gold of the stars'.

In the context of nationalism, the quest for distant and glorious roots is a concept frequently employed to mould a collective identity. Just before the First World War, Denmark used an illustration of a dolmen. In Spain, a 1938 issue reproduced the 'Dama a Elche', an antique bust rediscovered in 1897 and considered at the time as one of the finest examples of Iberian art. The same note presented a reconstruction of a Phoenician boat. In Italy, the glorious past of ancient Rome was a ready-made reservoir of inspiration for banks of issue; in the 1870s, for example, the Banca Romana's notes showed Romulus and Remus being suckled by a she-wolf. The Banca d'Italia returned to the theme during the Fascist era. In Greece too, the story of classical times had become an inseparable part of the nation's history – a kind of golden age. Since the inter-war period, the National Bank had issued more and more series recalling the splendours of the past through its most important remains: temples, statues, reliefs. The Acropolis and its various monuments were frequently given pride of place, doubtless because it was also a symbol of national unity, but we also find statues of Poseidon and Athene, or the Lion Gate at Mycenae.

Life expectancy of banknotes

The life of a banknote is intimately linked to its security: the costs involved in producing 'safe' notes are, in theory, recompensed by the fact that they will remain in circulation longer. Unfortu-nately, there are other factors to take into account; these can lead to the premature withdrawal of a note, a series or even all the paper money in circulation.

Changes in monetary units are macro-economic events that require a complete replacement of all banknotes in circulation. In Austria, the currency system was originally based on the florin, then, after the adoption of the gold standard in 1892, the crown, until that was ousted in 1924 by the schilling. Germany changed its currency unit three times in the nineteenth and twentieth centuries, Spain twice: in 1862, following the adoption of the decimal system, the real was replaced by the escudo, and in 1868 by the peseta. Denmark renewed all its notes on the adoption of the gold standard in 1875. When a republican government came to power in 1910, Portugal created the escudo in place of the real; however, notes printed in reals were not completely withdrawn from circulation until 1929. In 1958, after the third devaluation of the currency since the war, General de Gaulle decided to create a revalued French franc – known as the 'franc

50-franc or 10-belga note, Banque nationale de Belgique, 1927, obverse, by Anto Carte (1886–1954), 144 x 87 mm (5.67 x 3.43 in.). BNB. The invention of the belga, a monetary unit of account, during the efforts to stabilise finances in 1926, led the Banque nationale de Belgique to issue new notes.

45
MIRRORS OF THE NATIONS

Banknotes being exchanged in the concourse of a Paris bank, May or June 1945.
The replacement of notes above 50 francs in value was designed to neutralise the removal by the Germans of large amounts of French currency, and restore financial fortunes.

1,000-lire note, Banca d'Italia, 1897, obverse, by Rinaldo Barbetti (1830–1903), 225 x 121 mm (8.86 x 4.76 in.). BI. This denomination remained virtually unchanged for half a century, and was the work of a famous Italian sculptor and wood engraver who apparently drew his inspiration from the frescoes at Pompeii.

lourd': literally, the 'heavy franc' – in an operation designed to persuade the French that the national economy was now starting out afresh on a more solid basis. At first, notes in circulation were overprinted with the equivalent of their value in *nouveaux francs*; later fresh issues were produced in values of the new unit. In 1963, a similar measure was introduced in Finland: a new mark was created 'weighing in' at 100 old marks.

After the Second World War, the whole European system of fiduciary money was in chaos. Notes in circulation during the war passed side by side with those printed by Allied forces: Italian lire, German marks, French *francs complémentaires*, all of a very mediocre quality and easy to imitate and falsify. In 1944–5, vast operations of de-monetisation and exchange were set in train in certain countries, accompanied, for instance in Belgium and Finland, by the use of forced loans to bring money into government coffers. To accomplish these massive changes, the central banks had only a mixed bag of paper money at their disposal: reimpressions, with various degrees of modification, of notes that had circulated during the war; new series prepared during hostilities but under conditions which left much to be desired in the way of security; or reserve series, produced in the inter-war period and never yet released. It took until the 1950s for the situation to return to normal everywhere. More recently, the adaptation of notes for machines accepting or dispensing cash led to a blossoming of new series in the 1980s.

It should not be imagined that banks alter their notes for the sake of change or to avoid users becoming bored with a design. On the contrary, they have frequently had to yield to the conservatism of the general public. Certain types of note remain virtually unchanged over long periods; examples are the Bank of England's famous £5 note, the 'Svea' issues in Sweden (1890–1952), or the Italian 1,000-lire denomination that underwent little modification from 1897 to 1950. In Denmark, the 500-crown note was nicknamed 'the ploughman' since Gerhard Heilmann's 1910 design showed a man plodding behind a plough drawn by a pair of horses. At the time, the message, as might be expected, was the importance of farming to the Danish economy. In the course of time the note underwent several minor alterations, but the central design held good until 1964. Then, agriculture was no longer the only source of Denmark's revenue, and, especially, the tractor had replaced the horse. But still the public were unwilling to let their 'ploughman' go. After repeated hesitations, the Bank decided to issue a new note in homage to Christian Ditlev Reventlow, a leading figure in the agricultural reforms of the late eighteenth century. This choice allowed the designer to keep the time-honoured ploughman, who was placed side by side with the portrait of Reventlow. The new 500-crown note circulated from 1964 to 1974.

The custom of giving notes a nickname is common in the Netherlands, where each denomination has its own. The 100- and 1,000-florin denominations released between 1921 and 1924 were both known as 'Grietje Seel', after a girl who acted as the designer's model. As for Germany, new 100- and 1,000-mark issues were put into circulation at the end of 1884. They were typical pre-First World War German notes and are remembered in the country's monetary history under their popular names: the 'Blue' and the 'Brown'. They remained in circulation for almost forty years.

Portraits of the Ancestors

In the 1850s, two or three German notes appeared with portraits of historical figures. The oldest must be the 1851 designs of the small principality of Schwarzburg-Rudolstadt; in a medallion is a person identifiable as Count Albrecht VII, founder of the line of princes of Rudolstadt. Four years later, a private bank in Kassel experimented with two medallion portraits, including Johannes Gutenberg, in obvious homage to the founding father of the printing press.

Curiously, this kind of pictorial content failed to inspire any imitators in the German Confederation. When, in the 1860s, other notes appeared showing historical characters, it was no longer in Germany (at least until the inter-war era) but in the United States, Italy and Greece. On the Greek notes printed by the American Banknote Company of New York, the Greek National Bank chose to commemorate George Stavrou, chairman at the time of the Bank's founding in 1841. His portrait was to remain on all paper issued by the Bank until its restructuring in 1927! In Italy, the first series of notes produced by the Banca Nazionale nel Regno d'Italia (1866) took the audacious step of pairing Christopher Columbus with Camillo Benso, Count of Cavour. In the 1870s and 1880s, Italy's regional banks each chose an emblematical figure for their issues: the Banca Nazionale Toscana opted quite naturally for the poet Dante Alighieri, the Banca di Napoli for Cavour, Galileo, Leonardo da Vinci and Giovanni Manna.

But Spain was the first European nation to take a real interest in the great figures of its past and allot them a regular place on its banknotes. Paradoxically – and this was

50-escudo note, Banco de España, December 1871, obverse, 184 x 120 mm (7.24 x 4.72 in.). BEsp.
With its portrait of Don Gonzalo Fernandez de Cordoba, who distinguished himself by his victories against the Moors and in Italy, this is one of the first designs to celebrate the heroes of Spanish history.

100-escudo note, Banco de Portugal, 1918, obverse, by Eugene Mouchon (b. 1843), 209 x 130 mm (8.23 x 5.12 in.). BP.
From 1901, Portuguese notes tended to portray historical figures, especially the country's sovereigns, the viceroys of the Indies, and the sailors and conquistadors who made the fifteenth and sixteenth centuries a golden age for Portugal: Alfonso of Albuquerque (1453–1513), Henry the Navigator (1394–1460), Luis de Camões (1525–80) and Vasco da Gama were featured several times between 1901 and 1940.

1,000-peseta note, Banco de España, 1965, obverse, by Antonio Fernández. 146 x 91 mm (5.75 x 3.58 in.). BEsp; also fresco by Roque Meruvia showing the dictator Franco as St James, the saint and knight who delivered Spain from the Muslims. Archivo Histórico Militar, Madrid.
In Spain, relations between the Church and the Franco regime were such that several banknote designs included popular saints, here St Isidore of Seville.

A parable: the banknote that preached charity

Normally, the issuing banks steered clear of religious themes, except in Portugal and Spain, where Church and State had a long history of collaboration. There, banknotes were devoted to local saints: St Isabel of Portugal (1964) and St António of Lisbon (1965), the 'Catholic Kings' (Spain, 1958), St Isidore of Seville (1965). In the countries of northern Europe, such references are much rarer, being likely causes of dispute. In 1952, the Nederlandsche Bank issued a 25-florin note designed by Jan Sleper, showing King Solomon, and St Martin sharing his cloak. The artist, who was also working on two other designs involving St Francis of Assisi and the parable of the beggar Lazarus and the rich man, was eager to use banknotes as a means of inculcating strong moral values: altruism, charity and justice. The appearance of the note raised a hue and cry in the press – and even in parliament – with complaints about 'Romish propaganda', i.e. in favour of Catholicism. Other malcontents demanded to know why a view of the French city of Tours appeared in the background of a Dutch note? Once bitten, twice shy: the Bank dropped its plans to use Sleper's other designs. Furthermore, his 'Solomon' enjoyed only a brief life: it was replaced in 1961.

100-florin note, Nederlandsche Bank, 1950, obverse, by J.-B. Sleper. 168 x 98 mm (6.61 x 3.86 in.). DNB.
This note, depicting the parable of Lazarus, was never issued: a previous religious design by Sleper had aroused controversy.

unique in the story of the banknote – the first real-life, historical character to figure on a Spanish note (1871) was not a Spaniard, but Gutenberg. From 1871 to the First World War, the Banco de España published portraits of twenty-eight national figures: warriors, kings, politicians, churchmen, financiers, painters, sculptors, architects and writers. Most of these had lived in the sixteenth and seventeenth centuries, Spain's golden age, but the Bank did not hesitate to commemorate recently departed celebrities connected with its own history, such as Count Francisco Cabarrus (1752–1810), promoter of the Banco Nacional de San Carlos (1781) or Don Ramon de Santillan, the Banco de España's first governor in 1856. This penchant for honouring people linked with the Bank led it to take the previously unheard-of step of including a person still alive at the time of issue: in 1905, a note showed José Echegeray, winner of the 1904 Nobel Prize for literature, but also Minister of Finance in 1874 during an important reorganisation of the Bank. After the First World War, Spain returned to the great figures of the past.

In Sweden, the notes of some regional banks, between 1870 and 1893, depicted real-life persons from national history, hero-figures of the political arena. An exception was Carl Linnaeus, the famous naturalist, whose portrait illustrated an issue of the Smalands Bank.

Between the wars, several other banks of issue opened their ancestral 'portrait galleries' to commemorate the great and the good who had contributed to their success. In the 1930s, the Reichsbank circulated a series celebrating men of the arts, sciences and finance, like Siemens or Liebig, who had helped modernise Germany during the nineteenth century. A *Rentenbankschein* of the 1920s (Deutsche Rentenbank) adopted a more forthright political stance: it showed Baron vom Stein (1757–1831), a Prussian statesman, the epitome of German nationalism in the late nineteenth century and lynchpin of Prussian opposition to Napoleon. France tended to stay loyal to allegorical designs, though we glimpse the odd discreet exception, such as portraits of André Marie Ampère and Louis Pasteur (1927) and the Duc de Sully (1939). In Italy, the few profiles representing national history are to be found in the watermarks: Julius Caesar, Dante Alighieri, Leonardo da Vinci and Christopher Columbus.

From then on, the choice of historical characters occasionally caused the public to raise its eyebrows. In 1935, a Dutch journalist was wondering what had inspired the Nederlandsche Bank to include a past president, Willem Cornelis Mees, or a portrait by Rembrandt: 'Agreed, they were both eminent Dutchmen. But by what right are we circulating banknotes with the portraits of any particular person as official means of payment?' The criticism was not without its point. The choice of artist or politician is always arbitrary, and a section of the population may profoundly disagree with it. For the article's author, only one choice would be unanimous: the portrait of the sovereign.

The policy of featuring an artist in association with his

500-franc note, Banque de France, 1959, obverse, by Jean Lefeuvre, 183 x 97 mm (7.20 x 3.82 in.). BF. The Banque de France had a preference for designs featuring literary figures; here, Molière.

£1-note, Central Bank of Ireland, 1977, obverse, by Patrick Hickleep, 148 x 78 mm (7.24 x 3.07 in.). CBI.
Here the Irish bank has chosen a legendary character, Queen Medb or Maev, said to have ruled over the mythical realm of Connacht. This region in the west of Ireland is a bastion of Gaelic culture.

work originates from Spain. As early as 1874, the Banco de España decided on a design featuring Goya and another with the engraver Valenciano Esteve – painted by Goya. From that moment, the Bank realised that banknotes were a way of introducing a wide public to works considered landmarks in the nation's artistic heritage. So was born the idea of the banknote as a kind of cultural beacon. It was an idea with a great future. Well-known paintings were not merely a means of illustrating the lives of artists like Velasquez and Murillo; they could show the landings of the *Conquistadores* in uncharted territory, sovereigns dying in an aura of religious piety, or the victories of famous warriors. In fact, two things were achieved for the price of one, with the public receiving lessons in both art and history at the same time. Between the wars, the idea was adopted outside Spain by the Reichsbank, which illustrated a host of notes with fifteenth- and sixteenth-century German masters like Albrecht Dürer, Barthel Bruyn the Elder or Hans Holbein the Younger. And during the Second World War, anxious not to upset the German occupiers, the Nederlandsche Bank turned to seventeenth-masterworks of the 1600s.

From the 1960s, European banknotes were almost systematically illustrated with national figureheads from the fields of art, philosophy, literature and, to a lesser degree, science, For some countries, such as Austria, the Netherlands and Italy, this was something new and even in conflict with their traditions. Each country gave priority to one facet of its culture. France particularly honoured its writers: Chateaubriand, Hugo, Molière, Racine, Voltaire, Corneille, Montesquieu and Saint-Exupéry. Belgium, Spain and Italy favoured artists; in Belgium, Van Orley, Rubens, Meunier, Ensor, Permeke and Magritte; in Spain, Goya, Bayeu, Sorolla, Rusiñol, Rosnero and Zuolaga; in Italy, Michelangelo, Leonardo da Vinci, Titian, Antonello da Messina, Caravaggio and Raphael. Austria paid tribute not only to its musicians but also to its men of science: Auer von Welsbach, Sigmund Freud, Karl Landsteiner, Eugen Böhm von Bawerk, Erwin Schrödinger. Portugal for a long time stayed with former kings and men of letters, but has recently returned to an older tradition, devoting a whole series to its great explorers.

Among all the designs selected by European countries, we have to say that not one of them has been willing to honour a great man from another nation; despite all the disasters resulting from nationalism in the past, jingoism is not dead. There is one odd exception: Christopher Columbus, claimed by both Italy and Spain, who commemorated him in 1964 and 1992 respectively. Moreover, the figures selected were almost exclusively male. Belgium, Finland, Spain and Portugal have never, so far, devoted an issue to a famous woman – unless we count their sovereigns. German and Scandinavian countries have shown more interest in their womenfolk, concentrating on personalities in literature or the arts, and sometimes those active in women's liberation movements. In recent German and Danish series, one denomination in two has been reserved for a woman. In Germany, this desire to right the balance has gone beyond the matter of gender: the Bundesbank has also given consideration to the religious convictions of persons represented and their regional origins.

Experiment proved that there were alternatives to the commemorative note. So-called 'poetic' notes were issued in the Netherlands (1948) and in Italy (1977) with female portraits belonging neither to celebrities nor borrowed from familiar paintings. Between 1975 and 1980, the Danmarks Nationalbank reproduced six works by the artist Jens Juel, including five which clearly represent a return

200-mark note, Staatsbank der DDR, 1985, obverse. Kreditanstalt für Wiederaufbau, Berlin. Some of the DDR's notes showed Karl Marx and Friedrich Engels, others views of factories. This example, never issued, idealises the family; in the background, an apartment block, part of a scheme for cheap accommodation.

Preliminary design for 25-florin note, Nederlandsche Bank, 1947, reverse, by Jan Roozendaal, watercolour, pencil and gouache on paper, 309 x 175 mm (12.17 x 6.89 in.). Stichting Museum Enschedé, Haarlem. A specimen of what is known as the 'poetic' design.

THE COLONIAL ERA

Numerous European nations produced colonial issues. France, however, was the most prolific, designing and printing notes for Guadeloupe, Martinique, Guyana, Indochina, Algeria, Tunisia and West and Central Africa. Such colonial or post-colonial issues dealt with economic, historical or geographical matters specific to the colony concerned. Those of the overseas *départements* published after 1946 for the Caisse centrale de la France d'outremer (after 1955 the Institut d'émission des départements d'outremer) concentrated on the growing of sugar cane and exotic fruits. One issue was dedicated to Victor Schoelcher, who devoted himself to the fight against slavery in the nineteenth century. The archaeological resources of the colonies were also put to good use. In Indochina, a 1931 issue used the ruins of Angkor. In Algeria and Tunisia, various denominations for the years 1940–50 reproduced Trajan's triumphal arch at Timgrad or the triad of temples on the capitol at Sbeitla, possibly to underline the common past of metropolitan France and the colonies under the Roman Empire. The banks of Central or West Africa produced 'ethnographic' illustrations in the 1950s and 1960s involving the harvesting of regional products like coffee, cocoa and cotton, side by side with profiles of the natives or local animals.

Detail of 1,000-franc note, Bank of Indochina, Djibouti, 1938, obverse, by Lucien Jonas (1880–1947), 210 x 120 mm (8.27 x 4.72 in.). BF.

to the theme of feminine beauty. Finally, the notes issued in the 1980s by the Nederlandsche Bank renounced once and for all the tradition of honouring the great figures of the past, rather turning to abstract themes.

Economic themes may have been banished since the last war, but some notes, despite everything, still reflect or celebrate political events and developments. Several of the seven constitutional monarchies among the fifteen member states of the EU have continued to honour their reigning monarch. Two countries, Great Britain and Luxembourg, have done so on a regular basis; others – Belgium, Sweden and Spain – sporadically. For the last-named, the tradition re-established itself after the restoration of democracy. Conversely, the republics rarely illustrate their notes with their current presidents. The exception, Finland, has done it twice, in 1955 and 1975.

Directly or indirectly, a few notes have reflected political tensions, even in recent years. In Belgium, two series issued in 1945 and 1950 paid a handsome tribute to the House of Saxe-Coburg, which had occupied the throne since national independence, without, however, featuring the reigning king, Leopold III, whose behaviour during the occupation was a source of controversy. In Greece, strained relations with Turkey have continued to preoccupy successive governments. A number of Greek notes issued since the Second World War have carried portraits of heroes of national independence, or scenes of combat between Greece and the Ottoman Empire in the more distant past.

For the Finnish banknote specialist Tuukka Talvio, the modern habit of featuring celebrities reflects the values of contemporary society – pluralism and democracy – just as portraits of crowned heads once mirrored attitudes of the past. It is important to bear in mind that the choice of design usually lies solely with the issuing bank, which is obliged to consider the differing views of the population to avoid any possibility of arousing dissension – not always easy in the case of recently deceased figures. In France, 'essays' for a note to feature the Lumière brothers were abandoned when the central bank discovered that their attitude during the Second World War had not been without blemish. Indeed, even sovereigns are not beyond criticism. When, not so long ago, the Sveriges Riksbank decided to commemorate Charles XI, there were protests in the province of Scania, where he was remembered as a tyrant. The way personalities are chosen has its critics, for instance the French Internet correspondent who was recently wondering why 'a philosopher is worth more or less than a talented artist, himself momentarily valued differently in monetary terms to a scientist. We see a constant procession of portraits as a grateful posterity honours its

50-drachma note, Bank of Greece, 1978, reverse, 143 x 64 mm (5.63 x 2.52 in.). BG. The design shows a heroine of the war of independence, Laskarina Boumboulina, who played a leading role in the struggle against the Ottoman Empire in the 1820s.

5,000 escudo-note, Banco de Portugal, 1981, obverse, 170 x 75 mm (6.69 x 2.95 in.). BP. Such a design, with its portrait of a former Minister for Education, Antonio Sergio de Sousa (1883–1969), could never have appeared before the 1974 revolution; his opposition to Salazar's dictatorship cost him several years in exile.

10-mark note, Suomen Pankki, 1986, obverse, by Torsten Ekström, 142 x 69 mm (5.87 x 2.72 in.). SP. Finland demonstrated its originality by dedicating one of its issues to an athlete, the runner Paavo Nurmi, who won nine Olympic gold medals during the 1920s.

Apocryphal prospectus announcing a reduction in the value of René Magritte's paintings (1962) with a heading made up from a Belgian banknote and a photo of the artist. The Banque de Belgique lodged a complaint over this infringement of its rights by the Surrealist writer Marcel Mari?n (1920–93) and, years later, some of its directors only reluctantly accepted a design portraying Magritte.

heritage. We have Richelieu, Pasteur, de Gaulle and Delacroix, but never Rimbaud, the little homosexual, nor Modigliani, damned by his drink problem. A draconian system of selection is operated at the highest level by people who can unerringly put their finger on the perfect candidate – someone with mass appeal, squeaky-clean.'

Designs are not random choices. Banknotes, issued as they are by a source constantly interacting with departments of government, reflect values enjoying favour in the society which issues them: faith in progress, the virtue of work, social harmony, the greatness of a nation. Through their mass diffusion, they have been for two centuries a tool of communication, and analysing them allows us to examine, albeit indirectly, the great founding myths of Western society. But we need to keep our wits about us; often what is not said tells us more than what is, and it is impossible to ignore how self-censorship governs the choice of subject. Viewed like this, banknotes reveal themselves to be far more than just coloured pieces of paper money. The critical citizen, even today, needs to know how to decode them. In a democracy, the established order should never be taken for granted.

Emergency Issues 3

5-franc note issued by Giuseppe Mazzini (1805–72) to finance the Alleanza Reppublicana Universale, 110 x 230 (9.06 x 4.33 in.). BI. As a refugee in London during the 1850s, Mazzini launched a subscription fund to finance the armed struggle for Italian independence, especially the purchase of arms.

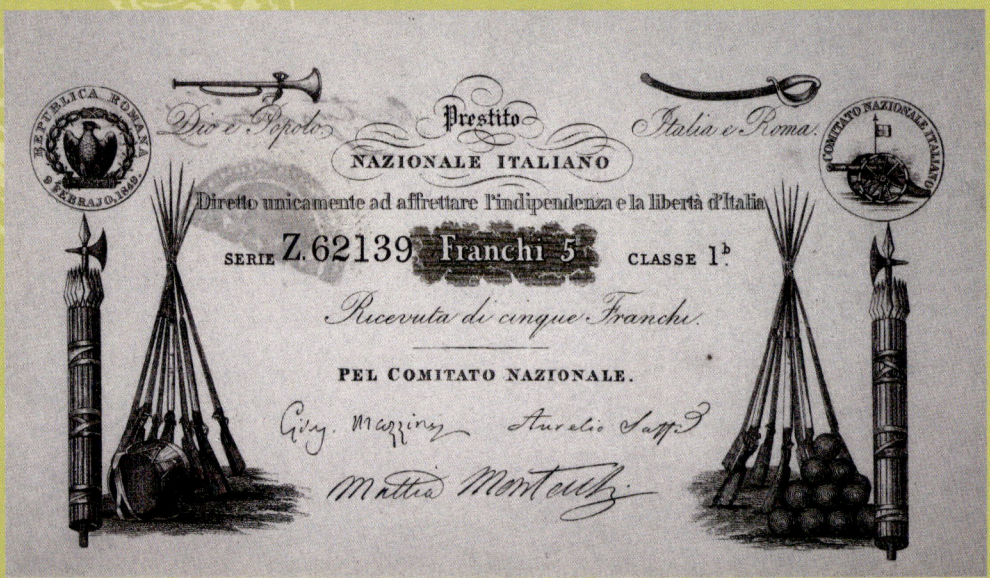

The technical term for these notes is 'obsidional money', but the Germans and Austrians call them *Notgeldscheine*; the British refer to them as emergency notes; the most common term in France is *billets de nécessité*; in Portugal, they are known as *moedas de troco* (money for barter), while for the Italians they are *biglietti fiduciari*, or notes of trust (although it remains unclear whether they inspire trust or instead demand it more than other banknotes). Emergency issues are a means of substitute payment, designed to compensate for a temporary dearth of banknotes or fractional currencies. They have been issued at various times not only by local or regional authorities, but also on the private initiative of businessmen and industrialists. They usually had only a limited value and were printed on a wide range of papers, and were only valid within a restricted geographical area and time period.

Such occasional issues obviously have a place in a work dedicated to banknotes, but they also reflect the crises of the last two centuries, both political – struggles for independence, military occupation, civil wars – and economic – financial collapses, periods of hyper-inflation.

Emergency 2-groschen note issued in 1813 by the town of Erfurt, with inscription 'Blokade von Erfurt'. DBB. The town was occupied by Napoleon's troops during the war between France and the coalition of Prussia, Austria and Russia.

THE FRAGILE EUROPE OF THE VIENNA CONGRESS

25 After the Napoleonic wars the European monarchies took measures to establish a durable balance of power at the Vienna Congress. However, this equilibrium was soon threatened by the upsurge of nationalism. New states were born in painful circumstances – Belgium, Greece, Italy, Germany – and the crises that marked their creation sometimes gave rise to numismatic curiosities.

Greece rose up against Turkish domination in March 1821 and declared its independence on 1 January 1822. In order to finance its struggle against the Ottoman Empire, the provisional government took out a loan, in the form of bonds with a value of 100 to 1,000 piastres that were legal tender for the acquisition of public assets. Although these bonds were not banknotes, they could circulate as if they were. The war of independence lasted six years, and it was punctuated by massacres, military victories and setbacks and internecine power struggles. A further series of government bonds was issued in January 1928 by the first president of the Greek state, Kapodistrias, in order to reward those who had fought for independence. The holders of these bonds were granted, as far as possible, the full ownership of land of an equivalent value. The president also set about laying the foundations of the country's economy by taking all the steps needed immediately to endow it with its own currency – the phoenix, the symbol of a state reborn from its ashes. In an era when transactions were usually made with Turkish piastres, this was one of the most appropriate ways of giving the country a real sense of independence. Phoenix coins were put into circulation in 1829, with banknotes following in 1831. In the meantime, the diplomatic negotiations between the great powers had led to the recognition of Greek independence (January 1830).

Elsewhere, on the Italian peninsula and in Hungary, the drive to independence also gave rise to the issuing of occasional banknotes. In 1848, the shock wave emanating from the events in Paris were strongly felt all over Europe, but most particularly in countries governed by foreign dynasties. Hungary proclaimed its sovereignty, with Kossuth's government declaring the deposition of the house of Habsburg and instituting its own currency. However, first Austrian and then Russian armies put to right these deviations from the established order, and in September 1849 the town of Komarom became the last one to surrender, after a siege of Homeric proportions. Kossuth, forced into exile, never completely gave up hope and issued banknotes in the United States intended to finance a new Hungarian revolution. There was a similar story in the Italian peninsula, where movements mixing liberal demands with nationalism emerged. The Bourbons were thrown out of Sicily and Austrian troops were

58
EMERGENCY
ISSUES

IOU for 1,000 piastres on behalf of the provisional government of Greece (1822). BG.

Eugène Delacroix (1798–1863), *Greece Expiring on the Ruins of Missolonghi*, 1826. Musée des beaux-arts, Bordeaux. Greece's struggle for independence aroused the sympathy of many intellectuals in Western Europe.

obliged to leave Venice by the local populace, while Pope Pius IX was forced to flee from Rome. Provisional governments were set up, and these put treasury bonds into circulation (with those of Venice bearing the slogan *Moneta Patriottica*). Emergency money was issued on a provincial basis in, among others, Ancona, Bologna, Pesaro and Rieti. The Roman republic was proclaimed in February 1849, with a triumvirate at its head comprising Giuseppe Mazzini, Aurelio Saffi and Carlo Armellini, who ordered the Banca Romana to issue new banknotes that were the only permitted legal tender. However, in August of that year French troops occupied the pontifical states and restored the Pope's worldly authority, while Venice surrendered to Austrian troops after a siege lasting five months.`

In 1859 Italy was seized by a new outbreak of independence fever. The 1848 scenario was repeated: every state on the peninsula was plunged into turmoil. In Venice, bonds were put into circulation to finance the fight against the Austrian 'occupiers', this time bearing the motto *Per l'Italia a Venezia*. Subscription bonds, signed by Garibaldi, were also issued to buy a million rifles for the fight against all the despots in Italy. The Sardinian army, backed by France, drove the Austrians out of Lombardy. In southern Italy, the expedition of the *Mille*, led by Garibaldi, succeeded in occupying first Sicily, then Naples. After the proclamation of the Kingdom of Italy, Garibaldi once again issued subscriptions, this time for the 'repurchasing' of Rome and Venice. This staunch partisan of a totally unified Italy was depicted on these 'banknotes', with, at his feet, the lion of Saint Mark, the emblem of Venice, and an eagle (Italy) protecting Romulus and Remus, symbols of the Eternal City.

However, in 1866 the financial upheavals accompanying independence obliged the young Italian government to proclaim banknotes as the only legal tender, with coins being taken out of circulation. At the time, the note with the lowest value was one of 20 lire. The government tried to put notes with lower values into circulation, but as they were of very poor quality they were immediately counterfeited and had to be cancelled. To make up for the lack of small change, hundreds of towns, districts and associations, as well as industrialists and businessmen, issued their own *biglietti fiduciari*, with a value of one lira or more. Unfortunately, speculators got into the act, with some individuals putting a large number of notes into circulation in the hope that a certain amount would never be presented for reimbursement. Merchants 'forgot' to put their address on their notes, while others left town after issuing large quantities of *biglietti fiduciari*. Some issuers refused to make cash reimbursement of sums under 10, 20 or even 100 lire. In the end, a great many issuers went bankrupt, and this pushed the government to take vigorous measures to put an end to the practice, by decreeing that emergency notes should be exchanged. This exchange was completed in 1876.

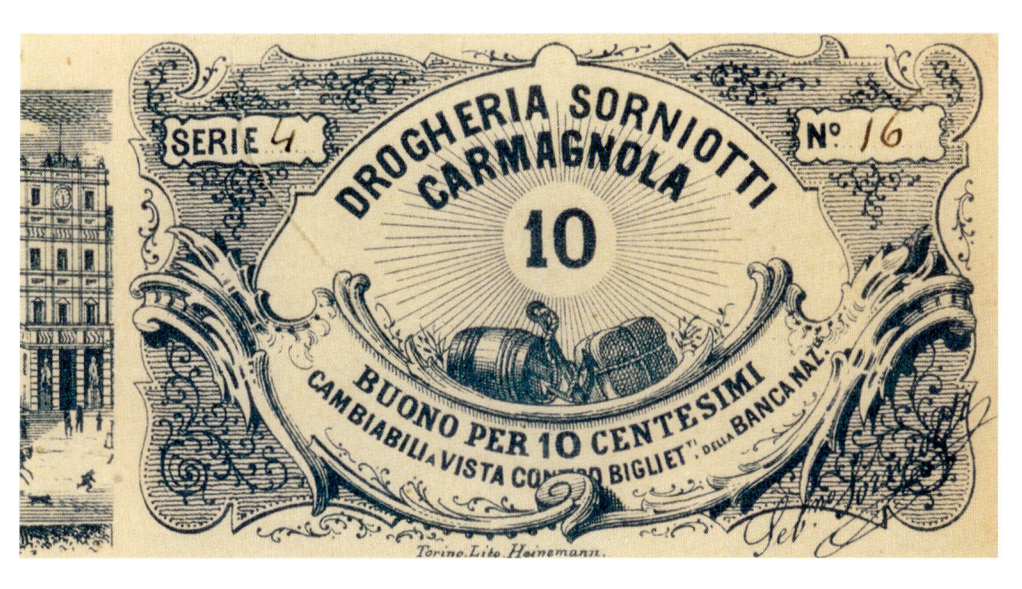

While some states achieved independence, for others it was still a dream. In 1865 the Fenian Brotherhood, the American branch of the Irish revolutionary movement, issued notes in the United States, with a value expressed in dollars, to support the Irish independence movement.

10-centime bill of 1893 by the Drogheria Sorniotti of Carmagnola, 89 x 45 mm (3.50 x 1.77 in.). Fondazione Cassa di Risparmio di Parma, Parma.
Issued to offset yet another lack of specie in Italy.

Sixty years later, the first president of the insurgent Republic of Ireland, Eamon de Valera, wanted to repay this debt of honour, but the remaining holders of these notes preferred to keep them as sacred relics.

Little by little, the work of the Vienna Congress started to come unstuck. The unification of first Italy and then Germany radically altered the balance of power in Europe. The Prussian victories in Sadowa (1866) and Sedan (1870) can be considered turning points in this respect. The war between Austria and Prussia led to extensive hoarding of fractional currency in Austria, and, despite the availability of banknotes of little value, many towns, businesses and factories, especially in Bohemia, resorted to issuing emergency notes – with a total of over a thousand different types! In France, the Franco-Prussian war unleashed serious economic disruption. The besieged cities of Belfort and Langres issued their own paper money. Many French towns in the occupied area, starved of capital and cut off from the Banque de France, were for a while forced to issue their own 'money vouchers' or 'circulation bonds'. In Sedan, for example, one of the banks printed notes of 1, 5, 10 and 20 francs. In his novel describing the events of the French defeat, *The Debacle*, Emile Zola paid tribute to this initiative: 'Sedan,' declares one of his characters, 'faced with a total lack of cash, would never have been able to confront the crisis, without the felicitous creation of local fiat money, paper money from the Caisse de Crédit Industriel, which saved the town from a financial disaster.' In all, there were more than 300 different issues of French paper money in the period 1870–73, printed not only by municipalities but also by industrial companies and chambers of commerce. To put a stop to this, the Banque de France put 5-franc notes into circulation in 1872 to replace any hoarded bonds.

Necessity knows no law:
the horrors of the Great War

The First World War marked the end of the world of the nineteenth century. This conflict, Dantesque in its extension, intensity and duration, was also an economic upheaval that resulted in the global leadership of the United States. From August 1914, fixed exchange rates for notes were proclaimed almost simultaneously in all the countries involved. In order for the Belgian economy to continue to tick over, the Banque Nationale put into circulation 'current account notes', available to all its account-holders. Small change soon became scarce as people hoarded even nickel coins, and the Mint was paralysed by the removal of all its stocks of precious metals. In order to reactivate financial transactions, more than 600 Belgian collectives, local authorities and businesses took the liberty of issuing emergency notes, only valid within a very confined area. To curb this proliferation, the Banque nationale de Belgique issued notes with a value of 1, 2 and 5 francs. Some weeks later, when the Germans moved into Brussels, they set a fixed rate of exchange for the mark to facilitate their requisitioning: they only needed to keep the printing press in operation to ensure that there was no lack of money, which considerably increased the fiduciary circulation of the occupied regions while also brutally destabilising their economies.

Large amounts of emergency notes were similarly issued in France, the Grand Duchy of Luxembourg and Portugal. Furthermore, special notes were used in prisoner-of-war camps, issued to ensure that inmates could never use them in any circumstances outside the camp. Each camp in Germany and France had its own notes, so there were hundreds of different types. The ones that circulated in the camps of Austria-Hungary were particularly colourful and attractive; this did not escape the attention of the military charity office in Vienna, which sold some series at their nominal value as collectors' items.

It was in Germany, however, that emergency notes were most numerous, and it was there that they also circulated for the longest period. From 31 July 1914, when Germany entered the war, the exchange of banknotes was actually suspended. The fixed rate of exchange for notes was officially proclaimed on 4 August. The hoarding of gold and silver coins by the local population very quickly provoked a crisis with respect to means of payment. The authorities tried to appeal to the patriotic spirit of German citizens by encouraging them to put the currency back into circulation, but to no avail. This scarcity was heightened by the financial needs of the soldiers at the front and the formation of stocks of basic commodities by many private individuals.

The Reichsbank authorised the *Darlehenkasse* (lending banks) under its administration to issue notes to

25-centime note issued during the First World War by the Premier groupement économique régional, comprising the chambers of commerce of the Nord and the Pas-de-Calais. Private collection.

German propaganda poster inviting subscriptions for the war effort, c. 1915. Deutsches Historisches Museum, Berlin.

André Huguenin, *Théâtre de la guerre européenne 1914–15*, 1915. Imperial War Museum, London.

a value of 1 to 50 marks, guaranteed by the commitments which these banks had undertaken (securities on merchandise and stock). Strictly speaking, these notes did not constitute money, but they were accepted as payment by all public cash desks and they circulated just like real money. Nevertheless, their introduction was not enough to compensate for the lack of small change. By the beginning of August, many municipal administrations, as well as saving banks and businesses, decided to issue emergency notes with values ranging from 1 to 5 marks. No doubt conscious of their affront to the Reichsbank's monopoly, these issuers were at pains to stipulate that this emergency measure was only temporary. Nevertheless, the periods for reimbursement were renewed regularly; in a war situation, any reprisals against local authorities and businesses were unthinkable. These notes, issued in exceptional circumstances, were printed on rough paper and sometimes bore only hand-written inscriptions. The town of Lopischewo, in East Germany, was content to cut up playing cards and put a stamp with the name of the municipality on each piece!

This first phase in the issuing of emergency notes, in which some 450 issuing bodies have been recorded, lasted until the middle of 1915. After an eighteen-month normalisation period, the printing of 'replacement notes' resumed in December 1916, following the minting of nickel coins, as part of the war effort. The first of these notes, with values of 10, 25 or 50 pfennigs, were unpretentious but they gradually gained in quality from 1918 onwards and acquired ever more elaborate designs. Some sported images of factories, but most boasted distinctive local features, such as beautiful buildings, artistic curios or historical events.

The end of the war did not usher in a return to normality; on the contrary, the political and economic situation became even more confused. The Communist Party threatened to take over the reins of power; thousands of demobilised soldiers returned home; Germany had not only been bled dry but was also obliged to cover the costs of the post-war 'reparations'. The hoarding of coins continued, and this was compensated to an ever greater extent by the issue of emergency notes. Even the Reichsbank's notes were hoarded, as the public feared a breakdown in the credit institutions; piles of notes were withdrawn from the banks. In order to avoid deepening the discontent of an exhausted population that was being targeted by revolutionary movements, in October 1918 the Reichsbank took the initiative of formally authorising local authorities, banks and businesses that were short of cash to make up for the lack of means of payment by printing notes of high value (from 5 to 100 marks). These notes had to be withdrawn from circulation by February 1919, as the Reichsbank was afraid that these high-value notes would be forged and wanted to prevent the Rhine states, which were being shaken by separatist movements, from taking advantage of this and grasping their autonomy in the financial sphere. In all, some 600 towns and companies benefited from the

Two emergency notes issued in 1921 by the League for the Promotion of German Culture, signed by the designer, Max Eschlé (b. 1890), 125 x 80 mm (4.92 x 3.15 in.). BNB.
'Nothing is sacred any more; vice prospers openly', laments one of the notes in a denouncement of the growing decadence of German society, while the other underlines the ruinous state of the nation.

authorisation to issue these high-value notes or *gro gel*. At the same time, the board of the Reichsbank hastily commissioned private companies to print new banknotes. One of these auxiliary notes, whose sole adornment was a black frame, earned the uninviting nickname of 'obituary notice'.

The German collectives that took the initiative to issue emergency notes became more and more diverse: villages, towns, hamlets, but also commercial companies, sports clubs, cultural associations, parties and hotels. Around 1,400 public or private issuers put over 6,000 notes into circulation between 1917 and 1922. While many displayed local tourist sites or featured symbols of an eternal Germany, such as Goethe or Frederick of Prussia, others conveyed a political message. Several openly criticised the Treaty of Versailles, the reparations which it imposed on Germany (132 billion gold marks) and the powers that had signed it. The city of Neuhaldensleben, famous for its crockery, issued a note decorated with locally produced chamber pots, with comments making it clear that the 'treaty of shame' should never have been signed. This note was widely considered a tasteless provocation and even gave rise to protests in Paris, to such an extent that the government ordered it to be withdrawn. While some emergency notes denounced the decomposition of German society, class conflicts, the arrogance of the *nouveaux riches* and the selfishness of profiteers, others vividly illustrated the dire poverty into which the population had been plunged, the need for city dwellers to look for food in the country and the boom in the black market. The Reichsbank, however, observed this massive and uncontrolled printing of emergency notes – and the excessive speculation it engendered – with increasing dismay, and in July 1922 the government banned the issue and circulation of this type of money, although it proved incapable of preventing its reappearance in the period of hyper-inflation from 1922 to 1924.

MAKING A VIRTUE OF NECESSITY

In 1918 emergency notes began to attract the attention of collectors willing to buy them at a price in excess of their face value. For towns with a chronic cash shortage, this could provide extra income that was not to be scorned, so more and more of them took pains to assuage the passion of collectors by offering well-crafted series and ensuring their distribution throughout the country. Many of the notes issued during the war were already impossible to find, but some municipalities were quick to produce reprints specifically aimed at collectors. Soon there were catalogues of emergency notes, special albums, collectors' clubs, specialist traders and fairs, exhibitions and even magazines. In Germany and Austria it seemed as though the entire population had become collectors. The craze for emergency notes was fomented by all those who could make a profit out of it, such as the artists commissioned to design them. The Schwartz printing works in Lindenberg employed the designer Heinz Schiestl full time, solely to create emergency issues. Some printers made this type of work their speciality and even solicited orders from towns that had not yet succumbed to the latest fashion. One opportunist put money into circulation without asking the permission of the municipality mentioned on the notes; another issued notes in the name of a town that did not even exist!

Emergency issue by the town of Papenburg, designed in 1921 by F. Berck, 104 x 77 mm (4.09 x 3.03 in.). BNB. It shows an average, decent German, recognisable by his hat: a victim of the rapacity of the tax system.

Inflation runs amok

The First World War, financed by the printing of banknotes, completely destabilised the economies of all the countries involved. None of them were spared the scourge of relentless inflationist tendencies. In Italy, where the postwar fiduciary circulation was five times greater than that of 1914, millions of banknotes were burned in an effort to revalue the lira. Inflation was particularly serious in Greece, which had been at war since 1912. First the Balkan war, then the fight alongside the Allies, earned the country substantial increases in territory (Crete, Macedonia, Epirus) but exhausted its economy. The watershed year was 1920: the country, already torn by internecine political struggles, was also obliged by Turkey to evacuate the coasts of Asia Minor. The expenses of the military operations were topped by the cost of transporting the one and a half million Greeks who were fleeing Ionia. In the course of one year the total value of the banknotes in circulation rose from 163 to 463 million drachmas. Nor did the printing presses remain idle after that, for the integration of the newcomers also required funds. In 1922 and 1926, two enforced loans were imposed on the population. The system used was entirely original: all the banknotes in circulation were cut into two pieces, one half going to the state as an enforced loan, the other provisionally serving as a means of exchange, but at half the nominal value on the note. The torn banknote was then changed for a new one with a reduced value. This measure allowed the government to put new money into circulation without increasing the number of notes available (the 'torn-note' technique was also used by Finland after the Second World War). Despite these drastic measures, inflation continued to soar: in 1927 the index exceeded 1,800 per cent with respect to the prices in 1914. At that point Greece appealed to help from the Society of Nations and successfully negotiated a stabilising loan, in return for major financial reforms.

It was in Germany, however, that inflation was particularly rampant. After the beginning of the war – financed almost entirely by the printing of banknotes on the German side – the value of money plunged with increasing speed. Between the end of 1913 and the end of 1919, the circulation of paper money increased tenfold and the value of the mark fell by over half. The country's long-term debt also rocketed over the same period from 4.8 billion to 92.8 billion marks, but the successive governments of the Weimar Republic were unable to get things back on an even keel. By the start of 1922 the mark's purchasing power had plummeted to one-fiftieth of what it was before the war.

In the autumn of 1922, the Reichsbank, whose printing works were on strike, once again proved incapable of providing the country with sufficient banknotes (and those that were made available relentlessly increased their face value). In September, barely two months after it had banned all issues of emergency money, the government

The effects of inflation on Germany: distribution of food.

The effects of inflation on Germany: practical problems of stocking notes at the banks, children playing with worthless banknotes.

reauthorised municipalities and businesses to print notes of a value of up to 1,000 marks. In January 1923 the situation deteriorated when the Ruhr was occupied by French and Belgian troops. The inhabitants of the region expressed their opposition to this measure by completely boycotting the foreign occupiers. The Ruhr's economy was soon totally paralysed and the population only survived with help sent from Berlin. As this help was financed by the printing of banknotes, the fall in the mark accelerated abruptly. The face value of the notes printed by the Reichsbank and the issuers of emergency notes rose steeply: 100,000 marks on 1 February 1923, 10 million on 25 July, 1,000 million on 5 September, 200 thousand million on 15 October.

In order to tackle the printing of an ever-growing body of banknotes – 57 different types between January 1922 and November 1923, a total of 10 thousand million notes in 1923 alone! – the Reichsbank had to turn to private printers. In the final phase of the apocalypse, at the end of 1923, 144 printing works were involved in the production of notes for the Reichsbank, requiring 1,783 printing presses and 30 paper mills! All that without counting the 5,000 or so public or private issuers of emergency notes, some of whom printed notes with a value of 100 billion marks! There was a shortage of paper, to such an extent that many issuers resorted to simple overprints to modify the face value of notes that had become worthless. Hyperinflation deregulated every area of the economy.

Commercial accountancy had become impossible. The figures on the balance sheet of a company like Bayer boasted 20 digits before the decimal point! A suitcase of money was needed for even the smallest transaction. Banking operations were completely chaotic: the elimination of expired banknotes and the delivery, storage and exchange of new ones posed increasingly complex problems. The endless variations in prices made the public extremely jittery. There was widespread unrest: looting of bakeries, riots in workplaces, scuffles in dole queues.

November 1923 saw the first appearance of notes valued in billions of marks. However, the introduction of the revalued mark or *Rentenmark*, guaranteed by a general mortgage of the nation's assets, and the stabilisation of the currency in the proportion of one trillion paper marks for a revalued mark brought an end to two years of financial nightmare. The effects of this disaster were nevertheless so profound that it was one of the main elements that fuelled the rise of Nazism.

Inflation also reached phenomenal levels in Austria. In September 1922 a 500,000-crown note was issued – the highest face value ever attained by an Austrian banknote. Loans were granted to Austria under the control of the League of Nations. It was not until the foundation of the Österreichische Nationalbank in 1923, and the launching of a new currency, the schilling, in 1924, that the Austrian economy managed to escape from the mire in which the war and the dismantling of the Empire had plunged it.

The political problems of the inter-war years

The peace treaties of 1919 established new frontiers in many parts of Europe, thereby creating new difficulties to replace the ones that were supposedly being solved. And in all the areas where the status quo was modified, the circulation of banknotes was one of the transitional problems that invariably cropped up.

The dismantling of the Austro-Hungarian Empire and the disintegration of the Russian Empire gave rise to the birth of several new states, such as Czechoslovakia, Hungary and Yugoslavia, where the notes of the old Östereichisch-Ungarische Bank were overprinted to serve as provisional funds until the issue of national banknotes. The dismembering of the Austro-Hungarian Empire, decided by the allied powers, was based on two premises: that Austria was no longer an element of equilibrium in Europe, on account of its alliance with the Reich, and that the best way of containing pan-Germanism was to build strong national republics on the ruins of the Empire. In practice, though, the whole of central Europe, apart from Czechoslovakia, turned out to be severely destabilised and suffered a deep financial recession.

Elsewhere, the dissolution of the Empire allowed Italy to recover border areas that had been claimed by the irredentist movement ever since the *Risorgimento*. Immediately after the war, Austrian banknotes were circulating in the territories annexed by Italy (South Tyrol and the Trieste region), overprinted with an Italian stamp. The Italian writer Gabriele d'Annunzio (1863–1938) objected to the post-war incorporation of Fiume, the Adriatic Port snatched from the Austro-Hungarian Empire, into Yugoslavia, even though this had been established by the London Ppact of April 1915. D'Annunzio led a handful of soldiers into the town to cordon it off. Disowned by his own government, he was obliged, in order to pay his troops, to put a *Città di Fiume* stamp on banknotes that had first been issued by the Östereichisch-Ungarische Bank. His escapade finally came to an end in January 1921, when Fiume was declared a free city in accordance with the treaty of Rapallo (November 1920).

Germany, for its part, lost Alsace-Lorraine to France, as well as a part of Schleswig-Holstein to Denmark. Some of the emergency notes issued in Germany in 1919 and 1920 are veritable manifestos against these territorial amputations, while others attacked the pretensions of Poland in Upper Silesia or criticised the occupation of the territory of Memel, beyond East Prussia, by the allies. Danzig and Sarre were entrusted to the high commissioners of the Society of Nations. Danzig was proclaimed a free city in 1919 and issued its own banknotes, first in marks then in florins. An autonomous bank of issue was founded there in February 1924, and its notes remained in circulation until Danzig's incorporation into the German

50-pfennig emergency issue from Soltau, 1921, 78 x 50 mm (3.07 x 1.97 in.). BNB.
It protests against the territorial annexations suffered by Germany at the time in Schleswig-Holstein, Alsace-Lorraine, the Dantzig corridor and the area around Memel.

1-mark emergency note issued by the commune of Broacker in 1919, reverse, 90 x 67 mm (3.54 x 2.64 in.). BNB.
It demands the retention of the town within German territory, and eagerly anticipates the failure of the plans to make it part of Denmark, whose flag appears in the design.

Reich in 1939. In Sarre, the all-powerful French company Mines Domaniales de la Sarre issued notes of low value, which circulated until 1930. This Land was returned to Germany by plebiscite in 1935.

This inter-war period was also characterised by another phenomenon: some national groups which had gained a brief spell of independence or autonomy – Catalonia, the Basque country, Finland – found this autonomy being challenged by the very states whose temporary weakness had permitted their emancipation. This was the case in Finland, which became independent of the Russian Empire in 1917 but was brutally attacked by the USSR in the winter of 1939–1940. The country's independence had been marked by a civil war lasting several months from 1917 to 1918, during which the country had been divided into two: the south was controlled by the Reds (Communists), the north by the Whites. In order to be able to pay its soldiers' wages, the 'White' government came to an agreement with a private bank in Vasa, the Vaasan Osale Pankki, which loaned it 20 million marks. Banknotes with this total value were put into circulation, reimbursable in notes from the National Bank after the war. They were illustrated by the artist Akseli Gallen-Kallela, who had already been responsible for designing the uniforms, ranks and decorations of the White army. Gallen-Kallela decorated all the notes with different types of lichens – maybe in reference to the Finnish nickname for banknotes: birch bark.

The brief adventure of Catalonia and the Basque country as autonomous regions was closely linked to the civil war that tore Spain apart from 1936 to 1939. The advent of the Republic in 1931 had endowed Catalonia, one of Spain's richest regions, with far-reaching autonomy. The Spanish Civil War broke out after the election of a 'Popular Front' government in 1936. A nationalist military junta, supported by the Right and the Church and sustained by outside help from Germany and Italy, sought to overthrow the republican regime. After the scission of the Spanish territory in July 1936, a Banco de España was set up by the nationalist forces in Burgos. In November it was announced that the nationalist government would not recognise any banknotes issued by the republican government after 18 July. Any notes issued before this date in circulation in areas controlled by the nationalists had to be stamped to distinguish them from those being used by the republicans. As the nationalists, like the republicans, did not have access to suitable printing equipment in Spain, their definitive banknotes were printed by the German company Giesecke & Devrient and exchanged for the stamped notes, although notes with a value of less than 25 pesetas were printed in Zaragoza to relieve the shortage of money, using inks and paper imported from Germany.

Meanwhile, what was happening on the republican side? The circulation of banknotes grew exponentially – a symptom of inflation. The government first put into circulation all the reserve notes in the coffers of the Banco de España, before releasing new issues commissioned from England. The notes manufactured by Thomas De La Rue & Co. and Bradbury, Wilkinson & Co. were transferred to the Banco de España's branch in Paris and then dispatched overland to the Pyrenees. Some regions occupied by the republicans were cut off from Madrid by areas held by the nationalists: this was the case of the Basque country, endowed with a provisional government and a relative autonomy since 1936, and the provinces of Santander and Asturias. In these regions, banks and saving banks issued open current account cheques payable to the bearer in the Banco de España. The Generalitat of Catalonia, which enjoyed greater autonomy, issued low-value notes to compensate for the absence of fractional currencies. There was also a widespread circulation of notes issued by municipalities, local political committees, cooperatives, trade unions and businesses. The number of issuing bodies has been calculated at around 2,000, and these were responsible for roughly 7,000 different types of note! A diverse range of materials were used, from parchment to celluloid, from wood to leather. Some notes unequivocally proclaimed the political radicalism of anarchist communities and adopted new units for counting: *entero* or 'whole' for the main notes, *grados* or 'degrees' for the fractional ones.

5-*pessetes* note issued by the Generalitat (Assembly) of Catalonia following a decree of September 1936, reverse, 167 x 70 mm (6.57 x 2.76 in.). BNB. A clear statement of the armed struggle between Catalonia and the forces of General Franco.

War, yet again

The degradation of Europe's political climate became noticeable in 1937. The following year Germany annexed first Austria, then some parts of Czechoslovakia. In September 1939 the German government, anticipating further military invasions of new territories, created an institute, controlled by the Reichsbank, to oversee the issue and circulation of occupation money, the *Reichskreditkassenscheine*. As soon as German troops occupied a new territory, the circulation of these bonds became legal and an exchange rate with the local currency was fixed. They were first used after the invasion of Poland, and subsequently circulated in Denmark, Belgium, Greece, France, Luxembourg, the Soviet Union, Norway, Yugoslavia and Italy. Later on, the Germans organised the issue of notes in local currency in the occupied territories. In Belgium, a Bank of Issue was substituted for the Banque nationale. In the Netherlands, Denmark and France, the banks of issue continued to work 'normally'. The occupiers formally prohibited the multiplication of emergency notes, and in that respect the situation became normal quite quickly. In contrast to what had occurred in the First World War, the exportation of Reichsbank notes outside German territory was forbidden. Some countries or territories were, however, both obliged to adopt the mark as the sole legal means of payment and annexed to the German monetary zone: for example, Luxembourg, the Eupen–Malmédy region and Alsace–Lorraine.

The treatment of the occupied areas was harsh: the economies of the conquered countries were destabilised by requisitions disguised as trading agreements. The occupation years were particularly hard for the famished population of Greece, where the daily food intake only amounted to 29 per cent of what the Red Cross then considered to be the minimum subsistence level. Tuberculosis caused a sharp rise in the death rate. On the financial front, the situation very quickly got out of hand. First, the Italian and German occupying forces put their own notes into circulation – 'drachmas' from the Cassa Mediterranea di Credito per la Grecia and 'occupation marks' for large sums. The occupiers then claimed the reimbursement of these occupation notes and demanded major contributions to the war effort. In order to pay for this, the Greeks had to resort to the printing of banknotes. The money circulation, which amounted to 19.3 billion drachmas at the end of March 1941, rose to 180 billion in September 1942 and 1,300 billion drachmas in September 1943. This surrealistic explosion in the currency circulation was accompanied by a systematic looting of the country. The capitulation of Italy in 1943 hardened the attitude of the German occupying authorities, and Greece's debt for enforced supplies to Germany went from 80 million mark, at the end of 1943, to 188 million in May 1944. This financial catastrophe had serious

100-crown note of the protectorate of Bohemia–Moravia issued by the occupying Germans in Prague, August 1940, reverse. Private collection.

Strike notes

Ireland was riven from 1919 to 1922 by violent confrontations between British troops and nationalist forces, which had formed a clandestine government in 1919. One curious relic of those troubled times is this 'strike note' issued by the city of Limerick. In April 1919, in the midst of the conflict between the independence movement and the British army, the latter declared the city of Limerick a military zone and turned it into a fortified camp, thus preventing its inhabitants from coming and going as they pleased. That month a general strike was decreed in the county of Limerick. The strikers, who demanded the lifting of martial law, propagated their own notes to enable them to make purchases, guaranteed by the confederation of trade unions and the workers' Party. They bore the legend 'General strike against British militarism'. The strike proved successful, but the open warfare between the British and the Irish was to last for another two years before Ireland was to achieve autonomy.

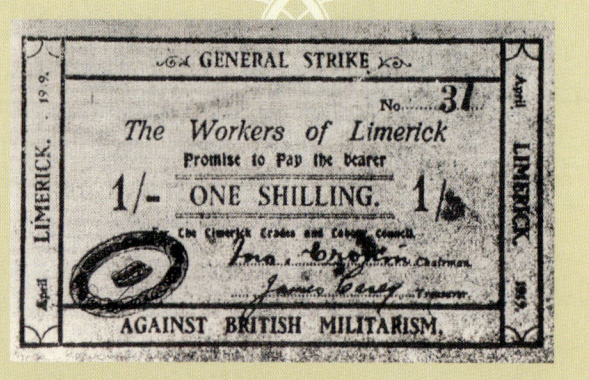

1-shilling note issued in 1919 by the trade unions of Limerick and calling for a general strike against the presence of British forces.

effects on Greece's economical and political evolution after the liberation. The parity with the pound, fixed at 600 drachmas in November 1944, was reviewed several times and by the beginning of 1946 20,000 drachmas were needed to make up one pound.

The Axis forces were, however, not alone in using occupation notes. When the allied military forces conquered Europe, they used Allied Military Currency notes expressed in the currency of the Axis countries. The reverse of the notes used in Italy from 1943 bears a summary of the allied powers' programme: freedom of speech, freedom of faith, freedom from want, freedom from fear. These notes were issued for large amounts, in excess of those issued by the Banca d'Italia. After 1946 they were no longer considered occupation money and, although they were printed in the United States, they had the same standing as issues from the Banca d'Italia and remained in circulation until 1950. After issuing occupation notes in Italy, the Allies repeated the process in Austria and Germany. In 1944 Yugoslavia rose up against the German occupiers and won back Istria, Fiume and the Slovenian coastline. Banknotes specific to this occupation period were issued in lire, with legends written in Croatian, Slovenian and Italian.

The nerve centre of a war is, by definition, also that of resistance. In some countries, resistance forces – the Italian partisans fighting the German troops at the end of

100-drachma note, Cassa Mediterranea di Credito per la Grecia, 1941, reverse, 110 x 54 mm (4.33 x 2.13 in.). Fondazione Cassa di Risparmio di Parma, Parma. Notes of this bank were forced upon the Greeks by the Italian occupiers.

Allied Occupation notes: 100-lire note, 1943, 155 x 66 mm (6.10 x 2.60 in.). Fondazione Cassa di Risparmio di Parma, Parma; 1 mark, 1944, 67 x 78 mm (3.07 x 2.64 in.), (private collection); 2 Austrian schillings, 1944, 59 x 115 mm (2.32 x 4.53 in.). ONB.

25-drachma note issued by the Greek resistance in 1944. BG.

the war, for example – managed to print their own notes. In 1944 the Greek civil committee for national liberation printed large quantities of notes to buy provisions for the partisan armies. When the resistance movements lacked their own notes, they often had to resort to robbery to obtain funds. The Belgian resistance attacked several branches of the Banque nationale. In 1942 the French *maquisards* seized a billion francs in new 1,000-franc notes, while they were being transported to Clermont-Ferrand train station. This feat was, however, undermined by the Vichy regime, which refrained from putting this type of note into circulation!

Other notes were specially printed for prisoner-of-war camps. Contrary to the practice of the First World War, the high command of the Wehrmacht ordered notes to be printed for the camps as a whole. In Italy, the camp notes were also identical, although they did each bear the number of a particular camp. In the concentration camps set up in Germany or the areas occupied by the Nazis, special vouchers were printed for the use of the inmates. Most of these were very crudely printed and only a few specimens are still in existence.

After the war, galloping inflation obliged the central banks rapidly to increase the fiduciary circulation. In 1947 the Italian authorities, confronted by strong monetary depreciation, put into circulation *titoli provvisori* or provisional bonds of 5,000 and 10,000 lire until the definitive banknotes for these sums could be printed. These remained in circulation until 1950. During this period of inflation, some banks printed on their own account *assegni circolari*, cheques for preprinted sums. Germany once again experienced a dearth of small change, which gave rise to the issue of emergency notes, exactly as had occurred after the First World War. Over 250 issues have been recorded, with values of 5 to 50 pfennigs, and they were mainly the responsibility of industrial, commercial and craft firms, banks and transport companies. Their circulation was forbidden by the allied occupation forces, but this prohibition was not always easy to enforce. When Austria adopted (or rather recovered) the schilling as its national currency, German fractional coins were not immediately withdrawn from circulation (no funds were available to strike them in schillings). The coins in circulation in Germany were abundant in Austria, as their purchasing power was far greater there. The haemorrhage was so intense that fractional coins became unavailable in some parts of Germany and, to make up for this shortfall, more than a thousand new kinds of local note were printed.

The history of European emergency notes did not come to a complete halt once the consequences of the war were overcome. Italy was again confronted by shortages of cash in 1966 and between 1975 and 1978. Various types of emergency money were then put into circulation: not only *assegni circolari* printed by banks, but also stamps, telephone tokens, plastic chips and printed notes issued by companies or trading associations. However, apart from these few isolated cases, circumstances of necessity have barely been seen since peace was restored in Europe. Is there any better argument in favour of the continent's economic and political unification? The notes we have discussed call for reflection. They should definitely be preserved as precious relics of the ideas, shortcomings and suffering of the generations that came before us. The Germans understood this when they set about collecting the *Notgeldscheine* after the First World War. In the words of one contemporary printers' magazine, 'In a hundred years or more an intelligently compiled collection of emergency money will bear witness to the anguish of our age.'

2-mark note, Diedenhofen POW camp, 100 x 58 mm (3.94 x 2.28 in.). BNB. During the First World War, each German camp issued its own notes.

5-franc note, Banque de France, 1944, 76 x 66 mm (2.99 x 2.60 in.). BNB. In 1944, the American forces brought with them French 'invasion' or 'liberation' money: notes designed to meet the needs of the allied armies, something which aroused the opposition of General de Gaulle. On the other hand, in June 1945, the Banque de France imported notes from England and the USA to replace those it was withdrawing from circulation. Here, an American truck in front of the Banque de France.

NOTGELD – A CLOSER LOOK

The German Notgeld series represents an extraordinary chapter in the history of paper money. In those times of exceptional suffering, some of these bills depicted a range of iconographic allusion to local mythology, tales and fables, misery and anguish, self irony and black humour, and displayed an intellectual and artistic freedom that is unique in the annals of the propaganda images of classical official money. Even though part of the production of Notgeld was intended for a large class of collectors, these notes are today often ignored and forgotten in archives – perhaps because of their sheer quantity and relative worthlessness. Here the artist Stephen Sack has recognised a rich source to explore. The notes are photographed to reveal the texture of the paper and cropped to remove the exact historical context. Sack strives to create a story book of images from his imagination. He uses the museum as an archaeological site sifting through the detritus of history to find aesthetic possibilities and symbolic significance. From the more than 20,000 existing German *Notgelder,* Sack concentrated on his personal vision of them: searching for the rare instances where he can revive images from the past to devise artworks that take on new emotions, form and significance.

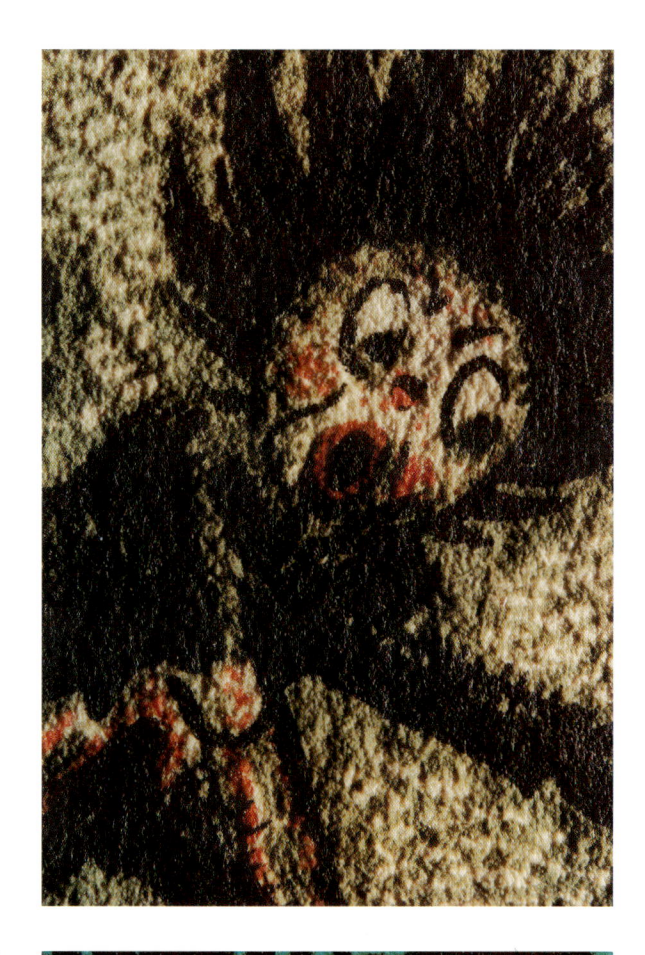

EMERGENCY
ISSUES

Security Measures and the War against Forgery 4

J. Louis Charbonne, *The Skinflints*. BNB.
In the nineteenth century, the genuineness of banknotes was even more subject to suspicion than that of specie.

Forgery and counterfeit notes

The Banque nationale de Belgique, in its review of 1905, stated, with reference to recent counterfeiting of its money: 'Every banknote incites counterfeiting, just as all wealth incites covetousness. No matter how relentlessly we pursue the struggle against forgery, our success will always be limited. Just as science exhausts all its resources to create a new banknote, that same science also reveals the secrets needed to achieve a criminal counterfeit. Today's inimitable banknote is tomorrow's counterfeit.' The bank concluded philosophically that the only way to do away with a forged note was to issue a new one.

From the eighteenth century onwards, counterfeiting was used not only as a means of illegal enrichment but also as a weapon against political enemies. In 1793 William Pitt's government in Britain helped French exiles to counterfeit *assignats* and smuggle them into France, via the insurgent Vendée and Flanders, in order to destabilise the regicidal Republic. The Comte d'Artois, who reigned in France between 1824 and 1830 after the Restoration under the name of Charles X, was one of the mainsprings of the production of counterfeit *assignats*. On several occasions he personally visited the mill that made the paper used for this counterfeiting to make new orders and offer advice on watermarks. Not that the British lacked experience in this field, as it had previously encouraged – or rather organised – the production of counterfeit dollars during the American Revolution (1775–83). The same tactic was subsequently used by Napoleon. When he occupied Vienna in 1806, he seized the templates for printing the *Banco-Zettel* issued by the Wiener-Stadt-Banco, and he was thus able to cover a good part of his expenses by reprinting these notes in Paris and Italy. The Emperor also ordered the counterfeiting of Russian banknotes and made plans to do the same with the notes of the Bank of England, although this project never came to fruition.

At the beginning of the nineteenth century, the Bank of England, confronted by emergency restrictions on the minting of coins, introduced notes with values of 1 and 2 pounds, thereby providing a great temptation for counterfeiters, as these notes were very roughly made. It was said, not entirely in jest, that some ten thousand engravers in the country were capable of reproducing one of these notes. Furthermore, they circulated very widely and their users, in many cases illiterate, were unaccustomed to handling banknotes. In 1807 alone, the Bank had to cancel over 4,000 counterfeit 1- and 2-pound notes; it also acted with the utmost severity to put a stop to this practice; several engravings from 1818 criticised the casual way in which the authorities hanged forgers. At the same time, the Bank created a special commission to study means of strengthening security with respect to banknotes, although it barely managed to reach any practical conclusions. Instead of gradually perfecting the notes – through more complex printing processes, for example – the Bank seemed to be searching for the ultimate weapon that would render forgery completely impossible. Impatient with this attitude, the Society for the Encouragement of Arts, Manufactures and Commerce, concerned that English notes were deficient not only in security but also in artistic quality, set up its own commission, to which printers and artists could send designs for banknotes. The best of these were published, thus giving rise to a public debate. In 1821, however, the restrictions on the minting of coins were lifted and the 1- and 2-pound notes were withdrawn from circulation; at the same time, the Bank of England's efforts to tighten up security also ground to a halt.

In the nineteenth century banks of issue often printed a warning to potential forgers on their notes, to the effect that the production and circulation of counter-

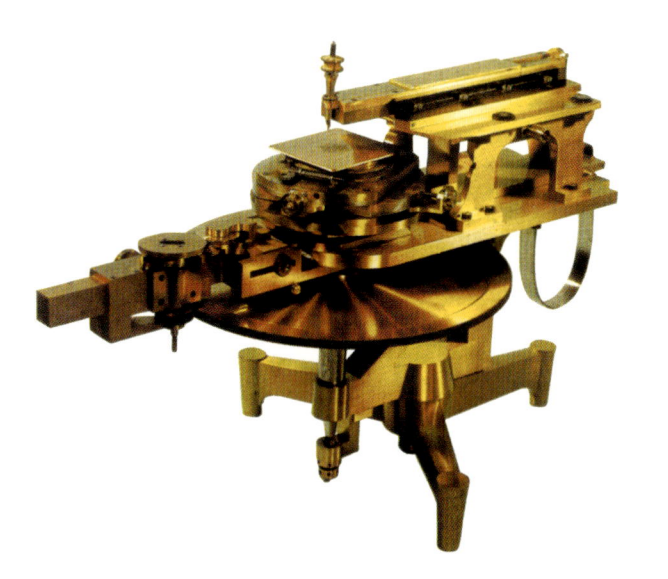

Chequering machine invented by Jakob Degen (1760–1848), *c.* 1820. ONB. This device allowed the engraving of regular *guilloche* patterns on metal. Other similar machines were developed during the 1800s, but a number of banks were reticent to accept mechanical engraving processes. The Bank of England only adopted the technology in 1928.

feit notes were statutory offences. The *assignats* announced that 'the Nation punishes counterfeiters and rewards those who denounce them'. (The death penalty for counterfeiting was, however, abolished in 1832.) The first notes of the Banco Español de San Fernando to bear the legend 'Death penalty for forgers' date from 1835. The earliest warning of this type in Austria appeared in 1841, stating that 'imitators and counterfeiters of the notes of the Bank (of Austria) are liable to the same penalties as the counterfeiters of paper money issued by the State. It is the duty of the authorities to locate, arrest and punish such criminals'. In 1856 a note issued by a German bank, the Geraer Bank, inserted an extract from the law on counterfeiting in a box illustrated with a prison wall, while, the following year, prisoners' fetters appeared on a note from the Hannoversche Bank. Notes issued by the Swedish Göteborg Bank in 1848 and 1852 declared that 'anybody who imitates or counterfeits this note will be punished in accordance with the law. Any denouncer of an imitator or forger will be rewarded'. The warning to counterfeiters on Finnish notes was printed in three languages: Russian, Swedish and Finnish. The counterfeiting of banknotes was a problem of international dimensions. In the 1820s English forgers copied notes issued in Prussia; the effect of this counterfeiting was so detrimental that in 1825 the Pommersche Ritterschaftliche Privat-Bank in Stettin printed 1-thaler notes bearing an extract, in English, from the British Act of Parliament of 11 August 1803, which prohibited the counterfeiting of foreign banknotes.

These warnings, however, did little to prevent forgery. In August 1845 the Privilegirte Österreichische Nationalbank came across some counterfeit 10- and 100-gulden notes of an extraordinarily high quality – so much so that only a handful of forgers could have been capable of such good imitations. Suspicion quickly fell on one Peter Ritter von Bohr, a known stock-exchange speculator who had been investigated by the authorities five years earlier after having been found in possession of a false banknote. This time his wife had recently used a forged banknote to buy a watch. Their house was searched, and an impressive collection of printing material was discovered. Von Bohr was unable to keep up his story that this equipment was justified by his artistic activities, as he had recently become almost blind. Even after his arrest, however, he denied all charges, but his wife was less resolute. Another search of their home unearthed large amounts of counterfeit notes. Found guilty of forgery, von Bohr attempted suicide, but he later collaborated with both the authorities and the Bank by showing them his counterfeiting techniques. He was sentenced to hang but was reprieved by Emperor Ferdinand and died in prison after serving two years of his sentence.

In his posthumous memoirs, Wilhelm Stieber, Bismarck's spymaster, described the fight against counterfeiters in the mid-nineteenth century. In 1852, as head of the criminal investigation department in Berlin, he was confronted with a massive diffusion of very skilfully forged coins and banknotes. An analysis of the materials used and the places where the forgeries had been discovered soon led Stieber to concentrate his attention on Rhineland and Westphalia. He managed to infiltrate the gang responsible by taking advantage of the resemblance between one of his officers and a gangleader; he dismantled several workshops and arrested some hundred people. This affair must have left its mark on Stieber. Years later, when Bismarck, the President of the Council of Prussia, asked him to set up a spy network to gather information on Austria's internal situation and its future plans in the event of a war with Germany, Stieber decided to finance this network with forged Austrian banknotes! His ideas were not lacking in ambition: he sought to flood Austria with hundreds of spies, generously grease the palms of journalists to take advantage of their contacts, bribe potential informers and stir up the minorities: 'I got an impressive bunch of specialists out of prison, all world-class professional forgers. We got down to work at once. An initial test carried out in Vienna proved that even experienced Viennese bankers could not distinguish our fake money from the real thing. Our printing presses worked flat out and we produced several million false Austrian banknotes.' The plan worked perfectly, and soon Bismarck was better informed on the state of mind of Austrian citizens than the Emperor Franz-Joseph himself. He was particularly able to ascertain the total absence of any plans for war among his neighbours, as well as their considerable shortfalls, with respect to Prussia, in the military field. That was in 1864. Two years later, Germany penetrated Austrian territory in Sadowa, bringing the Empire to the verge of collapse, and asserted itself as the uncontested leader of the Germanic confederation.

In the First World War, Austria believed that Britain was planning another inundation of its territory with false

Gabriel Cloquemin, *Convicts Being Fettered*, first half of nineteenth century. Musée Carnavalet, Paris.
From 1832, counterfeiters no longer risked the death sentence in France, the maximum penalty now being hard labour for life.

Marks of authenticity

In the eighteenth century various marks of authenticity – date, signatures and numbers – were added to each note by hand. However, they gradually came to be printed, as writing marks of authenticity with a feather pen was a time-consuming business. In the Banque de France, for example, signing notes by hand quickly became extremely burdensome. In 1820 its board authorised the signing to be shared between the Secretary-General and an employee; in 1827 and 1841 the book-keeper and the head cashier, respectively, were enrolled to help with this task. An average employee could produce 1,300 signatures in a day, but the most dextrous officials could manage twice that number. In 1848 signing machines were put into service for two of the three signatures on the 100-franc note. However, in 1857 this procedure was called into question, as some bank managers considered that a mechanically applied signature was tantamount to forgery. The partisans of printing, for their part, argued that the large number of people now being delegated to write signatures made it no longer possible to consider hand-written signatures as a mark of authenticity. In 1862 France finally decreed that all the signatures on its banknotes should be appended mechanically: by then, the increase in production had required ten employees to work full-time just signing banknotes.

At the Bank of England, £5-notes were still partially produced by hand in the mid-nineteenth century, 1845. BE.

banknotes, this time in order to destabilise the economy. In August 1918 a confidential memo was sent to all the branches of the Österreichisch-Ungarische Bank, alerting employees to this possibility. The information available seemed to indicate that the British would smuggle in these false notes under the cover of convoys repatriating wounded Austrian soldiers. This was not, however, the only threat to the Austrian currency in this period. In the spring of 1919, immediately after the disintegration of the Austro-Hungarian Empire, the Communist government in Hungary, headed by Bela Kun, was faced with an extraordinary proliferation of forged banknotes, to the values of 1, 2, 25 and 200 crowns, produced in private workshops with access to the original templates.

The situation was somewhat different in Finland, where, in early 1918, the Communist forces controlled the state bank's printing presses for several months and issued large amounts of notes of varying values. After the Civil War, the Finnish government wanted to cancel all the money printed by the 'Reds', but these banknotes only differed from the earlier ones in their series numbers. There followed a widespread circulation of notes with numbers modified, with varying degrees of expertise, by scratching them out or other techniques. The national bank finally decided to reprint its notes with new colours. Even this measure did not entirely discourage forgers, who set about dyeing the illegal notes.

After the First World War, counterfeiting mushroomed at a phenomenal rate. In 1923 an International Criminal Police Commission was founded in Vienna. (In 1946 it would be renamed the International Criminal Police Organisation, or Interpol). The fight against forgery was high on its agenda, along with action against fraud and drug-trafficking. One of the organisation's prime functions was to serve as a conduit for the exchange of information between its member countries, and it assembled an enormous dossier on counterfeiters and forged banknotes. The secretariat was initially established in Vienna, before being transferred to Berlin in 1938, after the *Anschluss*, and to Paris in 1946. The magazine *Contrefaçons et falsifications* (Counterfeits and falsifications), the official organ of the International Criminal Police Commission for the Repression of Counterfeit Money, first appeared in 1924. Its editor was Hans Adler, an expert adviser to the Commission. A French edition was published by the Belgian body responsible for the suppression of counterfeits and falsifications, a German version was distributed by the Association of Austrian Banks and Bankers, and a Dutch edition was sponsored by an Amsterdam company, the Financieel Archief (Systeem Keesing). The Commission collaborated with the judicial authorities of the fifteen countries that now make up the European Union (apart from Ireland), as well as the United States, the Baltic countries, Norway, Bulgaria, Hungary, Poland, Romania, Switzerland, Czechoslovakia and Yugoslavia. The issuing banks in over 60 countries were regularly asked to

80

THE WAR
AGAINST
FORGERY

Micrographic examination of minute particles from banknotes, *c.* 1921.

Counterfeiting inspired novels, films – and comic strips. The Belgian artist Hergé (1907–83) drew inspiration from news trivia for *The Black Island*, in which his hero Tintin routs an international gang of money-traffickers.

inform the rest of the world of any issue of new banknotes, seizures of forged notes and arrests of counterfeiters. In 1929 an international convention on the repression of counterfeiting was signed in Geneva, on the initiative of the Society of Nations.

The dossiers on counterfeiters made it clear that some of these offenders had a long history of recidivism. The case of Salomon Smolianoff serves as a good example. He was a Ukrainian who had been ruined by the October Revolution. In 1927 he checked into a hotel in Stockholm under a false identity and went on to pay his bill with a false English 50-pound note. The law caught up with him in Amsterdam, where he admitted his real identity and claimed that the forged notes that he had disposed of were in fact the work of another counterfeiter, an academy professor called Zaranski. Smolianoff himself had merely appended missing signatures and numbers. 'I kept the unfinished notes which I found in the professor's suitcases for a long time, without ever touching them. However, at the limit of my resources, and in a foreign country, I finally decided to complete them and use them'. It turned out that, although the two forgers did know each other well, the banknotes they put into circulation were not of the same type. In the course of the inquiry, 'Smolianoff' notes were also discovered in Stockholm, Oslo, Bergen, Amsterdam, Frankfurt, Baden-Baden, Munich, Prague, Vienna, Budapest, Berlin and Paris. Rather a lot for just one man! However, it was impossible to prove that Smolianoff had any connection with a criminal gang and he was only given a short prison sentence. Five years later, in 1932, a large number of false English 10-pound notes were identified in Rotterdam, Paris and Jerusalem. After a secret investigation, Scotland Yard and the Dutch police collared one Boris Sepkovich in The Hague in possession of 500 false 10-pound notes. Tracing the network up to the top, they ended up in Berlin, where in 1935 they arrested Smolianoff himself, who had been producing false banknotes in the German capital since 1930!

Several incidents of forgery between the two world wars implicated a private company commissioned to do printing work for a bank of issue. The most notorious case involved the English firm Waterlow & Sons and the Banco de Portugal. In February 1924, the Banco put into circulation a new 500-escudo note, decorated with a portrait of Vasco de Gama, and printed, as usual, by the English company. However, in December 1925, pairs of notes with the same numbers were discovered in Oporto. It turned out that Waterlow & Sons had passed on a series of banknotes, stamped with numbers that had already been released, to a gang that specialised in the production of falsified official documents. Without the knowledge of the Banco de Portugal, more than 200,000 notes to the value of 500 escudos had been reprinted, identical in every respect to those already in circulation. For a while, the 'false' notes circulated alongside the genuine ones. When the affair was made public, the Bank was concerned about how it was possible to separate the grain from the chaff – in other words, how to recognise the false notes. Waterlow & Sons indicated the technical means that could be used to distinguish the two issues, but the Banco de Portugal decided to honour all the notes in circulation and exchange them for new ones.

During the Second World War, the German secret services counterfeited pounds sterling on a massive scale. Himmler, acting on the idea of an SS officer, Alfred Naujocks, was apparently the instigator of this attempt to undermine Britain's financial stability. A high-ranking officer, Bernhard Krüger, a chemical engineer in civilian life, was responsible for the technical aspects, as well as providing the code name for the operation - 'Bernhard'. He recruited designers, engravers, typographers, printers and photographers by taking them out of the camps and prisons where they were being held as prisoners of war or common criminals. One of his 'employees' was none other than Salomon Smolianoff, whom we have already met. The printing workshops were hidden in Sachsenhausen concentration camp, near Berlin, and they succeeded in reconstructing almost perfectly the paper, watermarks and printed motifs of British banknotes. The Nazis disposed of these notes by making purchases in neutral or allied countries, although they also spent them on the black markets of occupied areas. The German secret services took advantage of these forgeries to buy arms and foreign currency. It was said, moreover, that they were used to pay both the famous spy Cicero and Otto Skorzeny, who rescued Mussolini from San Grasso in 1943. Nevertheless, only a small part of the money produced in the Sachsenhausen workshops – which provided work for 144 people in 1944 – could be used before Germany's surrender. According to some sources, a mere 7.5 per cent of the output was dispersed. At the end of the war, just as Smolianoff and a small team were about to start a massive production of fake dollars, the Germans evacuated the camp at Sachsenhausen. The stocks of unused notes were dumped in Lake Töplitz, in Austria. Since then, part of this 'treasure' has been recovered by intrepid divers – and some of these rescued counterfeits have been bought by collectors at their face value!

In the second half of the twentieth century the falsification of banknotes became once again the domain of private individuals, either organised in gangs or working as lone amateurs. Large-scale counterfeiters often draw on professional printers with access to specialist machinery, although they sometimes have to make do with equipment that has been merely cobbled together. This 'industrial' counterfeiting can prove dangerous as large amounts of forged money in circulation are liable to erode a country's credit in the long term. As for the amateurs, they have varying degrees of skill and attempt often extremely rudimentary procedures in their homes. Counterfeiters of this kind are rarely dangerous, partly because their production is limited – and frequently only used to cover their personal domestic needs – and partly because the majority of their output can fool only the most gullible consumer.

Nevertheless, these amateurs have included the odd genius. Several incidents demonstrated this after the Second World War – the Karl Peglow affair in Germany, for example, or the Bojarski affair in France. It was once said that 'in the history of counterfeiting, one talks of a Bojarski in the same way as one talks of a Cézanne in painting'. This Polish-born engineer had married a French woman and led a bourgeois life in a beautiful house in Vic-sur-Cère. It was there, in 1964, that French police, led by the head of the Sûreté Nationale's Office for the Repression of Counterfeiting, Emile Benhamou, discovered a fully equipped counterfeiting workshop, hidden by a trapdoor. However, what really stunned the police was that the subsequent inquiry demonstrated that Bojarski had reconstructed, step by step, without any outside help,

Bank of England £20-note forged by the Germans during the Second World War, 210 x 130 mm (8.27 x 5.12 in.). BNB.

every phase of the banknote production process, with near-perfect results. He had worked out a way of making pulp by dissolving leaves of cigarette paper and tracing paper in bleach; he had engraved copper plates with all the skill of a professional; he had copied the watermarks of the notes of the Banque de France, of which it had been – with reason – so proud; he had made up the inks required for his masterpieces, on the basis of commercially available products. This affair, exceptional in many ways, became even more so when the management of the Banque de France announced its intention to reimburse holders of false 'Bojarski' notes who had received them as payment in good faith. What greater tribute could the Banque pay to the genius of this forger? Moreover, in his cell Bojarski dreamt of breaking with his past and working for the Banque!

However, such cases are the exception to the rule. And, in fact, there is often no need to be a genius to deceive plenty of people. In 1957 the German Chief of Police, Heinz Müller, explained that the technical perfection applied to banknotes would be futile as long as the general public accepted the most rudimentary forgeries so unthinkingly. And he gave some examples. Police in northern Germany had recently seized some 50-mark notes, drawn by hand, on which a humorous forger had written, in place of the warning to counterfeiters: 'counterfeiting notes is often worthwhile, as it's very difficult to get by these days'. Another rival to the issuing banks, who designed 20-mark notes, was proud to inscribe, in capital letters, '20 FALSCHE MARK' instead of '20 DEUTSCHE MARK'. (A question of honour, no doubt). Others put into circulation advertising leaflets imitating the image of a banknote, photographic reproductions, in black and white or in garish colours, or notes printed on writing paper with a simple rubber stamp. And all of these found a taker!

More recently, issuing banks have been confronted by a fashion for forgeries made by amateurs with the help of a colour photocopier. This type of reproduction has required new answers. It is often necessary to remind the public, and particularly young people – via poster campaigns in schools, for example – that it is illegal to reproduce banknotes 'for fun' or 'to see what it comes out like'; this very act presumes the intention to create fake money, and a reproduction does not have to be of high quality to constitute punishable counterfeiting. The printing of numbered banknotes is therefore absolutely forbidden. On an international front, the fight against forged banknotes still occupies part of the resources of Interpol, although for the last few years the falsification of credit cards has often been of greater concern than that of paper money. Every year Interpol produces a new edition of its counterfeiting dossier, published in eight languages: German, English, Arabic, Chinese, Spanish, French, Italian and Russian. The first part of this register, giving descriptions of the most notorious forgeries, is reserved for institutions specialising in the fight against counterfeiting.

500-escudo note, Banco de Portugal, 1922, obverse, 188 x 111 mm (7.40 x 4.37 in.). BP. This issue, with its portrait of Vasco da Gama and printed by Waterlow and Sons in London, was at the centre of the largest counterfeiting scandal in Portuguese history.

Poster advertising discounts at German Konsum stores, c. 1949. Deutsches Historisches Museum, Berlin.
Nowadays, strict legislation governs the use of banknotes on publicity material.

Scraps of paper

The need to fight against forgery has obliged banks of issue to summon up all their inventiveness and continuously question their most basic assumptions and most tried and tested techniques. As we shall see, production methods have become ever more complex, with respect to the composition of the paper, the colour of the illustrations and printing techniques.

In the early days the paper did not present any distinctive characteristics, but in the second half of the nineteenth century, the banks of issue, prompted by improvements in watermarks, started to use rag papers of increasingly special quality. The pulp was obtained by crushing rags and old clothes selected from those collected by ragmen. Linen or hemp would be added to increase a paper's resistance, while cotton made it more supple. The time taken for the crushing was of crucial importance: if it was too long, the solidity of the paper was endangered; if it was too short, the pulp would not be homogeneous enough and the quality of the watermarks would be diminished.

Fiduciary paper has very special requirements: good resistance to traction, folding and perforation. It must have a constant, precisely defined weight and a smoothness that can be recognised by touch. The latter is achieved by satinising, a process that consists of squeezing the paper between two cylinders.

The manufacturing process gradually became more complex and more automated. When paper mills could no longer obtain sufficient amounts of rags – particularly rags without synthetic fibres – they started using untreated cotton. The final decades of the twentieth century saw the introduction of continuous paper in large rolls, and a production process that incorporated the creation of the watermarked support and the immersion of the security thread into the sheet, as well as drying, gluing and satinising.

Where possible, issuing banks sought to obtain their paper supply from their own country through paper mills that were under their direct control. In 1754 the Riksens Ständers Bank set up its own paper mill in Tumba, not far from Stockholm, and the first paper for banknotes was produced in 1759. Private Swedish banks also took advantage of the Tumba paper mill, at least until 1852, when part of their supply began to come from England. The paper for the first Finnish banknotes was sometimes provided by the local Tervakoski company, but it more often came from abroad (Germany and Sweden). From 1886 onwards, however, a Finnish paper mill was able to satisfy almost all the demands of the state bank. All the banknotes in the Netherlands, from the first 'roodborstjes' in 1816, have been printed on paper manufactured within the country, mostly by the Van Houtum & Palm company in Ugchelen. Spain began to manufacture paper for banknotes in Burgos in the early 1950s. The Bank of England has entrusted its supply to the Portals company for many

Burning banknotes at the Banque nationale de Belgique, first half of the twentieth century. BNB. The disposal of used notes has long been a headache for issuing banks.

Issuing banks have devised various technical means to test the strength of their paper. Two pictured here are a Schopper pliagraphe for measuring resistance to folding, and a Lhomme & Ardy extensometer to test tear strength. BF.

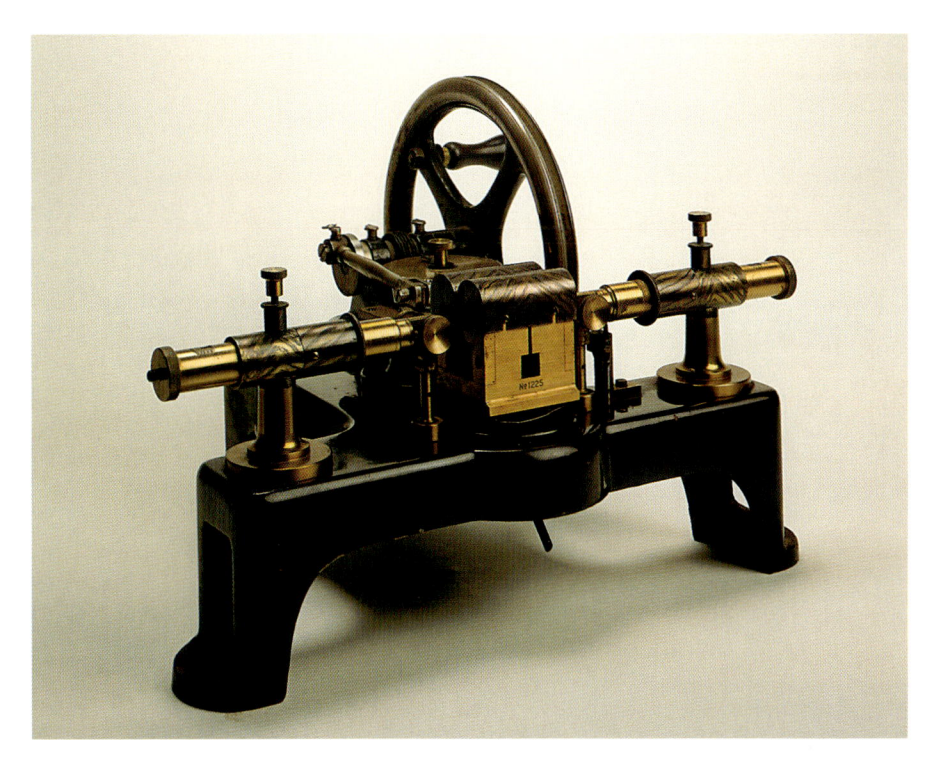

years. The German Reichsbank used the products of the Spechthausen mill, near Eberswalde, for a long time, although in times of crisis it had to resort to many other suppliers.

The Banque de France first turned to the Guyot paper mill in Buges, which had already provided the paper for the *assignats*. In 1811, it switched to the Papeterie du Marais, but it was already contemplating the creation of its own paper mill. After several vain attempts to do so, in 1875 the Banque finally built a mill at Biercy (Seine-et-Marne) – although it was only capable of handling its 1,000- and 500-franc notes. Private companies continued to supply the bank with the paper for lower-value notes. In 1890 the head engineer at the Biercy mill proposed replacing the rag paper used until then with paper made with ramie, a fibrous plant native to China, which would make its paper more opaque and give it a distinctive feel when touched. France took up this proposal in 1902 for its larger banknotes. In 1920 a new paper mill and a new printing house were put into operation on the outskirts of Clermont-Ferrand. Today this paper mill, now fully modernised, produces continuous watermarked paper, based on untreated cotton and furnished with its own security thread.

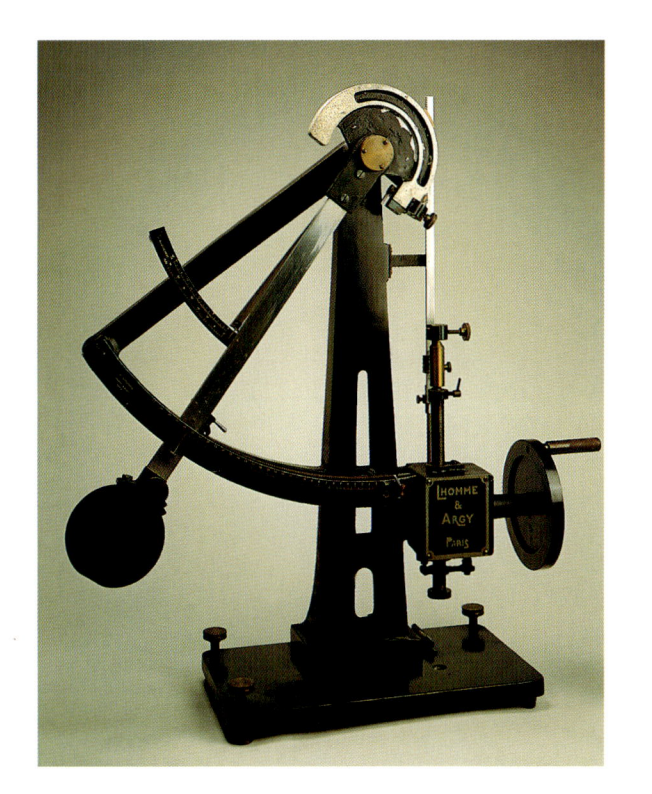

Other countries have long depended on paper from outside. For reasons of quality, the Banque nationale de Belgique started to place orders with the Papeterie du Marais mill in France in 1869. The manufacturing of the paper was supervised by a representative of the Banque de France. In 1906 Belgium stopped using handmade paper, which was uneconomic for making notes with lower values, and turned to watermarked paper made with machines in the French Perrigot mill in Arches. In 1925 there was a further change: the Banque now placed its orders with the British Portals company, which supplied the Bank of England. In Portugal, the Banco de Lisboa used paper provided by a local firm until 1834, then it resorted to English mills, with a demand for paper 'similar to that used by the Bank of England for its own notes'. From 1875 onwards, the Banco de Portugal turned to a series of foreign mills, particularly French ones (Blanchet Frères & Kléber, Masure et Perrigot, Papeteries d'Arches, Papeterie du Marais and Papeterie de Sainte-Marie).

The format of the banknotes issued in Europe has obviously depended on the period and the country concerned. Up until the First World War, notes were printed in large formats, but this practice had its disadvantages: faster deterioration, the abundance of multiple folds that could obscure the face value and the increasingly high cost of the support. Increased production and a drive to save paper, particularly in the years between the two world wars, caused European banknotes to shrink almost everywhere. Nowadays, the notes in circulation come in various types of format. In most countries they vary in length and breadth according to their face value, to make them easier to distinguish from each other, although the notes in the Netherlands, Denmark, France, Luxembourg and Austria are all of the same width, but with varying lengths, to economise on paper and adapt to the printing equipment available. Finnish and English banknotes are all of the same format.

10-riksdaler note, Sveriges Rikes Ständers Bank, 1859. SRB.
With rectangular notes, it is not always the horizontal dimension which is the longer. There are also some square formats.

Dupont machine for the industrial production of watermarked paper, c. 1875. BF.

The watermark

The oldest security device still in use, apart from the signature of the issuer, is the watermark: texts, numbers or images visible when held up to the light, due to variations in the thickness of these parts in the pulp. The process originally involved placing a wire, fashioned to form an image in relief, on the mould used to make the paper: once it had dried, the paper was thinner at this point. As early as 1666, a watermark reading 'Banco' could be seen on some *kreditivsedlar* from the Stockholms Banco. In the first half of the nineteenth century, the elements selected to appear on watermarks were the name of the bank or its initials, the value of the note in letters or figures or geometric forms. More complex designs, such as the coat of arms of the issuing country or plants, were less common, although in 1847 the notes of the Banco de Isabel featured a watermarked portrait of Queen Isabel II. The mid-nineteenth century witnessed the development of the shaded watermark technique in Europe. This consisted of stamping the metallic mesh that supports the pulp with a matrix: the ridges had a thinner layer of pulp and the hollows had a thicker one, which made it possible to achieve papers that presented finely shaded images against a back light. The shaded watermark technique was first used in England in 1855. In 1862, the Banque de France produced an innovative shaded watermark of a human head. Other European countries gradually showed interest in this idea. The human head was first used in Spain in 1871, in Belgium and Portugal in 1894 (in a period when both countries were supplied with French paper), in Germany in 1908, in England on two notes issued in 1928, in Austria in 1930 and in the Netherlands in 1931. However, even after they adopted this motif, some countries, such as the Netherlands, went on to make variations with animals (bees, seagulls), fruit or crowns.

Wax Hermes used for the watermark on a 100-franc note of the Banque de France, 1862, BF. To make the copper matrix which stamps the paper and produces the watermark, a design is engraved on a wax model backed by a glass sheet. The transparent nature of the material and the backing allow the assessment of variations in light and shade.

The evolution of printing techniques

The first banknotes were often drawn up by hand, at least in part. When the Bank of England tried to put completely pre-printed notes into circulation in 1695, a forgery was immediately discovered! The Bank reacted by decreeing that on all its notes, the value, the name of the person to whom it was made out, the registry number and the cashier's signature would henceforth all be written with pen and ink. The printed text was composed in italic, in order to establish a degree of similarity with the entirely hand-written notes that had been in circulation until then.

For the printed part of the notes – whether text, decorations or an engraved vignette – the issuing banks had a choice between black-line relief engraving and intaglio. In the former, the ink is only retained by the parts in relief. In the nineteenth century, wooden blocks were used to apply this technique to some notes, such as those of the Kingdom of Prussia, issued in 1806, which had an outer margin printed from a wooden matrix. However, this type of material wore out too quickly, so for large runs steel or yellow copper plates were preferred. The Banque de France made steel typographical matrices to use the relief-engraving technique on its very first banknotes. For a while, a single plate served to print each type of banknote; in this way, some 175 notes could be printed per day (at that time, the banks of issue used manually operated presses). The increase in the amount of notes put into circulation, however, forced the Bank's management to put more presses into operation: the original plates for the notes were then reproduced by electrotyping. This procedure involves making a wax mould of the imprints of the plates, then plunging this mould into a tub saturated with copper salt and connecting it to the two poles of an electric battery. After a few days, the copper has settled on the mould and has assumed its shape to form a perfect double of the steel template. This method was also used by some issuing banks to duplicate wooden typographic plates in copper (this was the case for the late nineteenth-century notes of Denmark).

Outside France, only the Banque nationale de Belgique and, from 1855, the Bank of England have systematically employed typographic printing based on relief engraving. Other countries mainly used intaglio engraving. Dating from the fifteenth century, this process consists of transferring onto paper, through pressure, the ink remaining in the incisions in a metal plate once it has been engraved and inked and then had its surface wiped clean. This produces sharper printing than typography. Intaglio engraving was used from the end of the seventeenth century for the notes of the Bank of England. In France, the notes issued by John Law's Bank between 1716 and 1720 were printed using either intaglio or typography.

80-florin note, Nederlandsche Bank, 1814, known as the *roodborstje*, 210 x 95 mm (8.27 x 3.74 in.). DNB. Notes of the Netherlands from 1815 to 1860 featured only typographical characters. The printer Enschedé constructed a security framework from a font known as *parelmuziek*, designed in the 1700s for – you've guessed! – printing musical scores. Only Enschedé possessed this font. But the device proved too crude to prevent the appearance of false *roodborstjes* in 1853.

The decorative elements on some *assignats* were printed in intaglio: the portrait of Louis XVI engraved by Augustin de Saint-Aubin (1736–1807), for example, or the eagle with outspread wings designed by Nicolas Marie Gatteaux (1751–1832) and engraved by Pierre Alexandre Tardieu. In Spain, the *cédulas* or bonds of guarantee of the Banco de San Carlos, dating from 1783, were printed in intaglio from etched copper plates. The Netherlands adopted intaglio printing in 1860.

Up until the end of the eighteenth century, the engraved plates used for intaglio printing were normally made of polished red copper, with a thickness of one to three millimetres. The Banco de Lisboa was still using these copper plates to print notes in 1822, but they wore out very quickly. Their replacements always bore new motifs, which explains why there was such a great diversity of designs for a relatively small volume of banknotes. At the beginning of the nineteenth century, the American Jacob Perkins perfected a technique for printing on steel that gave rise to much more resistant plates. This process was introduced in Austria in 1841, on the initiative of Franz von Salzmann, who was in charge of the printing of banknotes, and its first use in Denmark seems to date from 1834.

By around 1860, therefore, almost all the countries in Europe – apart from England, France and Belgium – had adopted intaglio printing. In 1857 the Banque de France studied the possibility of converting to it as well but eventually ruled it out. It was true that some of its executives acknowledged that the process had certain aesthetic advantages, but at that time intaglio could not be used on both sides of a note, and the Banque would have been

The play of light

In the eighteenth century most notes were not printed on the reverse side, which served for endorsements or successive transfers, added in pen. The first notes printed on both sides in Finland date from 1840; in Portugal, from 1847; in the Netherlands, from 1860; in Austria, from 1863; in Spain, from 1868. The notes issued in 1806 by the Wiener-Stadt-Banco represented an innovation, as they introduced a new double-sided printing technique invented by Johann Ferdinand Edler von Schönfeld: when the note was put up to the light, the illustrations on both sides fitted together perfectly. The same trick was used by the Banque de France from 1813 to 1863, but with considerably more complicated images. Between 1818 and 1821, the Bank of England investigated the possibility of making 'identical' notes, with the reverse side of the note bearing the inverted image of the obverse. The Bank finally rejected this idea, but the process was soon put into practice elsewhere. Several German banknotes from the years 1849 to 1855 bore illustrations that could be found, inverted, on the other face. The same technique was also used in Belgium for the first notes issued by the Banque nationale in 1851. On the Spanish note of 1868, it is the lithographed background that is reproduced in an inverted form. The trick of identical printing was, however, quickly mastered by forgers and became almost obsolete in the 1860s.

5-florin note, Duchy of Nassau, printed by C. Naumann of Franfurt am Main, 1847, reverse. DBB. To make counterfeiting more difficult, some engravers attempted relief effects.

1,000-mark note, Suomen Pankki, 1918, reverse, by Eliel Saarinen (1873–1950), 200 x 120 mm (7.87 x 4.72 in.). BNB. All the notes of the 1909 series by Saarinen (slightly modified for a new issue in 1918) were designed with a vertical axis of symmetry.

Printer's plate for Banque de Flandre notes of the 1840s. BNB.

obliged to abandon its identical printing. It should also be noted that in times of crisis, or when funds were low, the time-consuming procedure of intaglio was rejected in favour of typographic printing. This occurred in Germany, for example, during the hyperinflation from 1921 to 1924. Sometimes, intaglio was only used to print the notes with the highest values, as was the case in Denmark in 1875.

In the nineteenth century, printers of banknotes rarely took advantage of lithography, a planographic printing process invented in 1798 by the Bavarian Aloys Senefelder and based on the repulsion of greasy inks and water. There are some exceptions, however: the notes issued in 1844 by the Banco de Isabel, or those issued in 1847 and 1868 by the Banco Español de San Fernando, subsequently the Banco de España. In Germany, the Kurhessische Leih- & Commerzbank in Cassel put a lithographic note into circulation in 1855. In 1856 the Nederlandsche Bank conducted research on polychromatic lithography, but an experiment undertaken by the lithographer Charles Rochussen proved to be a failure. The process was basically restricted to the reproduction of artistic or humorous drawings.

Many banks sought to combine several printing techniques on their notes. Many of the banknotes produced in the mid-nineteenth century by the Giesecke & Devrient company used typography on the obverse and intaglio on the reverse. The notes issued by the Banco de España in 1862 combined three printing processes: lithography, intaglio and typography.

Printing equipment was gradually improved over the course of the nineteenth century. In the early days, manual intaglio pressing was a slow process that required two workers: one to ink the plate, another to wipe it. The paper was then put into position, in line with markers, and the press was operated by hand. In the middle of the century, steam presses made their first appearance. The ones used by the Reichsdruckerei in Berlin in the 1890s were manned by two teams of two employees, working simultaneously; this procedure made it possible for each machine to produce runs of six to eight hundred sheets of four banknotes in one day. In 1904 the Reichsdruckerei acquired semi-automatic intaglio presses, which inked and wiped the printing plates mechanically. The next phase began in 1928: completely automated printing machines were introduced by the Reichsdruckerei, in conjunction with the Koenig & Bauer company from Würzburg. The inking and wiping of the plates, the feeding of the sheets of paper, the printing and the final collection were all undertaken without any human assistance.

In 1934 the Banque de France finally adopted intaglio printing; the perfecting of an original dry printing technique made it possible to use intaglio printing on both sides of very thin paper, permitting a very precise alignment and exact juxtaposition of the motifs printed on the obverse and the reverse. The 5,000-franc note printed that same year was evidence of this: the main motif, printed in four colours, was identically reproduced on both sides.

Printing methods continued to evolve in the second half of the twentieth century, not only by incorporating different printing methods into a single process, but also

Printing department of the Banque nationale de Belgique. BNB.
Most European issuing banks print their own notes.

Intaglio plate for a 5,000-franc note of the Banque de France, 1934. BF. In 1933–4, the Banque de France adopted intaglio printing on dry media.

by progressing from a system of printing in separate sequences on presses that were fed paper sheet by sheet to a system of continuous printing on presses equipped with rolls of paper. In the 1950s, the Sveriges Riksbank and the Bank of England collaborated with the Goebel company in Darmstadt and with Thrissell in England to develop machines for continuous printing. After a period of trial and error, the first Swedish notes printed on this type of press were issued in 1961, and the first English ones appeared the following year. In the early 1960s the Bank of England also investigated a system of electronic screening, designed to discard any defective notes before they went into circulation. Electronics was still in its infancy, however, and the experiments were abandoned in 1967.

With respect to continuous printing, other countries followed the lead of Sweden and Britain. The Goebel machine used in France since 1989 can print four notes at a time. The notes are printed obverse – reverse in a single sequence, in trichrome intaglio and coloured offset, at a rate of 120 m (400 ft) of rolled paper per minute!

Automation has also changed the operations used to monitor notes once they are returned to the bank of issue. The Bundesbank installed a machine in 1977 that made it possible to process notes withdrawn from circulation at a rate of eight per second. The machine discards any notes in bad condition and checks their authenticity by reading codes on the paper.

Banknote checkers at their desks, c. 1920. BNB.
The manual checking of notes – still carried out today – allows faulty specimens to be rejected. These, however, are eagerly sought by collectors.

100-schilling note, Österreichische Nationalbank, 1949, reverse, by Erhard Amadeus-Dier (1893–1969), 176 x 85 mm (6.93 x 3.82 in.). ONB.

SECURITY HANGING ON A THREAD

The incorporation of foreign bodies into the pulp is a long-established security measure. In 1822 the Banque de France was already dreaming of making forgers' lives more difficult by inserting metallic elements into the paper. A wire crossed the entire breadth of a Spanish note issued in 1871, and, in the following years, the Banco de España inserted strips of cotton, one centimetre wide, across the breadth of its notes! This practice was abandoned at the beginning of the twentieth century, when the bank went back to printing its notes abroad. In Germany, the *Reichskassenscheine* notes of the 1880s were printed on a new type of paper invented by the American Russ Wilcox, with coloured vegetable fibres mixed into the pulp. Red and blue fibres were similarly embedded in the paper used for banknotes in the 1890s to form a strip running across the entire note. The French paper mill in Arches used the same process in 1903 for paper commissioned by the Banco de España. In 1906 the Giesecke & Devrient company applied for a patent for a procedure that incorporated strips of coloured paper into the pulp. The strands of silk embedded in the paper supplied to Portugal in 1938 by the English Portals company were only visible when the note was exposed to ultraviolet light.

A metallic thread was first inserted into a British banknote in 1940. This system of a security thread (made of metal or plastic) was then adopted by most other European countries: by Germany and Austria in 1949, by Belgium and Spain in 1978 and by France in 1990. The principle has recently been modified to prevent coloured photocopying of banknotes. In 1984 the Bank of England came up with the idea of inserting a metal strip which appears on the surface of one of the faces at regular intervals. This strip comes out badly in photocopies as a discontinuous black line which stands out at first glance. This new process was also taken up by most banks of issue in the 1990s.

The choice of printer

Most European banks of issue strive to be independent as far as printing is concerned, but some are obliged by financial and technical factors to resort to private printing houses. The notes of the Banco de España, for example, were printed in Spain from 1868 to 1875, from 1885 to 1905 and from 1941 onwards, but before 1868 and in the remaining intervals they were printed by British or American companies. The Banco de Portugal, which had its own printing workshops in the nineteenth century, turned to British printers in 1903. The Bank of Ireland only acquired its own printing works in 1970, as Greece had done in 1949. The Finnish Suomen Pannki created a printing department in 1885, under the supervision of a German-born lithographer, but it was not until 1922 that the engraving and printing of banknotes was completely undertaken in Helsinki itself.

The most important companies specialising in fiduciary paper were created in the middle of the nineteenth century. In England, Bradbury, Wilkinson & Co., Ltd., founded in 1824 by William Bradbury, specialised in printing from steel matrices. In 1861 Bradbury teamed up with the engraver Robert Wilkinson and sought business printing banknotes. The firm worked not only for several English banks but also for the national banks of Greece – in 1885, 1897 and 1917 – and Finland – in 1897 – as well as the Banco di Napoli from 1870 to 1880 and several Swedish banks. In the twentieth century it was one of the firms entrusted with the printing of Spanish banknotes, from 1906 to the Second World War, and it was responsible for the bulk of Portuguese notes from 1903 onwards. The Bradbury company has, however, faced competition from other English companies. The Thomas De La Rue company, which produced its first banknote in 1859, took over some issues of the Banco de Portugal after 1945. As for Waterlow & Sons, its output included notes issued by the Ionian Bank in 1898 and in 1914; 100- and 25-drachma notes issued in 1916–17 by the Bank of Crete; some of the Banco de Portugal's notes in the 1920s; as well as the Legal Tender Notes issued in Ireland between 1928 and 1959.

The notes produced prior to the unification of the Reich in Germany were the work of various companies, one of the most prolific being C. Naumann in Frankfurt (later Dondorf & Naumann). This firm's notes displayed a whole series of security measures which were extremely modern at that time: mini-letters, relief engraving, highly detailed backgrounds with geometric designs ornamented with guilloches; and identical printing. In the 1870s Naumann made some notes for foreign banks of issue, particularly the Italian Banca Nazionale and the Banque nationale du Luxembourg. Another German printing house, Giesecke & Devrient, was founded in 1852 in Leipzig by Hermann Giesecke and Alphonse Devrient. It soon began to specialise in engraving from copper and steel matrices. It produced a note for the Leipziger Bank in 1855, and two years later it did work for the Hannoversche Bank. Over the course of time this highly specialised production took on a growing importance, and between 1860 and 1875 it worked successively for some twenty German banks of issue, such as the Bank für Süddeutschland in Darmstadt, the Sächsische Bank in Dresden, the Leipziger Bank and the Bayerische Hypotheken-und Wechsel-Bank. When the Reichsbank was founded in 1875 it turned to foreign customers, supplying banknotes to Luxembourg, Switzerland, Portugal, Germany's African colonies and several Latin American countries.

These European firms faced competition from the American Banknote Company, founded in 1858. The notes that came off its presses were highly distinctive, with margins ornamented with guilloches and numbering with a unique appearance. They never bore a watermark. The American Banknote Company mainly worked for the Greek national bank – from 1867 to 1928 – the Banca Nazionale nel Regno d'Italia – from 1866 to 1872 – and the Banca Romana, in the 1870s.

Logo of the British printers Bradbury, Wilkinson & Co., 1935. Private collection.

1,000-peseta note, Banco de España, 1907, reverse, by Enrique Vaquer, 145 x 108 mm (5.71 x 4.25 in.). BESp. This is the last note produced by the Banco de España's press before the Second World War.

500-peseta note, Banco de España, 1876, reverse, 170 x 97 mm (6.70 x 3.82 in.). BESp. The style of individual presses is immediately recognisable. This note is by the American Bank Note Company.

The colour of money

In the early nineteenth century banknotes were still printed in black. Ink of this colour was the most stable and its manufacturing had been perfected, as it had already been used to print the paper money that had been issued in the eighteenth century. Red ink was far less common, although it was used in the production of some *assignats*. The first notes printed by the Nederlandsche Bank in 1814 were also printed in red, earning them the nickname of *roodborstjes*, or 'robins'. Some Austrian notes issued in 1806 by the Wiener-Stadt-Banco, and in 1825 by the Privilegirte Österreichsiche National bank, were printed in two colours (red and black). A note issued as early as 1777 by the Royal Bank of Scotland went one better: the text was in black, the value in blue and the bank's seal in red.

The new invention of photography forced issuing banks to pay closer attention to the question of colour. The search for an exact, automated means of reproducing reality had been underway for some time. The discoveries of Niépce (1826), Talbot (1835) and Daguerre (1837) had made possible the 'immediate capturing of forms by a sensitive plate'. Photography was initially considered a mere scientific curiosity; in only a few years it became an industry, a means of communication and even an art form in its own right. Several photo-engraving techniques were developed over the course of the nineteenth century, adapted to the different printing methods (relief, incision or flat) and all based on the effect of light on photosensitive surfaces. The halftone technique made it possible to reproduce photos on relief supports. Intaglio photo-engraving was made possible by the development of helio-engraving. These processes made the task of banks of issue more complex as they provided counterfeiters with remarkable tools for reproducing banknotes exactly and cheaply. In 1849 the Paris Academy of Sciences raised the alarm by alerting governments of the danger that could be posed by new techniques for the mechanical reproduction of texts and engraved images. It was now no longer necessary to call on the services of an engraver or designer. An inquiry undertaken in 1850 on false 200-franc banknotes implicated a 'maker of daguerreotype portraits'.

Two ways were open to the issuing banks: increasing the detail of their designs (intaglio made possible renderings of extreme precision, which photo-engraving would not manage to attain for many years to come), or developing the use of colour, less photogenic than black and white. In Portugal the two sides of a note issued in 1847 were printed in different colours. In 1851 the Banque nationale de Belgique started printing its provisional notes in black with security backgrounds of blue, red or green, depending on the value of the note. In 1853 the Bank used a blue ink for the main motif of its new 1,000-francs – even though this cobalt blue apparently caused the printers great difficulties. (The same colour was taken up by the Banque de France in 1862, as the counterfeiting of notes printed with black ink was becoming more and more common.) This blue ink, chosen for its resistance to various chemical reactions, came from the Schneberg royal manufacturing house in Saxony. However, the results were only partially successful as the note's highly detailed motif had been designed for printing with black ink, and the public complained about the faintness of the texts, which were sometimes hard to read. From 1871 to 1873 the Banque de France recruited the chemist Berthelot to experiment with the simultaneous use of two colours. The board finally opted to combine the cobalt blue of the main motif with a bistre colour reserved for the security backgrounds. Its first two-coloured note, with a value of 20 francs, was put into circulation in 1888. It also displayed a vignette printed with invisible ink, made up of ornamental motifs and bearing the inscription 'the law punishes the counterfeiter'. This warning was only supposed to appear under the effect of intense heat.

In 1856 the Königliche Preussische Kassen-Anweisung printed 1-thaler treasury notes with a warning to counterfeiters repeated on the reverse over fifty-three lines and printed in five different colours, which made the note impossible to forge. Unfortunately, the printing process turned out to be so complicated that a large number of notes had to be destroyed due to manufacturing defects.

Four-colour printing was perfected at the end of the nineteenth century. In 1897 the Banque nationale de Belgique issued a four-colour note printed on Lambert typographic presses, which made it possible to print one whole side of a note in a single passage through the machine. The Banque de France developed its first four-colour note in 1897, but the vignette designed by François Flameng was criticised for its excessive number of motifs; it was not until 1910 that a four-

One of the earliest cameras used by Nicéphore Niépce, c. 1820–30. Musée Nicéphore Niépce, Chalon-sur-Saône. The invention of photography placed a question mark over the future of notes printed in black on white.

100-franc note, Banque de France, 1862, obverse, by P. Brisset and H. Cabasson, 180 x 109 mm (7.09 x 4.29 in.). BF. The first French note printed in blue ink; it was also the first to use the shaded representation of a head as a watermark.

20-franc note, Banque nationale de Belgique, 1894, obverse, by Louis Titz (1859–1932). 137 x 88 mm (5.39 x 3.46 in.) BNB. The first four-colour Belgian note, released in 1897.

colour French banknote actually went into circulation. Some issues presented degradations of colour that made them look like rainbows. This was the case, for example, with most of the Austrian notes issued between 1904 and 1927. The 1,000-mark notes issued by the Reichsbank from 1876 were printed in black and brown, with numbering in red, but the Reichs-bank only made moderate use of colour in the other values before the turn of the century. Only a few distinctive markings, such as the order number or the state seal, stood out in red against the dominant blue or brown. The same is true of Austria at this time. The first coloured notes issued by the Bank of England – in 1928 – were those of 1 pound and 10 shillings, and they remained in circulation until 1960.

The technical factors involved in the creation of a banknote have always been complicated. In order to gain the confidence of users and stand up to coins – as paper has hardly any intrinsic value – banks of issue have implemented ever more diverse security techniques. Unfortunately, counterfeiters have consistently kept up with them by updating their own methods of reproduction. The development of scanners and photocopiers worries today's banks of issue in the same way that the appearance of photography troubled their predecessors. Reflective surfaces have now been added to some banknotes. Inks are mixed in such a way that their spectrum analysis wavelengths are the ones most difficult to reproduce with electronic machinery. Invisible inks are put into the body of the note and can only be seen under black light: this is the principle behind the machines that detect fake banknotes. The war against forgery continues.

10,000-lire note, Banca d'Italia, 1976, obverse, by T. Cionini. 133 x 69 mm (5.24 x 2.72 in.). Fondazione Cassa di Risparmio di Parma, Parma.
This example, which carries a portrait of Machiavelli, is proof of the remarkable advances made by modern colour technology.

Lambert machine for the colour printing of banknotes. BNB.
This was a French device, used particularly by the Banque nationale de Belgique.

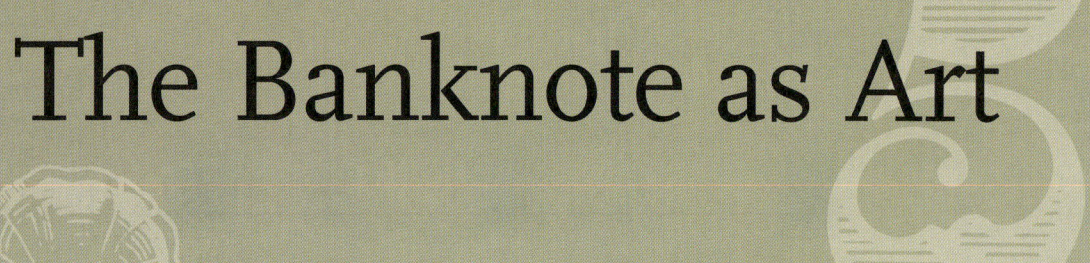

The Banknote as Art

Portraits of the Artists

Although it may be arguable whether banknotes can be considered works of art, it cannot be denied that they are all influenced by the personality of their creators, their country of origin and their times. Moreover, the aesthetic aspects of the banknote, which had already been taken into account in the French *assignats* of the late eighteenth century, evolved over the course of time until they gradually became a determining factor in their conception. Nevertheless, few art historians have bothered themselves with banknotes, even when they were produced by well-known artists.

Issuing banks have traditionally worked with two types of artist: draughtsmen and engravers. The former were responsible for the motifs that appeared on the notes, while the latter reproduced them on steel or copper plates ready for printing. In a few exceptional cases, a single artist was capable of combining both skills: the medal-maker Jean-Jacques Barre (1793–1855) designed and engraved the 500- and 1,000-franc notes issued by the Banque de France in 1842. In Belgium, Joseph Pierre Braemt (1796–1864) and the sculptor and medal-maker Léopold Wiener (1823–91) drew up and engraved the first notes to be issued by the Banque nationale de Belgique, between 1851 and 1856.

The engraving techniques used have varied according to the era, the country and the artists concerned. The fine lines and precision of dry-point engraving reflected a strict, classical approach to art. In the nineteenth century, Spanish issuing banks often used aquafort engraving. The engravers Raphael Esteve (1772–1847), Bartolomé Maura (1842–1926) and the latter's protégé Enrique Vaquer were renowned master aquafortists who worked successively for the Banco Español de San Fernando and the Banco de España. Esteve worked with Goya and is particularly famous for his engravings based on the paintings of famous Spanish artists.

In the nineteenth century, many of the engravers working on banknotes were specialists in the production of medals and coins. In France, for example, Barre was appointed the 'chief coin-engraver' of the Kingdom of France in 1840; André Galle (1761–1844), the engraver of the 500-franc note issued in 1817, worked extensively on the the first decimal coins, while the creator of the same year's 1,000-franc note, the Bordeaux engraver Bertrand Andrieu (1761–1822), was similarly versatile. In Belgium, Braemt and Wiener were the two top engravers in the Brussels Mint. In Spain, the first note issued by the Banco Español de San Fernando, in 1830, was engraved by Mariano González Sepúlveda, head of the engraving section in the Royal Mint. In Portugal, the Banco de Lisboa employed Francisco de Borja Freire, one of the senior engravers in the Portuguese Mint from 1820 to 1840. In Sweden, Carl-Abraham Broling (1798–1851) was an official of the Royal Mint in Stockholm before being appointed the official engraver and head of the Sveriges Rikes Ständers Bank's printing shop in 1830. These are just some of the many examples of this two-pronged approach.

There were other engravers, however, who preferred to work with wood. One of these was the Belgian Adolphe François Pannemaker (1822–1900), one of the pioneers of halftone block engraving (used to reproduce halftones with a paintbrush). Pannemaker is famous for his vast body of illustrations (particularly countless wood engravings commissioned by Gustave Doré) but he also worked with the Banque nationale de Belgique, on three notes issued in 1869, and with the Banque de France, on two notes issued in 1862 and 1863. In Germany, where there was a significant revival of interest in wood engraving after the introduction of end-grain engraving, one of the most active promoters of this technique, Heinrich Neuer, designed and engraved a note for the Bayerische Hypotheken-und Wechsel-Bank in 1850.

5-franc coin of the Kingdom of Belgium, 1865, silver, obverse, with portrait of Leopold II, 37 mm (1.46 in.). Private collection; and 100-franc note, Banque nationale de Belgique, 1856, obverse, 170 x 98 mm (6.70 x 3.86 in.). BNB. Both the coin and the note are by Leopold Wiener (1823–91). Even in the nineteenth century, it was rare for a designer of notes to double as engraver. This is what happened here, as the Banque nationale de Belgique required a master engraver to see the whole process through. Like many engravers involved in the manufacture of notes, Wiener worked for the Monnaie nationale.

Before the work reached the engravers, however, draughtsmen had to create the motifs that were going to appear on the banknotes; these artists were recruited from various fields. The banks often turned to 'academic' painters working as teachers in official institutions. In Germany, for example, Paul Thumann (1834–1908), a teacher in the Weimar art school who was admitted to the Berlin Academy in 1880, designed the first 100-mark notes issued by the Reichsbank in 1883. He was a painter of historical subjects, renowned for his skill as a portrait painter and illustrator. Arthur Kampf (1864–1950), a genre painter equally adept in portraits and military scenes who was appointed a professor in the Berlin Academy in 1898, was also responsible for a note issued by the Reichsbank in 1916. In Holland, the Nederlandsche Bank started systematically to recruit freelance artists in 1860; in 1900, for example, it hired Nicolaas van der Waay (1855–1936), a professor in the Royal Academy and acknowledged master of allegorical painting. In Belgium, Henri Hendrickx (1817–94), known for his historical paintings, was head of an art school in Saint-Josse, a suburb of Brussels, as well as working for twenty-five years for the Banque nationale de Belgique, where he created at least eight notes between 1869 and 1893. Meanwhile, the Privilegirte Österreichische Nationalbank (in 1878 to become the Österreichisch-Ungarische Bank) entrusted the design of their banknotes to recognised painters working in a variety of genres: history, domestic scenes, portraits and landscapes. The painters they used – such as Peter Franz Fendi (1796–1842), Peter Johann Geiger

2-drachma note of the National Bank of Greece, 1885, obverse, by Bradbury, Wilkinson & Co., London; 100-drachma note, National Bank of Greece, 1867, by the American Bank Note Company, New York; and 10-drachma note of the exclusive issuing Bank of Epirothessalia, 1882, obverse, by the Imprimerie filigranique G. Richard et Cie, Paris. BG.
Three Greek notes from the same era, three different printers, and three separate, quite distinct, styles.

(1805–80), Carl Joseph Geiger (1822–1905), Ferdinand Laufberger (1829–81), Jozef von Führich (1800–76), August Eisenmenger (1830–1907) and Rudolf Rössler (1864–1954) – may have fallen into obscurity today, but their banknotes were always distinguished by their elegant design.

Quite a few of the artists employed to design banknotes had architectural training, especially in the first half of the nineteenth century. In Germany these included Wilhelm von Kaulbach (1805–74), who produced notes for the Brunswick bank in 1854 and 1869; Leo von Klenze (1784–1864), the creator of the earliest notes of the Bayerische Hypotheken- und Wechsel-Bank in 1836, and Karl Friedrich Schinkel (1781–1841) and Friedrich August Stüler (1800–65), who drew up Prussian Treasury notes in 1835 and 1851. Other examples are, in France, Charles Percier (1764–1838) and Charles Normand (1765–1840), who designed the first notes for the Banque de France, between 1800 and 1817, and, in Finland, Eliel Saarinen (1873–1950), who was contracted by the Suomen Pankki in the early years of the twentieth century.

In the nineteenth century, when a high proportion of commissions still came from official sources, the creation of banknotes fell under the category of 'official art'; in other words, it was entrusted to well-established artists who were in favour with the authorities. Charles Percier obtained a wide range of official commissions, including the conversion, in collaboration with Pierre Fontaine, of the Malmaison into the residence of the first Consul Bonaparte and the design for the Carrousel triumphal arch. Bertrand Andrieu faithfully served as a medal-maker for the Republic, the Empire and the Restoration. During the Restoration, Jean-Jacques Barre engraved a number of commemorative medals portraying royalty or official, patriotic ceremonies, and he was subsequently chosen to sculpt the coat of arms of the Second Republic in 1848 and the portrait of Napoleon III that appeared on the coins of the Second Empire. In Portugal, the creator of the first series of notes for the Banco de Lisboa was an official court painter, the draughtsman and aquafortist Domingos Antonio de Sequeira, who was nevertheless obliged to go into exile in 1823 for his political beliefs. In Belgium, Henri Hendrickx was also an 'official' artist who designed triumphal arches and the Ommegang chariots. In the Netherlands, Nicolaas van der Waay made the panels that decorated the golden carriages presented as a coronation gift to the young Queen Wilhelmine. None of the German architects mentioned above were lacking in official commissions: Schinkel drew up the plans for the New Guard, the theatre and the Old Museum in Berlin, while Stüler was responsible for, among others, the New Museum; Kaulbach worked on the decoration of the palaces of King Louis II of Bavaria, and Klenze, the Bavarian court architect, built the Old *Pinakothek*, the *Glyptothek* and the royal residence in Munich, as well as the famous Walhalla near Ratisbonne.

A good number of the artists who designed banknotes also received another type of official commission: the creation of postage stamps. Barre, for example, was responsible for the first French postage stamps. The painter Clément Serveau (1886–1972), who produced several French banknotes in the 1930s and 1940s, shared this interest in philately. His compatriot Louis Eugène Mouchon (born in Paris in 1843) designed dozens of stamps, not only for France but also for Belgium, the Netherlands, Luxembourg, Greece, Portugal, Argentina, Persia and Abyssinia. The Belgians Anto Carte (1886–1954) and Maurice Poortman (1890–1954), the Finn Signe Hammarsten-Jansson (1882–1970), the Austrian Koloman

104

THE BANKNOTE
AS ART

Lucas Cranach the Elder, *Portrait of Dr J. Scheyring*, 1529. Musées royaux des beaux-arts de Belgique, Brussels; and 1,000-mark note, Deutsche Bundesbank, 1960, obverse, by Max Bittrof (1890–1972). DBB.
Two examples of how note designs can also be lessons in the history of art.

Moser (1868–1918), the Dutchman Carl Adolf Lion Cachet (1864–1945) and the German Heinrich Nüsser (1821–83) all designed both banknotes and postage stamps.

Many of the banknote artists were even more versatile and explored a wide range of decorative arts. Such is the case in Austria of Koloman Moser, who designed a particularly elegant note in 1910, and Berthold Löffler (1874–1960), who produced one in 1927. As members of the Wiener Werkstätte, they were both responsible for a vast range of work: stained-glass windows, jewellery, decorative objects, furniture, pottery, theatre costumes, posters and toys. Carl Adolf Lion Cachet, who designed many notes for the Nederlandsche Bank in the 1930s, was also one of the most famous and versatile interior decorators in the country, and was particularly renowned for the dozens of boats that he fitted out. In the years between the two world wars a new type of artist appeared on the scene in some countries: the graphic designer, whose artistic skill was coupled with an appreciation of not only the technical limitations of a banknote but also the impact of images on the public imagination.

Apart from the fact that many of the banknote artists belonged to the circle of 'official artists', how did the banks choose them? Around the end of the nineteenth century competitions (either open to all comers or just to a few artists selected by the issuing banks) were held from time to time. In 1888 the Banque nationale de Belgique requested some preliminary studies from the artists Amédée Lynen (1852–1938) and Joseph Stallaert (1825–1903), but nothing specific came out of this rivalry. The Bank applied the same system in 1894, when the Bank assessed two design proposals they had demanded from the painters and illustrators Louis Titz (1859–1932) and Herman Richir (1866–1942).

Competitions, however, often yielded disappointing results. In 1926, after the mark had stabilised, the Reichsbank organised a competition for a new series of notes: 166 projects were presented, twelve of which were awarded prizes, but in the end none of them were used. The Suomen Pannki (Bank of Finland) organised an open competition in 1907 for the design of a new 1,000-mark note. A five-person jury was formed to examine the thirty-eight projects that were presented but none of these were considered up to standard. The bank then turned to two famous local artists, the painter Akseli Gallen-Kallela (1865–1931) and the architect Eliel Saarinen, and it was the latter's design that was finally used. In 1920, the Suomen Pannki turned to Saarinen once again, although the notes of 1939 and 1945 were designed by two members of the bank's printing team. In 1946, the Suomen Pannki tried the competition format again, despite the disappointing outcome of its last attempt in 1907. This time a major artist, Tapio Wirkkala (1915–85), was declared the winner by a jury of three, and he went on to design three notes, in a very simple style, that were issued in 1955. In 1981 the Suomen Pannki mounted another competition, but on a very restricted basis: only the graphic designer Erik Bruun and a few artists attached to the bank's printing department were allowed to take part.

The competition system was also tried in the Netherlands. In 1939, when the Nederlandsche Bank's usual designer approached retiring age, it asked four candidates to submit designs; three were chosen by teachers at the Rijksacademie in Amsterdam, the fourth by the Bank itself. The prize winner did eventually produce a banknote, although it had nothing to do with his original presentation. The same system was applied in 1946 and 1965, to launch other series of notes. In England, competitions were abandoned in 1968, when the Bank of England broke with its habit of using freelance artists for new notes and instead turned to their own draughtsman, Harry Eccleston, who had been put on the payroll in 1958 as an expert adviser. The most recent notes from the Bundesbank have also been entirely conceived in-house. In Belgium, all the notes issued between 1978 and 1982 were drawn up by artists unconnected to the Banque nationale, after a 'competition of ideas' open to all the country's artists, but the series issued in the 1990s were produced by the Bank's own staff.

Issuing banks have mainly tended to draw on local artists, but there are a few exceptions to this rule. In Portugal the penchant for all things French was keenly felt throughout the nineteenth century. The first engraver hired by the Banco de Lisboa, in 1843, was the Frenchman Auguste Fernand Gérard. History repeated itself in 1897, when the head of the issuing department of the Banco de Portugal, Joseph Leipold, employed the French draughtsman Louis Eugène Mouchon – who produced designs for countless banknotes that were realised by Portuguese engravers – as well as the German Otto Reim (a specialist in printing on steel plates) and the American George Tell MacCaskie (who had previously worked for the Federal Reserve Bank). In France, however, when the Banque de France took on the Italian engraver Romagnoli (also known as Romagnol) at the beginning of the twentieth century, some newspapers voiced their disapproval: were there not enough good artists in France? The same doubts were expressed in Finland, where in 1907 the Suomen Pannki resolved never again resort to foreign draughtsmen or engravers. It is only recently that the European banks have reconsidered artists from beyond their borders, as they have started to pay greater attention to artists' curriculums and experience with fiduciary paper. It was on this basis that the design of the Belgian notes issued in 1962 was entrusted to the Italian Florenzo Masino-Bessi, and a complete French series was assigned to the Swiss designer Roger Pfund.

If banknotes are original works of art, should they therefore bear the name of their creator(s)? This has in fact been standard practice in Belgium since 1851. In Spain, however, banknotes with an acknowledgement of the artist are hard to find, although the first instance of this seems to be the notes designed by Ribera and engraved by Martínez in 1869. Some later examples were signed by Bartolomé Maura in the 1890s, and by Enrique Vaquer in the twentieth century, but that is all. In Portugal, some notes from the 1830s issued by the Banco Commercial do Porto were signed by their draughtsman, J.B. Ribeiro, and their engraver but, once again, such cases are few and far between, although Mouchon only agreed to work for the Banco de Portugal on the condition that he could sign his work. In the Netherlands, Jacob Jongert's 'Minerva' note, put into circulation in 1930, was the first in which the names of the designer and printer were not mentioned;

since then most Dutch notes have borne their creators' names. In contrast, at about the same time in France, where the names of draughtsmen and engravers had been mentioned ever since the Revolution, this practice was abandoned. In 1927 the Banque de France decided to go ahead with a project for a 50-franc note drawn up in 1905 by the painter, the late Luc Olivier Merson (1846–1920). The launching of this note gave rise to a legal battle with the painter's heirs, who reproached the Banque de France for the modifications made to the original design. Since then, all the designs and preparatory drawings are retained by the Banque de France as a matter of course and its notes no longer feature the names of their creators. In Italy, most of the notes issued by the Banca d'Italia since 1897 have been attributed to a draughtsman, while in Germany the artist remains anonymous. As for the notes printed by private companies like Bradbury or the American Bank Note Company, these display not the name of an artist but the company's corporate name.

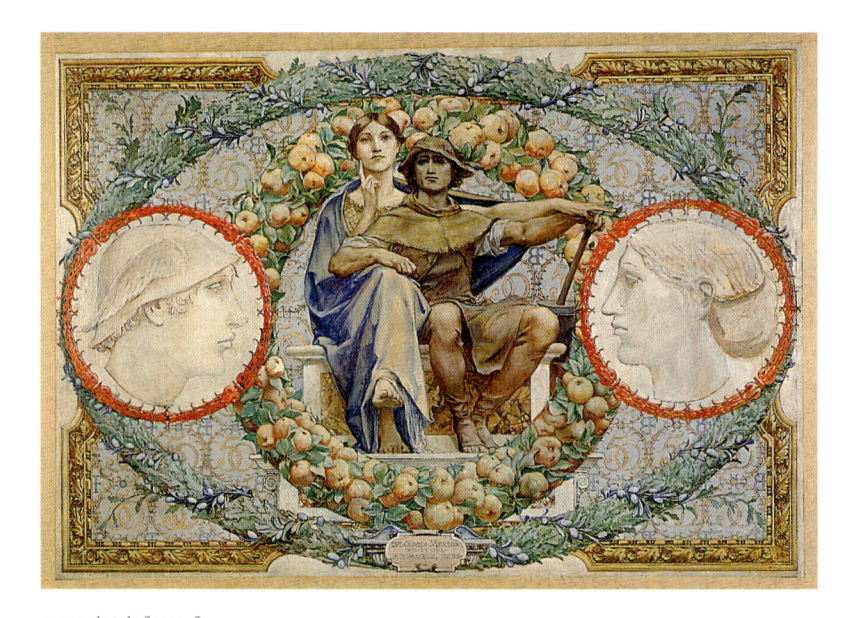

1905 sketch for 50-franc note of the Banque de France, issued 1927, reverse, by Luc Olivier Merson (1846–1920). BF. When, in 1927, the Banque de France modified the twenty-two-year-old sketch for release, the artist's legatees objected.

107

THE BANKNOTE AS ART

1,000-franc note, Banque de France, 1842, by Jaques Jean Barre (1793–1855), 230 x 125 mm (4.92 x 9.06 in.). BF; and 500-franc note, Banque nationale de Belgique, 1852, obverse, by Leopold Wiener (1823–91), 106 x 198 mm (7.80 x 4.17 in.). BNB.
One of the best examples of one note influencing another.

The sources of inspiration

In the early 1800s, official art often drew its inspiration from Neoclassicism, whether the Empire style in France or Belgium or the 'Biedermeier style' in the Austro-Hungarian Empire. Artists' infatuation with the art of Antiquity knew no bounds. Charles Percier, for example, borrowed decorative motifs from the paintings of Pompeii for the first banknotes issued by the Banque de France (in 1800 and 1806). Charles Normand, responsible for the banknotes issued by the Banque de France in 1817, had written several pieces on ornamentation in the ancient world. Peter Fendi, who produced a series of notes in the 'Biedermeier' style for the Privilegirte Österreichische Nationalbank, had devoted several years of his life to compiling an illustrated inventory of collections of Greek and Etruscan vases. It was therefore hardly surprising that the art of antiquity also found its way into banknotes well into the nineteenth century. In Belgium the security background of an 1883 Belgian note shows a bas-relief with a prominent image of a Roman chariot. François Flameng (1856–1923) also included a bas-relief with a classical theme on his 1,000-franc note, finished in 1897 but never issued. When the painter Camille Chazal (1826–75) was preparing his 20-franc note for the Banque de France in 1873, he found inspiration in the numismatics of the ancient world and designed a background of coins.

However, Neoclassicism was far from being the sole source of inspiration for the creators of banknotes. In the nineteenth century many artists in the thrall of Romanticism were intent on protecting or reviving their 'national' art. Banknotes from several European countries bore evidence of this concern, especially in Central Europe. In the middle of the nineteenth century, for example, most German notes renounced Neoclassicism in favour of either the Baroque style (volutes, asymmetrical cable moulding) or Neo-Gothic or medieval subjects (heraldic motifs, figures seated on mandorles). In the Netherlands, the Reliëfrand notes issued in 1860 were decorated, in the absence of any specific local ornamental style, in a manner typical of many German notes, with motifs that had in fact been designed by a Berlin artist, F.G. Wagner. The directors of the Nederlandsche Bank, however, considered that priority should be given to Dutch artists and promptly commissioned the Rotterdam painter, draughtsman and lithographer Johannes Hendericus Morriën (1819–78) to design the lower-value notes (25, 40 and 60 florins). Since then the design of Dutch banknotes has been entirely entrusted to local artists.

In Finland, the German stylistic influence was very strong in the nineteenth century: the 25-rouble note issued in 1840, designed by a German artist, was unequivocally rococo; the ones issued in the 1860s are typical of Central Europe (figures on medallions, heraldic motifs), and the 500-rouble note of 1877 bore witness to the breakthrough of Romantic inspiration in nineteenth-century German and Scandinavian decorative arts. In the latter years of the nineteenth century, the Suomen Pannki turned to outside experts, who undoubtedly had an influence on the style: for the 1886 note, it was Professor Wanderer from Nuremberg; for that of 1889, a Berlin artist, Emil Döpler; and for that of 1894, Danois Fristrup. Nevertheless, the Suomen Pannki was determined to imbue their notes with a genuinely 'national' character, and it found its opportunity to do this in the decorative motifs: branches of fir, silver birch or other Nordic trees and interlacing patterns typical of 'Viking' or 'ancient Finnish' art. Archaeological discoveries led to a greater appreciation of genuinely Scandinavian art, not only in Finland (the same type of 'Viking' decor can be seen on many notes issued by private Swedish banks between 1870 and 1890). In 1907 the architect Eliel Saarinen, commissioned to produce a new series of Finnish banknotes, was asked to modify his initial designs in order to create 'something more characteristic of our country.'

10-schilling note, Österreichische Nationalbank, 1927, obverse, by Berthold Löffler (1874–1960), 125 x 70 mm (4.92 x 2.76 in.). ONB. The artist has portrayed his wife on both faces of this Austrian note: on the obverse, as Mercury, and on the reverse as a nymph of the River Danube.

Original drawing for 100-crown note, Österreichisch-Ungarische Bank, 1910, obverse, by Koloman Moser (1868–1918). ONB.
From 1840 to 1938, most Austrian notes bore female portraits.

The stylistic evolution of banknotes is slow, as it is subject to the hesitant pondering of the issuing banks; the confidence of the populace, so hard to acquire and so easy to dissipate, must not be put to the test by abandoning an important symbol or making formal innovations. In Austria, for example, almost all the notes issued between 1841 and 1934 were adorned with one or two women. These were originally emblematic representations of Austria and Hungary, but at the beginning of the twentieth century some artists used them as an excuse for artistic experimentation. Most were no longer shown full-length, only their head being visible within a rounded frame. Several well-known artists, such as Koloman Moser, Berthold Löffler and Artur Brusenbauch (1881–1957) took part in this search for an idealised portrait. By confining these artistic variations to a tried-and-tested theme, however, the issuing bank limited the affront to conservative popular tastes and made daring artistic innovations more acceptable.

Since the Second World War, the portrait has come to the fore and realism has reigned supreme almost everywhere, but this conformity has meant that, from an artistic point of view, contemporary banknotes have become somewhat mundane. This monotony has, however, inevitably provoked reactions; in the Netherlands, for example, efforts have been made for some thirty years to cast off the yoke of realism – to great success, as Dutch notes have generally been well received by the public and have even become popular icons in terms of design.

Constraints and criticisms

Designing a banknote entails a degree of frustration for a contemporary artist. First of all, the subject is imposed, then a number of elements have to be incorporated for legal reasons or to discourage counterfeiters: signatures, the value of the note, the watermark, microtext, *guilloches* and so on. Then, the artist has to take into account the printing method, which has to be suitable for production in series. The paradox is that a banknote must be hard to imitate, yet it must also be readily identifiable. So the technical departments of the central banks tend to veer between highly detailed designs that are more difficult to counterfeit and those that deliberately opt for a greater simplicity and clarity.

The artist does not work alone, however: he or she is just a cog in a production process involving many other people, some of whom often have the final word. The printers – whether attached to a bank or independent – play a vital role by constantly recalling the technical criteria that the notes must satisfy of necessity. A systematic study of the Dutch banknote revealed that, in many cases, all the originality or fantasy that the artist poured into the design was lost in the course of engraving and printing. The author of this study, Jacob Bolten, even claims that the artist's creative work is sometimes totally disregarded; all too often, the original ideas are modified

50-florin note, Nederlandsche Bank, 1930, obverse, by Jacob Jongert (1883–1942), 142 x 101 mm (5.59 x 3.98 in.). DNB. One of the best examples of a Dutch note rising above technical constraints.

Luc Olivier Merson (1846–1920), *Truth*, early twentieth century. Musée d'Orsay, Paris. Like many designers and artists commissioned to work on banknotes, Merson, a classical painter, had also produced large-scale works, such as tapestries and frescoes for the Palais de Justice, Paris.

to such an extent that the spirit of the work is lost. Some projects for banknotes, successful on aesthetic grounds, have never seen the light of day on account of opposition from a printer. In 1910, for example, the head of the Rijksacademie in Amsterdam, Antonie Der Kinderen, drew up a project for the Nederlandsche Bank based on an episode from the legend of Mercury. This project was, however, overruled by the printer Enschedé, who considered that the relentless advance of the techniques for photographic reproduction made it unsuitable for issue: the representation of Mercury was too stark, and therefore too easy to copy. After six years of debate, the board of the Nederlansche Bank decided in favour of Enschedé and the project was abandoned. It passed into the history of the Bank under the unflattering epithet 'Mercury in the Sea of Ice', referring to the decor on the note, which featured rocks emerging from water.

According to Bolten, only a few Dutch designers have succeeded in pushing through their personal visions, at least partially, right to the end. One of these was R.D.E. Oxenaar, who managed, in the 1960s, to produce an original treatment of an initially forbidding subject: the five national glories. Ater a constructive dialogue with the printer, who viewed the matter from a strictly technical standpoint, Oxenaar successfully defended the originality of his work throughout the process. This is an exceptional case, however. The collaboration between the artist and the printer is not usually so understanding: the printer does not negotiate, he merely exercises his power of veto. This impasse has led some issuing banks to appoint an assessor on artistic matters, to champion the cause of this important aspect of the banknote.

More recently, artists have been further restricted by demands for not just single notes but whole series. The idea of the series emerged in the nineteenth century, particularly in Spain and Belgium, but it is in the last few decades that it has become widespread. The notes in a series must present a unity of form and style, so it is more and more common to find a whole series entrusted to a single artist.

One of the main difficulties confronting artists is the limited format. This problem must have been particularly acute for the not inconsiderable number of banknote artists with a background in monumental painting, like the Frenchmen Paul Baudry (1828–86), François Flameng and Luc Olivier Merson; the German Wilhelm von Kaulbach; or the Belgians Constant Montald (1862–1944) and Emile Vloors (1871–1952), idealists who considered that art had a role to play in the edification of the masses. The transfer of their large-scale compositions to a miniature format was sometimes fraught with problems. They produced their designs on a much larger scale than that of the note itself, and the beauty and precision of these studies is often startling when compared with the final product.

The banknote has often proved too small for the big names in art, perhaps because it presented too many technical constraints, but also because the boards of national banks were reluctant to take a leap from worthy classicism to unbridled artistic research. When great artists were called upon, their work rarely left the drawing board! In Austria, Gustave Klimt (1862–1918) was commissioned to design a 10-crown note but his project was not taken up. The Banque nationale de Belgique, for its part, called on established artists on several occasions and obtained some preliminary studies, but most of these contacts went no further. In 1906, for example, the Bank entered into a stormy relationship with the Symbolist painter Fernand Khnopff (1858–1921) after it commissioned him to present preliminary studies for a 1,000-franc note. When his drawings were examined by an *ad hoc* commission, they engendered harsh criticism: the composition was considered outmoded and lacking in decorative appeal, the poses and rendition of the figures were found to be baffling and the decor 'was too reminiscent of illustrated postcards'. In the end, the commission could not even imagine the artist to be capable of amending his design and was asked 'not to continue'.

The use of 'trendy' artists was not always a happy experience either, and it could even sometimes lead to disruptions in the money supply. In August 1906 the newspaper *L'Indépendance belge* strongly criticised the note designed by Montald, now considered a small masterpiece of Art Nouveau, by chronicling the misadventures of a merchant in Brussels: he had wanted to buy a horse with these new notes but the horse dealer, doubting their authenticity, had rejected them outright. The newspaper fulminated indignantly: 'The Banque nationale is totally to blame for worrying so little about the moral peace of country folk close to the heart of the government.' To top it all, the note was intended as a celebration of agriculture!

Public opinion has not only been forthright in its criticism of aesthetic considerations, it has also proved implacable in the defence of morality and the nation's spiritual well-being. In the nineteenth century, there was a veritable deluge of *putti*, or cherubs, on banknotes in Belgium, France, Spain, Italy, Portugal, Austria and Germany. They often served as a foil to allegorical female figures by surrounding them and endowing them with maternal virtues. On other occasions they were more active and became allegories for human activities. However, no matter how much these cherubs were invested with the innocence of childhood, their nakedness could still sometimes shock upright citizens. In most cases designers and engravers – anxious to avoid any polemic about the sex of angels – made sure to keep the genitals of cherubs well out of sight, but woe betide anybody who did not resort to this stratagem! The 20-mark *Reichskassenschein* or Treasury note, put into circulation in the entire German Empire, by virtue of the law passed on 30 April 1874, was widely criticised – despite the prior approval of Emperor Wilhelm – because it showed two chubby-cheeked young boys bearing bunches of grapes head on, in their birthday suits. In France, at the beginning of the twentieth century, a design for a banknote by Luc Olivier Merson was also vilified for its depiction of a naked boy. It should be pointed out that around this time the style of banknotes was becoming more realistic, and that the more lifelike use of colour undoubtedly fuelled the flames of the scandal.

For some people, however, nudity had its virtues. Franz von Salzmann, an official of the Privilegirte Österreichische Nationalbank, was convinced that the depiction of people without clothes could prevent falsifications, arguing that naked bodies attracted the attention of the users of banknotes and so any alterations to them would be more quickly detected. Notes decorated with scantily clad young women are not uncommon in the nineteenth century. Many bare breasts were justified by their capacity to provide nourishment or merely evoke the fertility of the land or the creativity of science, industry or art. Other naked breasts belong to 'noble savages', as in the 1,000-peseta Spanish note of 1876 commemorating Columbus's arrival in America. Notes with an erotic charge are, however, relatively rare: a 10-thaler note issued by the Danziger Privat-Actien-Bank in 1857, featuring a lascivious allegorical figure representing the Baltic Sea; a 5,000-real note from the Banco de Portugal, dating back to 1901, on which Mouchon drew an extremely sensual winged allegorical figure; the 25-drachma Greek note from 1888, where a languorous bare-breasted young woman lies voluptuously in a natural setting.

The Finnish notes designed by Eliel Saarinen in 1920 boast some of the most astonishing artwork in the history of the European banknote. Their economic message fades into the background as the eye is inevitably drawn to the pagan procession of naked people – men, women and children, all young and beautiful, mingling together. This nudity, which would be considered shocking on a banknote even today, stirred up a flurry of debate in the press but it was eventually accepted as the artist's declaration of faith in a glorious future. It was said that Saarinen had left his figures naked to any social distinctions, but in fact this nakedness was apparently intended to emphasise the vitality of the Nordic race. In this period the idealisation of the race expressed itself in various movements like naturism and eugenics, which were then established all over Europe, particularly in England, France, Switzerland and the Scandinavian countries.

In the last few years the use of computers has modified the design process for banknotes. In 1985 a CAD (computer-aided design) system was installed in the workshops of the Bank of England, after many years of trial

Design for 10-florin note, Österreichisch-Ungarische Bank, by Gustav Klimt (1862–1918). ONB. Buried in the archives of issuing banks are a number of preliminary designs commissioned from famous artists, but never used.

1905 sketch of 50-franc note, obverse, Banque de France, 1927, designed by Luc Olivier Merson (1846–1920). BF. Putti were ubiquitous on European notes in the 1800s, but became much rarer after the First World War.

and error. This made it possible to create or reproduce all types of images, from geometric motifs similar to the ones hitherto drawn by *guilloche* machines to subtly nuanced portraits based on the drawings of artists. Once these images had been processed they were passed directly onto diazo film, which was used to make the plates. In the late 1980s the Banque de France also introduced a computer-aided graphic design process, the Adagio system. Artists' designs are digitised and broken down into four colours before a technician creates the screens. The screened images in each colour are recorded on a magnetic tape and then passed through the scanner to produce the films.

The artistic aspects of the banknote are, however, less likely to be threatened by these technological developments than by the increasing number of constraints imposed on the grounds of security. For its most recent series, issued between 1994 and 1997, the Banque nationale de Belgique decided not to commission outside artists and entrusted the design to the artists in its printing department: 'These days banknotes require a veritable battery of security techniques in the printing process. This increasing complexity has obliged us entirely to entrust their creation to the artists in our printing shop, who are fully acquainted with the technical constraints and have mastered today's highly sophisticated graphic equipment.' Roger Pfund, who has produced notes in both Switzerland and France, maintains, however, that graphic artists are capable of coming to terms with the complexity of the brief for a banknote: 'There's nothing more interesting than a banknote. It's the most wonderful job for an artist, the most intense, the most dense, the one that stretches him most in both the graphic and the technical aspects. The more complicated the brief, the better, because it's within all these constraints that liberty is possible.'

1,000-mark note, Suomen Pankki, 1922, obverse, by Eliel Saarinen (1873–1950), 204 x 120 mm (8.03 x 4.72 in.). SP. Shows an astonishing procession of naked men, women and children; nostalgia for lost innocence?

1,000-franc note, Banque de France, 1897, reverse, by François Flameng (1856–1923). Never issued. 235 x 128 mm (9.25 x 5.04 in.). BF.
Fortune's somewhat scanty attire aroused some criticism.

115

THE BANKNOTE AS ART

5-crown note, Sveriges Riksbank, 1965, (reverse). SRB.
Guilloche work began by being a technical limitation, as its mechanical nature rendered it unattractive. It was not long, however, before designers turned it into a real work of art.

The Future is in the Euro

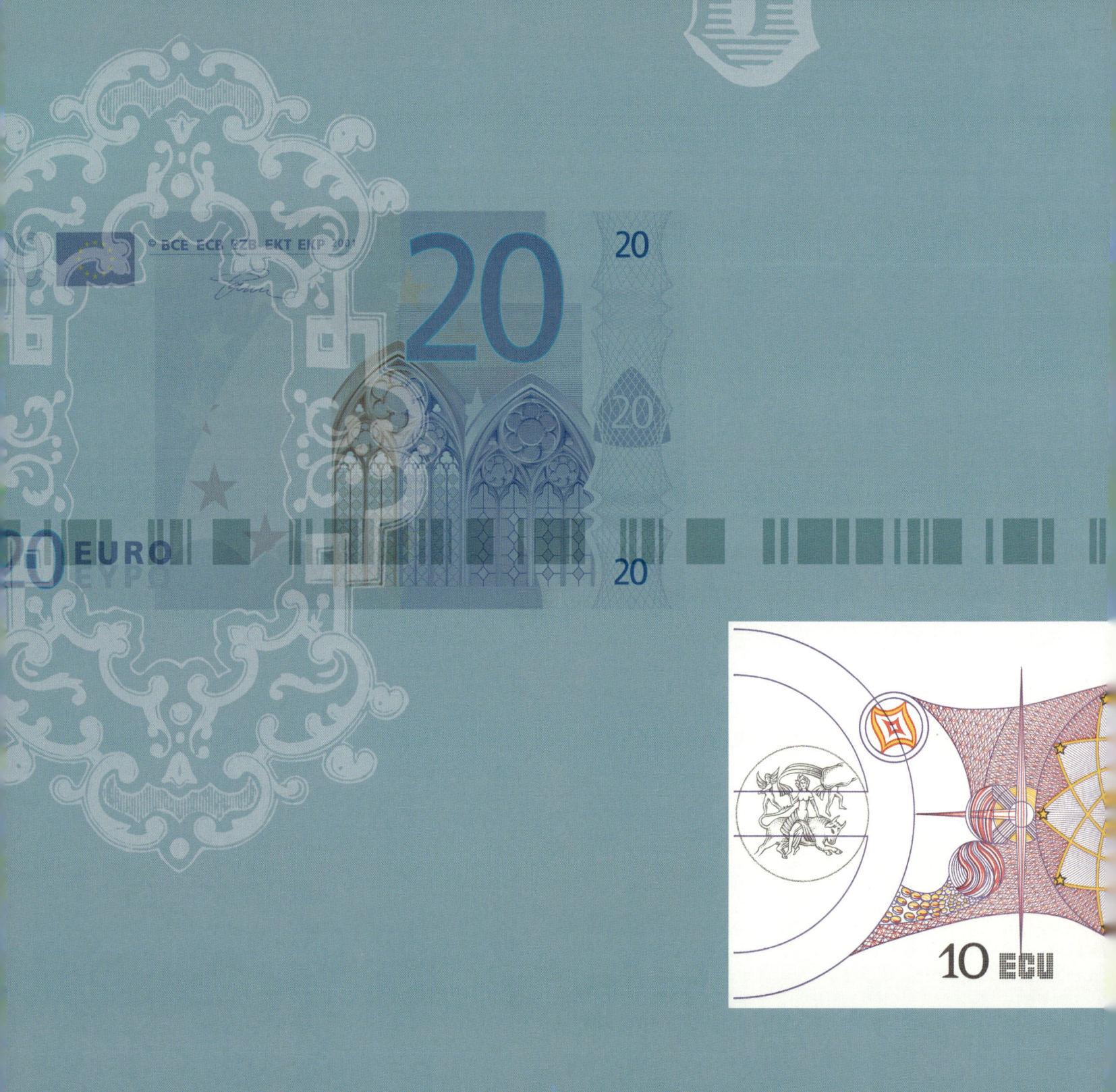

Enter the '€'

Between the two world wars some enlightened souls began to talk of Europe's need for a single currency, seeing it as an indispensable condition for the Old Continent's economical survival. After the Second World War, all financial experts were agreed on the urgent need to re-establish the convertibility of currencies. The British economist John Maynard Keynes dreamed of creating for this purpose a world-wide currency – the bancor – defined in relation to gold; this would serve as a yardstick for expressing the exchange rates of national currencies. This idea was not taken up. At the Bretton Woods Conference, the Americans imposed, in effect, a system of fixed parities between gold and the various currencies, although these parities would be susceptible to readjustment. There was, however, a huge gap between the ideal system formulated at Bretton Woods and the economic reality of a world emerging from the chaos of war; although the exchange rates were stable in theory, international trading and payments were burdened with restrictions that impeded any relaunching of the economy. The United States reacted to this situation by, on the one hand, unfreezing aid to kick-start the European economic machine (the Marshall Plan) and, on the other, by encouraging European countries to tighten up their financial collaboration. In 1950, a European Payments Union was founded to set up a multilateral payments system in Europe, in the hope of boosting trade. Under the auspices of this organisation, a counting unit common to all its members was created as a basket of European economies, designed to be the equivalent of 1 dollar. Furthermore, the United States had been urging Europe down the road to monetary unification ever since the Marshall Plan. However, the debate was still very much a theoretical one. Even a visionary such as Paul Henri Spaak, while admitting in 1947 that the idea was 'highly praiseworthy', considered it was only foreseeable after 'a very long wait'. And the gestation of a monetarily unified Europe did in fact last over half a century, if its starting point is considered to be the agreements made by the European Payments Union in 1950. The problem is that a currency is an essential instrument of sovereignty: for a state to renounce an independent policy in this field represents a real loss of autonomy. The founding text of the Common Market, the Treaty of Rome (1957), made no mention of the monetary union of its members.

It was not until the summit in The Hague in 1969, and the Werner report, published in late 1970, that the member states of the EEC came to see the culmination of the Treaty of Rome as monetary union. Nevertheless, this project was indefinitely postponed due to the financial upheavals provoked by the economic crisis of the 1970s, when the emphasis was put on attempting to maintain or re-establish a system of stable parities between the different currencies – a European Monetary System (EMS) – whereby the ratios between the currencies could not go beyond certain limits. At the same time, a European currency unit, the ecu, was introduced on the basis of a 'basket' of currencies in circulation within the Community; this unit was barely used, however, outside a few international financial transactions.

It was only in 1985, when the European Community established the target of a single European market for 1992, that it became apparent that there was a pressing need to strengthen economic unity by creating a common currency and constituting a central European bank. The advantages of such a union were obvious. The elimination of both the costs of conversion and the uncertainties of exchange – along with the easier comparison of prices – would make commercial transactions simpler. In a wider context, a single currency would expand markets, make them more fluid and, therefore, make it easier for European businesses and public bodies to find financial backing. On an international level, the use of a European currency in commercial operations would avoid any passive submission to variations in the rate of the dollar. Those who feared that the creation of a single currency would diminish the sovereignty of the member states in the economic sphere were met with the retort from the partisans of a single currency that this sovereignty had long since become illusory, as in practice the various currencies were dependent on the dollar or the mark. Monetary union, in contrast, made it possible to share this sovereignty.

The various phases marking the road to this monetary union were laid out in the Delors report in 1989, which was ratified by the leaders of twelve member states in December 1991: the Maastricht treaty decided to transform the Community into an Economic and Monetary Union (EMU). Britain was granted a special dispensation, allowing it to defer any decision on the single currency. The need for the national

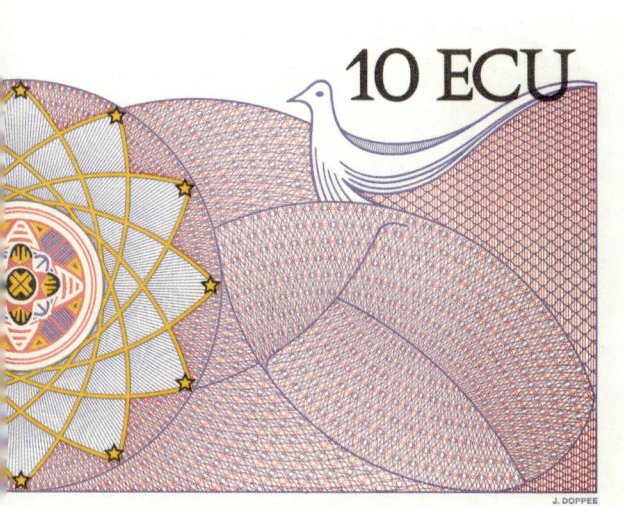

Special issue, with value in ecus, by the European Savings Banks Group to mark the 1992 World Fair in Seville. Private Collection.
In fact, the single European currency would be known as the euro. This was because the word 'ecu', for Germans, sounds like 'ein Kuh' (a cow), which was somewhat ridiculous. The term 'euro' was adopted in 1995.

economies to satisfy the criteria for economic convergence – stability of prices, healthy public finances, low interest rate, and so on – obliged the European authorities to spread the process of monetary integration over a period of eight years. A European Monetary Institute (EMI) was created in 1994 to prepare the ground for the single currency. The statutes of the central banks of the member states were amended in order to guarantee their independence with respect to the political authorities. More particularly, this meant that the finance ministers of the twelve participating members had to renounce their right to exercise an influence on the establishment of key interest rates, which would now fall to the future European Central Bank (ECB). In 1998 the ECB took the place of the EMI and set about defining a common monetary policy. Eleven countries adopted the single currency on 1 January 1999: Belgium, Germany, Spain, France, Ireland, Italy, Luxembourg, the Netherlands, Austria, Portugal and Finland. The twelfth member, Greece, adopted the single currency on 1 January 2001. Three European Union countries – the United Kingdom, Denmark and Sweden – decided not to join the Eurosystem for the time being as they considered that the single currency would entail too many political and economic problems. Some opponents of the euro argued, in effect, that the dissociation of monetary power from economic power and its entrustment to a single authority would give rise to an unbalanced situation, where this authority could easily impose its criteria over national budgetary powers.

In January 1999 the ECB, in conjunction with the monetary authorities of each country, fixed the exchange rates between the euro and the eleven national currencies that were about to disappear. The euro was then solemnly christened and began to be used, especially in large-scale financial operations (currency transactions, inter-bank operations and so on). All that remained to do was to give Euroland its own monetary signs, before the deadline of January 2002.

Klaus Staeck (b. 1938), *Europe: More than Just a Financial Entity*, 1984, Editions Staeck, Heidelberg.
In the construction of a single Europe, economics have always taken first place, much to the chagrin of certain intellectuals.

5-mark note, Bank Deutscher Länder, 1948, obverse, by Max Bittrof (1890–1972), 120 x 60 mm (4.72 x 2.36 in.).
In the aftermath of the Second World War, the construction of a united Europe seemed the only way to avoid future conflicts.

10-franc note, Grand Duchy of Luxembourg, 1967, reverse. BIL. The subject is the pont Grand-Duchesse Charlotte, a bridge linking the city of Luxembourg to the Kirchberg plateau, site of various EU institutions.

A MIRROR OF EUROPE

The preparation of euro coins and notes was started back in 1992 by a working party answerable to the committee of the governors of the central banks of the member states. The task was continued by, successively, the European Monetary Institute and the European Central Bank. All the participants in this process agreed, right from the start, that the iconography of the notes should transcend any specific national traditions. A number of themes were put forward, all determinedly neutral: European wildlife and plants, myths and legends common to the whole continent, the great founding fathers of Europe. In the end, however, when the competition for the graphic design of the notes was launched in 1996, the candidates were offered just two themes: pure abstraction or the evocation of 'eras and styles of Europe'. The competition was only open to graphic artists selected by the governors of the central banks. Forty-four projects were presented, and the prize finally went to Robert Kalina, a 41-year-old graphic designer employed by the Oesterreichische Nationalbank, who came up with a series dedicated to the architectural styles of Europe. This theme made it possible to evoke the cultural heritage common to all the Union's member states, thereby fulfilling one of the dreams of Robert Schuman, who had longed to base a European Union on cultural foundations.

What is the message transmitted by Kalina's banknotes? The obverses of each note show windows, porches or portals in the styles of different periods of European history: they symbolise openness and cooperation within the Union. The reverse presents various types of bridge, similarly arranged according to the 'seven ages' of Europe. On a metaphorical plane, these bridges represent the links between the peoples of Europe, and between Europe and the rest of the world. They also head towards the future, as the launching of the euro marks the beginning of a new phase in the construction of Europe. Robert Kalina was once asked, in an ironic tone, if he did not think that the vulnerability of these types of bridge would in-crease the fragility of the euro. In reply, the artist assured that an engineer had been consulted as a precautionary measure to check that there was no architectural detail that could prejudice the stability of the works in question.

The notes do not reproduce existing buildings; they are stylised depictions. This did not prevent Kalina from having to revise several of his designs after some observers thought they could see a resemblance with the Rialto bridge in Venice on the 50-euro notes, the Neuilly bridge in Paris on those of 100 euros, and the Normandy bridge on those of 500 euros; without mentioning the fact that other spoilsports have insisted that the ancient aqueduct on the 5-euro note can only be the Gard bridge, the last of its kind to have survived until today. The 500-euro note has also unleashed a different kind of controversy: its particularly high value has been decried in some quarters, on the basis that it could become the object of criminal contraband.

Two graphic elements that appear on all the notes are particularly worthy of comment. On the reverse, a map based on satellite photographs shows a Europe without frontier that extends well beyond the borders of the fifteen member states. Is this the anticipation of an

Celebrations to mark the launching of the euro at Frankfurt, January 1999. In the background, the towers of the European Central Bank.

enlarged Union? The other striking element is the European flag printed on the obverse of each note. It was undoubtedly considered necessary for Europe to strengthen its collective identity in the hearts of its citizens by using its strongest symbol. This flag, which underpins a programme that is both political and economic, was preferred to the euro symbol, which is too strictly limited to the financial sphere. There had been a proposal to put the flags of all the member states of the European Union on the notes, but this idea was dropped. Moreover, only a few countries – Finland, Austria, Germany – have included any national emblem on their own notes before the launching of the euro.

The introduction of euro notes has represented a huge logistical challenge for the ECB and the national central banks in the euro zone; there are 15 billion notes in all, with a total value of around 650 billion euros. Two thirds of these will be put into circulation immediately, the others will form a reserve. The printing started in the spring of 1999, when the ECB decided on the definitive technical specifications for the notes. Germany is the country that has printed the highest total number of euro notes – around 4,300 million, as against 2,570 million in France and only 56 million in Luxembourg. Greece, which was a latecomer to the Eurosystem, only started to print its stock in October 2000, and sought help from Finland in order to meet the deadline. The most common notes will be those of 50 and 20 euros, with runs of 3,670 and 3,600 million notes, respectively. The average life of each note in circulation has been calculated as being around a year and a half.

These notes will be among the best protected in the world, as they concentrate virtually all the security measures in operation in the various member states, including, for example, the use of special inks that permit the printing of motifs with colours that vary according to the angle at which they are observed. They also bear holograms, of the kind that have already been used on notes in Austria, Germany, Finland, Britain and Sweden. All in all, then, euro notes will be infinitely more complicated to imitate than dollar bills, whose manufacturing processes have become outdated. Nevertheless, it must be supposed that the

ELECTRONIC MONEY: THE DEATH KNELL FOR THE BANKNOTE?

Does the banknote still have a future as a paper support for money? In the medium term, at least, electronics threaten to banish it to the dustbin of history by replacing it with pre-paid cards, the electronic purse, the Internet and the credit card used from a payment terminal. The dematerialization of payment operations is clearly one of the cornerstones of today's banking strategies, for four reasons: increased speed and efficiency in processing; savings in administration costs; greater security; and the chance to create new services for consumers.

In fact, fiduciary money is already a marginal means of payment. Ninety-five per cent of the money supply is now comprised of representative money, even though in absolute terms fiduciary circulation is growing. Banknotes are still favoured by the public, however, for a good number of everyday transactions. What is astonishing, though, is the extent of the disparity between different countries in this respect. In 1993, the value of notes and coins in circulation amounted to 2,638 dollars per inhabitant in Switzerland, as against 1,511 in Germany, 1,164 in Belgium, 749 in France and a mere 455 in the United Kingdom. The number of notes in use per inhabitant can double from one country to another (twenty-one in Finland, for example, as against more than fifty in Austria).

In 1996 there were 12.7 billion banknotes in circulation in the fifteen member states of the European Union. Furthermore, the European Central Bank (ECB), which monitors and analyses the development and use of pre-paid cards and electronic money, has reported that the role of banknotes over the last five years in the monetary aggregate – which includes notes and coins in circulation, short-term deposits and other very liquid assets – has been remarkably stable in most countries in the euro zone: 'Banknotes offer numerous advantages. In particular, the costs of using them are negligible and they constitute an effective, universally accepted means of payment.'

Presentation of euro coins and notes in their final format in September 2001. Left to right: Wim Duisenberg, President of the European Central Bank; the Belgian Finance Minister, Didier Reynders; the Governor of the Banque nationale de Belgique, Guy Quaden. The symbol for the single currency derives from the Greek letter epsilon, with reference to the origins of European civilisation, the two horizontal bars suggesting the euro's stability.

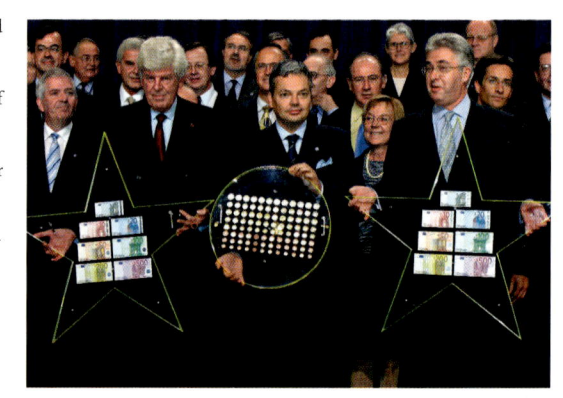

temptations to forge euro notes will be manifold, mainly because of the size of the geographical expanse in which they will circulate, the development of reproduction techniques and consumers' lack of familiarity with the new money. In anticipation of this risk, the member states signed a convention in December 1998 with Europol, a body created in 1995 to develop cooperation between European countries in the fight against all forms of international crime; the scope of Europol has been widened to cover the counterfeiting of money and other means of payment.

How will the notes be received by the citizens of Europe? Robert Kalina, who designed some Austrian models a few years ago, has no illusions: nostalgia will work in favour of the notes that have disappeared – and it will swell the ranks of collectors of old banknotes. More importantly, it is obvious that from now on the euro will be a decisive factor in the environment of the twelve member states concerned. It is too early to say whether this *rapprochement* in the economic sphere will have a knock-on effect in the political one. What is certain, however, is that these notes – the first tangible signs of the Union – will strengthen European citizens' sense of belonging to something that has for too long been considered merely an intellectual construct or an administrative machine: Europe.

Warning by the Danmarks Nationalbank against counterfeiting. Danmarks Nationalbank, Copenhagen.
The future of the banknote is threatened not only by the proliferation of credit cards and 'virtual' money, but also by modern methods of image reproduction, such as colour photocopying. This poster was distributed to every school in Denmark.

Relics of the past

Once a banknote has been withdrawn from circulation, it loses its function as fiduciary paper to be catalogued by archivists under the documents known as 'ephemera': visiting cards, playing cards, train or theatre tickets, advertising slips, electoral pamphlets – all remnants of a previous era that pack a great emotional punch when they are rediscovered a couple of generations further on.
Despite the huge runs of banknotes, many are now impossible to find and even the national banks have problems in assembling complete collections of their production.
Banknotes have been collectors' items for decades. We have already seen how the Germans became interested in the emergency notes issued in their own country after the First World War. The collecting bug spread after the Second World War, albeit slowly at first. It was only after the publication of specialist studies that collectors became interested *en masse* in paper money.
In this respect, the first edition of a world catalogue of paper money by the German enthusiast Albert Pick in 1974 was a milestone of cardinal importance. According to Claude Fayette, one of France's leading authorities on paper money, the collector is an aesthete, a lover of beauty and rarity. He or she has a mission in society – that of constructing the heritage of the future by valuing the present or the near past: 'It is never too late to start a collection. Some of today's issues will be great rarities tomorrow.' However, there are more collectors every day and the prices keep on going up …

A flutter of banknotes

Catalogue

The following pages represent an exhaustive catalogue of banknotes in current use (30 November 2001) by member states of the European Union. For security reasons, they are reproduced in reduced format. However, selective details have been enlarged to enable the reader to appreciate both the quality of engraving and printing and the measures taken to combat counterfeiting. All notes are shown on the same scale to permit realistic comparisons.

The countries are listed in the order adopted by EU protocol, which corresponds to the alphabetical order of their names in their official language. Besides the notes in use in the twelve countries agreeing to the single currency, we have also included those of the three member states which have, for the time being, declined to adopt the euro: Denmark, Sweden, and the United Kingdom. On the other hand, only the notes of public issuing banks will be found here, and not, for instance, those circulated by private establishments in Scotland, Northern Ireland and Luxembourg.

For each note, details (as far as are known) are given in the following order: face value in national currency, year of adoption (often distinct from year of issue), name(s) of designer(s), actual dimensions, description of motifs (obverse and reverse), watermark designs and security measures.

The catalogue is completed by the set of euro notes which will enter circulation in January 2002.

BELGIUM BELGIQUE – BELGIË

100 BEF *by Kenneth Ponsaers* – 1995 – 139 x 76 mm (5.47 x 2.99 in.)
OBVERSE Portrait of post-impressionnist painter James Ensor (Ostend, 1860–1949); details of paintings; Ensor's signature
REVERSE Detail from painting *Bathing at Ostend*, 1890
WATERMARK Head and signature of James Ensor.
SECURITY FEATURES Intaglio printing; colour details alter on reproduction; windowed, silver security thread with denomination; latent image; microtext; blind recognition features (tactile ink)

Certain details of Belgian notes – here the eyes and mouths of the masks – change colour when photocopied.

200 BEF *by Monique Golaire* – 1995 – 144 x 76 mm (5.67 x 2.99 in.)
OBVERSE Portrait of Adolphe Sax (Dinant, 1814–Paris, 1894), instrument-maker and inventor of the saxophone; musical notation, saxophones; Sax's signature.
REVERSE Profile of three saxophonists; stylised view of Dinant, Sax's birthplace.
WATERMARK Head and signature of Adolphe Sax.
SECURITY FEATURES Idem 100 BEF.

Belgian notes – like those of many other European countries – carry raised markings that allow those with eyesight problems to identify the denominations. The 200 BEF note has two horizontal bars and one vertical.

500 BEF *by Monique Golaire* – 1998 – 149 x 76 mm (5.87 x 2.99 in.)
OBVERSE Head-and-shoulder portrait of surrealist painter René Magritte (Lessines, 1898–Brussels, 1967); details from work; artist's signature.
REVERSE Detail of Magritte's work.
WATERMARK Head and signature of René Magritte.
SECURITY FEATURES Idem 100 BEF + OVI (optically variable ink) feature.

By using minimally differing shades of grey, the Banque nationale de Belgique makes the task of counterfeiters more difficult, as the tones alter and merge when photocopied.

1,000 BEF *by Kenneth Ponsaers and Nathalie Paquot* – 1997 – 154 x 76 mm (6.06 x 2.99 in.)
OBVERSE Portrait of the Flemish expressionist painter Constant Permeke (Antwerp, 1886–Ostend, 1952); details from work (fishing boat and trees beside canal); Permeke's signature.
REVERSE Fragments from paintings by Permeke (field, sleeping peasant).
WATERMARK Head and signature of Constant Permeke.
SECURITY FEATURES Idem 500 BEF + see-through feature; fibres/motifs visible under UV.

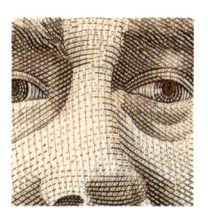

The use of portraits on many modern notes is principally to deter counterfeiters. Smiles and facial expressions are difficult to imitate precisely, making any alterations more readily identifiable.

2,000 BEF *by Kenneth Ponsaers* – 1994 – 159 x 76 mm (6.26 x 2.99 in.)
OBVERSE Portrait of the architect Victor Horta (Ghent, 1861–1947), 'grand master' of art nouveau in Belgium; architectural details; Horta's signature.
REVERSE Ornamental details in art nouveau style, from drawing by Horta.
WATERMARK Head and signature of Victor Horta.
SECURITY FEATURES Idem 1000 BEF.

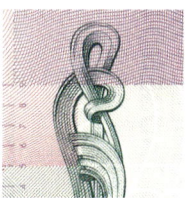

Art nouveau motif by Victor Horta. An essential part of banknote production is research; a few revealing details are required to conjure up an individual's personality, his or her achievements and historical background.

10,000 BEF *by Monique Golaire and Véronique Boland* – 1997 – 169 x 76 mm (6.65 x 2.99 in.)
OBVERSE Portrait of the royal couple Albert II (Brussels, 1934) and Queen Paola (Forte dei Marmi, 1937), King and Queen of Belgium since 1993; stylised view of map of Belgium overprinted with patchwork of coloured geometrical shapes; stylised representation of benches of Belgian Parliament; royal monogram.
REVERSE Stylised representation of plants and royal hothouses at Palace of Laeken.
WATERMARK Head of King Albert II and royal monogram.
SECURITY FEATURES Idem 1000 BEF.

Monogram of King Albert II. In Belgium, a federated state, the monarchy acts as a uniting force, and the ruler's portrait has appeared regularly since 1919.

DENMARK DANMARK

50 DKK – 1997 – 125 x 72 mm (4.92 x 2.83 in.)
OBVERSE Portrait of writer Karen Blixen (Rungstead, 1885–1962), known principally for memoirs *Out of Africa* (1937) and short story *Babette's Feast* (1950).
REVERSE Centaur, from sculptural motif in Landet church, Tasinge.
WATERMARK Geometric design in form of rosette.
SECURITY FEATURES Colour-variable, windowed security thread; blind recognition features (tactile ink).

Nowadays, European issuing banks tend to illustrate their notes with recently deceased figures – here, Karen Blixen, who died in 1962.

100 DKK – 1997 – 135 x 72 mm (5.31 x 2.83 in.)
OBVERSE Portrait of composer and conductor Carl Nielsen (Nörre-Lyndelse, 1865–Copenhagen, 1931), chiefly remembered for his efforts to restore Danish folk-music traditions.
REVERSE Basilisk, from sculptural motif in Tommerby church, Jutland.
WATERMARK Geometrical design in form of rosette.
SECURITY FEATURES Idem 50 DKK.

Those with poor eyesight can identify Danish notes by their length, but also by the bright geometrical pattern on the upper left-hand corner of the reverse. 100 crown notes are marked with a diamond design.

200 DKK – 1997 – 145 x 72 mm (5.79 x 2.83 in.)
OBVERSE Portrait of Johanne Luise Heiberg (née Pätges) (Copenhagen, 1812–90), one of the greatest Danish actresses of nineteenth century, later director of Denmark's Royal Theatre.
REVERSE A lion, from a sculptural motif in Viborg cathedral.
WATERMARK Geometrical design in form of rosette.
SECURITY FEATURES Idem 50 DKK.

The search for cultural roots remains a favourite theme with issuing banks. A good example is Denmark, which uses sculpted motifs harking back to the country's earliest conversion to Christianity in the tenth and eleventh centuries.

500 DKK – 1997 – 155 x 72 mm (6.10 x 2.83 in.)
OBVERSE Portrait of physicist Niels Bohr (Copenhagen, 1885–1962), father of quantum mechanics, Nobel Prize-winner in 1962 for theory of atomic structure.
REVERSE Man armed with sword and shield fighting dragon, from scene on font of Lihme church.
WATERMARK Geometrical design in form of rosette.
SECURITY FEATURES Idem 50 DKK.

The watermark is a transparent image produced by varying the thickness of the pulp during the manufacture of the paper.

1,000 DKK – 1997 – 165 x 72 mm (6.50 x 2.83 in.)
OBVERSE Portrait of artists Anna (Skagen, 1859–1935) and Michael Ancher (Bornholm, 1849–1927), against background of ships' anchors, after portraits by Peder Severin Krøyer (1884). Both artists specialised in genre scenes, especially of Jutland fishermen.
REVERSE Knights jousting, after sculpture in Bislev church.
WATERMARK Geometrical design in form of rosette.
SECURITY FEATURES Idem 50 DKK.

On this Danish note featuring the Anchers, a palette is used to identify them as artists. The designer has also taken the liberty of including a visual pun: the background decoration consists of anchors, alluding to the artists' names.

GERMANY DEUTSCHLAND

5 DEM – 1991 – 122 x 62 mm (4.80 x 2.44 in.)
OBVERSE Portrait of writer Bettina von Arnim, née Brentano (Frankfurt, 1785–Berlin, 1859), aged 24, known principally for her correspondence with Goethe; cornucopia; historic buildings of Berlin.
REVERSE Brandenburg Gate and handwritten extract from Bettina von Arnim's correspondence; cornucopia, symbolising her many interests and enormous output.
WATERMARK Head of Bettina von Arnim and denomination.
SECURITY FEATURES Intaglio printing; blind recognition features (tactile ink); windowed, silver security thread with denomination; see-through feature (D for *Deutschland*); latent image (denomination); microtext; fibres/motifs visible under UV.

The architectural background on the reverse shows various monuments in Berlin: Bettina von Arnim's residence, the City Hall, the Friedrichsbrücke, the Wiepersdorf Building, the Gendarmenmarkt Theatre and the Friedrichswerdersche Kirche.

10 DEM – 1989 – 130 x 65 mm (5.12 x 2.56 in.)
OBVERSE Portrait of mathematician, astronomer, geodesist and physicist Carl Friedrich Gauss (Braunschweig, 1777–Göttingen, 1855), aged 63; graph based on Gauss's equations; historic buildings of Göttingen.
REVERSE Sextant used by Gauss in research; background symbolises motions of the planets; lower right, map of Weissfeld prepared by triangulation.
WATERMARK Head of Carl Friedrich Gauss and denomination.
SECURITY FEATURES Idem 5 DEM.

When highly enlarged, the printing on the reverse reveals a tangle of mathematical signs and symbols.

20 DEM – 1991 – 138 x 68 mm (5.43 x 2.68 in.)
OBVERSE Portrait of poet and writer Annette Elizabeth von Droste-Hülshoff (Haus Hülshoff, near Munster, 1797–Meersburg, 1848), aged around 23; laurel branch, symbol of Anna's art; historic buildings of Meersburg.
REVERSE Pen and tree, recalling her novella *Die Judenbuche* (*The Jew's Beech*); stylised book.
WATERMARK Head of Annette von Droste-Hülshoff and denomination.
SECURITY FEATURES Idem 5 DEM.

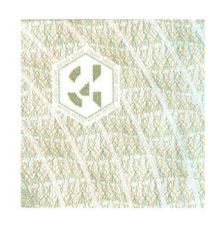

On several European issues, for instance the British £10 note devoted to Dickens and this 20 DEM denomination honouring Freiin von Droste-Hülshoff, a pen features as a natural symbol of the writer's profession.

50 DEM – 1997 – 146 x 71 mm (5.75 x 2.80 in.)
OBVERSE Portrait of Baroque and Rococo architect Johann Balthazar Neumann (Eger, 1687–Würzburg, 1753); instrument used to determine size of columns; historic buildings of Würzburg.
REVERSE Architectural details of ecclesiastical and secular buildings by Neumann: Benedictine abbey at Neresheim, staircases from *Residenz* at Würzburg; Chapel of the Holy Cross at Kitzingen-Etwashausen.
WATERMARK Head of Johann Balthazar Neumann and denomination.
SECURITY FEATURES Idem 5 DEM + Kinegram.

Device for determining the size of columns. Numerous European notes feature technical drawings or scientific instruments, all requiring the most careful research and meticulous draughtsmanship.

100 DEM – 1996 – 154 x 74 mm (6.06 x 2.91 in.)
OBVERSE Portrait of Clara Schumann, née Wieck (Leipzig, 1919–Frankfurt am Main, 1896) composer who also taught piano, from miniature of 1840; wife of Robert Schumann; stylised lyre, symbolising music; historic buildings of Leipzig.
REVERSE Concert grand piano; the Frankfurt Conservatory where Clara Schumann taught for many years; tuning fork.
WATERMARK Head of Clara Schumann and denomination.
SECURITY FEATURES Idem 50 DEM.

The complexity of the coloured background makes counterfeiting more difficult.

200 DEM – 1996 – 162 x 77 mm (8.38 x 3.03 in.)
OBVERSE Portrait of physician and serologist Paul Ehrlich (Strehlen, 1854–Bad Homburg, 1915) who discovered arsphenamine (Salvarsan), so-called 'magic bullet' in fight against syphilis. Shared Nobel Prize for medicine with Metschnikov in 1908; stylised cell structure as symbol of medicine; analysis of radiological structure of arsphenamine; historic buildings of Frankfurt.
REVERSE Microscope; stylised depiction of viral and bacterial structures; caduceus and cornucopia.
WATERMARK Head of Paul Erlich and denomination.
SECURITY FEATURES Idem 50 DEM.

The architectural details of the 200 DEM note are derived from the city of Frankfurt; the principal buildings are Ehrlich's house, the main railway station, Goethe's house, the cathedral, St Paul's church, and medieval facades overlooking the Römerberg, the city's central square.

500 DEM – 1991 – 170 x 80 mm (6.70 x 3.15 in.)
OBVERSE Portrait of Maria Sibylla Merian (Frankfurt, 1647–Amsterdam, 1717), of evangelical persuasion, who illustrated numerous works on botany and zoology; drawing of wasp; historic buildings of Nuremberg.
REVERSE Engravings from scientific works illustrated by Anna Maria Sibylla Merian (flowers, butterflies, caterpillar).
WATERMARK Head of Anna Maria Sibylla Merian and denomination.
SECURITY FEATURES Idem 5 DEM.

Caterpillar's head. Anna Maria Sybilla Merian, woman artist and naturalist, travelled widely, especially in the Dutch colony of Surinam, returning with a wealth of information on the fauna and flora of the country.

1,000 DEM – 1991 – 178 x 83 mm (7.01 x 3.27 in.)
OBVERSE Portraits of Wilhelm (Hanau, 1786–Berlin, 1859) and Jacob Grimm (Hanau, 1785–Berlin, 1863), professors of philology at University of Göttingen. Compiled record of Germany's linguistic and cultural heritage, but best known for collection of German folk-tales and legends.
REVERSE German dictionary by Brothers Grimm; façade of their workplace, the Royal Library in Berlin; facsimile of Jacob Grimm's handwriting; illustration for fairy-tale *Die Sterntaler* (*The Star Thaler*).
WATERMARK Heads of brothers Grimm and denomination.
SECURITY FEATURES Idem 5 DEM.

The most original background of the German series, consisting of crowns and frogs, is to be found on this note commemorating the brothers Grimm.

GREECE ΕΛΛΑΔΑ

100 GRD – 1978 – 158 x 67 mm (6.22 x 2.64 in.)
OBVERSE Theme of education: head of Athene Promachos, after statue discovered in the Piraeus; neo-classical building of Athens University.
REVERSE Portrait of writer Adomantios Koraes (Smyrna, 1748–Paris, 1833), whose literary studies contributed to winning of Greek independence, after portrait in the National History Museum, Athens; façade of monastery church at Arkadi, Crete.
WATERMARK Head of Charioteer of Delphi.
SECURITY FEATURES Security thread; intaglio printing.

On Greek notes, cultural and religious features are important identifying factors, and many examples depict an Orthodox church.

200 GRD – 1996 – 129 x 65 mm (5.08 x 2.56 in.)
OBVERSE Portrait of Rigas Velestinlis-Pheraios (1757–1798), after painting by D. Tsokos of Zante; champion of national independence, depicted declaiming his patriotic ode (*Thourios*).
REVERSE *The Secret School*, after work by Nikolaos Gyzis; one of clandestine schools run by Orthodox clergy during Ottoman occupation.
WATERMARK Head of King Philip of Macedon.
SECURITY FEATURES Security thread; fibres visible under UV; see-through feature.

Greece is the only EU country not to use Latin characters.

500 GRD – 1983 – 158 x 72 mm (6.22 x 2.83 in.)
OBVERSE Portrait of Joannis Capodistrias (Corfu, 1776–Nauplia, 1831), first president of Greece (1821) after war of independence, known for his contribution to the development of national agriculture; a house, supposedly his birthplace in Corfu.
REVERSE Citadel of Corfu, after period engraving; olive branch and bunch of grapes.
WATERMARK Head of the Charioteer of Delphi.
SECURITY FEATURES Idem 100 GRD.

Two clasped hands: a tried and tested motif, found on notes as far back as the French *assignats* of the late 1700s.

1,000 GRD – 1987 – 158 x 77 mm (6.22 x 3.03 in.)

OBVERSE Head of Apollo, copy of marble head (probably by Phidias) from Temple of Zeus at Olympia; two faces of silver stater from fourth century BC, showing Zeus and his emblem, the eagle.
REVERSE Ruins of Temple of Hera at Olympia, site of original Olympic Games; Myron's statue of the Discobolos.
WATERMARK Head of Charioteer of Delphi.
SECURITY FEATURES Idem 100 GRD.

Detail of the stater shown on reverse: references to coins form a constant theme dating back two centuries.

5,000 GRD – 1997 – 147 x 74 mm (5.91 x 2.91 in.)

OBVERSE Portrait of General Theodoros Kolokotronis (Ramavouni, 1770–Athens, 1843), hero of Greek war of independence; Byzantine church of the Holy Apostles, Calamata.
REVERSE Landscape from Carytaina, scene of victory by Kolokotronis, after watercolour by K. Rottman.
WATERMARK Head of King Philip of Macedon.
SECURITY FEATURES Idem 100 GRD + OVI (*optically variable ink*) feature; see-through feature; latent image (initials of Bank of Greece: TE); fibres visible by naked eye.

If you hold this note against the light, the detail of the stater on the obverse is completed by a similar design on the reverse, allowing you to check that the two faces correspond.

10,000 GRD – 1995 – 153 x 77 mm (6.02 x 3.03 in.)

OBVERSE Portrait of George Papanicolaou (Kymi, 1883–Clinton, New Jersey, 1962), physician who acquired worldwide reputation for contribution to diagnosis of bone-marrow cancer ('Pap smear'); laboratory instruments.
REVERSE Statue of Aesculapius, god of medicine; marble votive offering found in the Amphiareion.
WATERMARK Head of King Philip of Macedon.
SECURITY FEATURES Idem 5,000 GRD.

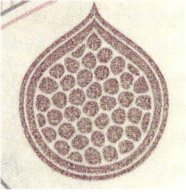

The colour of this motif varies according to the angle at which the note is held.

SPAIN ESPAÑA

1,000 ESP – 1992 – 130 x 65 mm (5.12 x 2.56 in.)

OBVERSE Portrait of Hernán Cortes (Medellin, 1485–Seville, 1547) who set out to conquer Mexico in 1518 and crushed the Aztec empire in 1521. Became governor-general of conquered territory; map of American continent; Aztec figure.
REVERSE Portrait of the conquistador Francisco Pizarro (Trujillo, 1475–Lima, 1541) who conquered Peru and founded Lima in 1535; terrestrial globe; astrolabe; helmet and sabre of Spanish *Tercios*; Lima cathedral; arms of Spain.
WATERMARK Head of Montezuma, Aztec king.
SECURITY FEATURES Intaglio printing; fibres/motifs visible under UV; security thread; OVI (*optically variable ink*) feature; see-through feature (compass rose).

The compass refers to the conquests of Pizarro and Cortes. As in the nineteenth century, Portugal and Spain use their notes to honour the explorers and conquistadors who built their overseas empires.

2,000 ESP – 1995 – 138 x 68 mm (5.43 x 2.68 in.)

OBVERSE Portrait of botanist José Celestino Mutis (Cadiz, 1732–Santa Fé de Bogota, 1808) observing a flower; map of the American continent. Studied flora and fauna of New World, discovered anti-malarial properties of quinine, and was equally distinguished as mathematician and astronomer.
REVERSE Entrance to Royal Botanic Gardens, Madrid, of which Mutis was president; floral motifs (particularly stylised fleur de lys); title page from his posthumous *Historia de los Arboles* (1869); arms of Spain.
WATERMARK Portrait of José Celestino Mutis.
SECURITY FEATURES Idem 1,000 ESP + microtext.

Signatures, in theory, remain a means of authentication for banknotes. Admittedly, though, few users pay attention to them.

5,000 ESP – 1992 – 145 x 71 mm (5.71 x 2.80 in.)

OBVERSE Portrait of Christopher Columbus (Genoa, 1541–Valladolid, 1506); map of American continent; compass rose; caravels from expedition; royal couple (Catholic monarchs Isabella and Ferdinand).
REVERSE Armillary sphere (navigational device); ship's compasses; autograph of Christopher Columbus; profile of caravel in background.
WATERMARK Portrait of Martín Alonso Pinzón (1441–1493), captain of the *Pinto*.
SECURITY FEATURES Idem 1,000 ESP.

Not surprisingly, Columbus' caravels feature on this note, issued to mark the 500th anniversary of the crossing of the Atlantic by the vessels *Pinta*, *Niña* and *Santa María*.

10,000 ESP – 1992 – 154 x 74 mm (6.06 x 2.91 in.)

OBVERSE Portrait of King Juan Carlos (Rome, 1938) who ascended throne on death of Franco, 1975; under him, Spain acquired democratic institutions and later joined European Community. To his left, Institute of Hispanic Culture, former Linares Palace.
REVERSE Portrait of Spanish sailor, astronomer and geographer Jorge Juan y Santacilia (Novelda, 1713–Madrid, 1773); sectional view of ship's prow, alluding to his *Treatise on Mechanics as Applied to the Construction of Vessels*; sailing ship.
WATERMARK Portrait of Antonio de Ulloa de la Torre-Guiral.
SECURITY FEATURES Idem 1,000 ESP.

The arms vary in colour according to the angle at which the note is held.

FRANCE

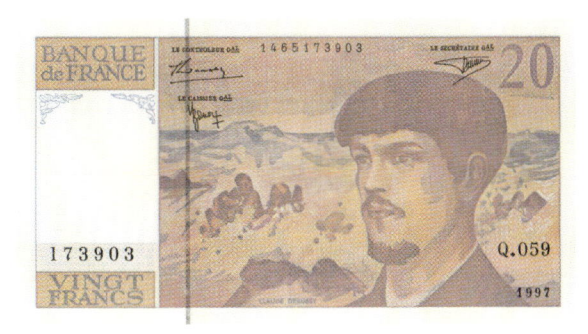

20 FRF – 1980 – 140 x 75 mm (5.51 x 2.95 in.)
OBVERSE Portrait of composer Claude Debussy (Saint-Germain-en-Laye, 1862–Paris, 1918) whose innovative techniques sounded the death-knell for conventions of tonal music, after work by Marcel Baschet; sea in background, allusion to symphonic sketches completed 1905.
REVERSE Debussy, after portrait by Michel Baschet; landscape in the Midi.
WATERMARK Head of Claude Debussy.
SECURITY FEATURES Security thread.

Nowadays, most watermarks echo the principal motif of a banknote, usually the portrait on the obverse, as with this example devoted to Debussy.

50 FRF by Roger Pfund – 1993 – 123 x 80 mm (4.84 x 3.15 in.)
OBVERSE Portrait of aviator Antoine de Saint-Exupéry (Lyons, 1900–Mediterranean, 1944), author of *The Little Prince*; background depicting two of his flights; aircraft silhouette (Latécoère 25).
REVERSE Saint-Exupéry's Bréguet 14 aircraft against backdrop of desert and sky with clouds; compass rose.
WATERMARK Head of Antoine de Saint-Exupéry.
SECURITY FEATURES Intaglio printing; blind recognition features (tactile ink); microtext; security thread; OVI (*optically variable ink*) feature (boa digesting elephant); windowed metallic, reflective 'strap'; motif in colourless ink (sheep); see-through feature (The Little Prince, from book of same name).

In the series of French notes by the Swiss artist Pfund, all the figurative elements on each denomination refer to the featured personality. On the Saint-Exupéry example, the variable-colour motif represents a boa constrictor digesting an elephant.

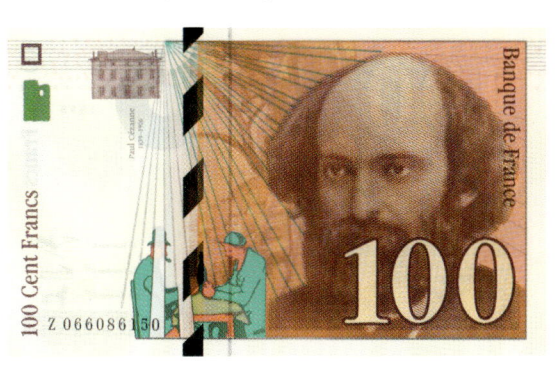

100 FRF by Roger Pfund – 1997 – 133 x 80 mm (5.24 x 3.15 in.)
OBVERSE Portrait of post-impressionist artist Paul Cézanne (Aix-en-Provence, 1839–1906); background recalling painting *View of L'Estaque*, 1878–9, when Cézanne was distancing himself from impressionism; view of the family home, le Jas de Bouffan, recurring in several works
REVERSE Reproduction of still life *Apples and Biscuits* (c. 1880); interpretation of colour circle.
WATERMARK Head of Paul Cézanne.
SECURITY FEATURES OVI (*optically variable ink*) feature (Cézanne's palette); motif in colourless ink (mountain of Sainte-Victoire); see-through feature (*The card-players*); other features, idem 50 FRF.

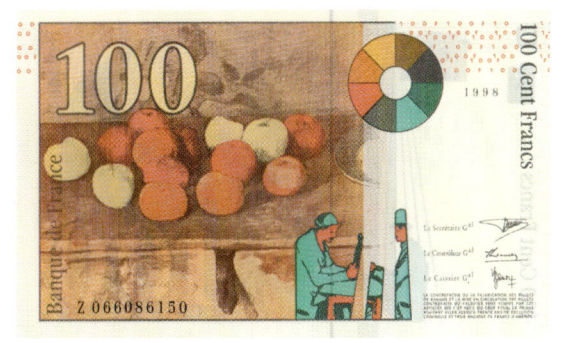

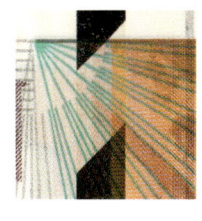

French notes are the only ones in the EU with a 'strap' – a wide metallised band incorporated in the paper – which appears black when photocopied.

200 FRF *by Roger Pfund* – 1996 – 143 x 80 mm (5.63 x 3.15 in.)
OBVERSE Portrait of engineer Gustave Eiffel (Dijon, 1832–Paris, 1923); Garabit Viaduct constructed by Eiffel in Auvergne, 1880–4; detail of metal framework of Eiffel Tower; sectional view of Nice Observatory.
REVERSE View of base of Eiffel Tower and Champ du Mars at time of Exposition universelle (Paris, 1889); in the background, dome of Palais des beaux-arts and glass roof of Galerie des machines.
WATERMARK Head of Gustave Eiffel.
SECURITY FEATURES OVI (*optically variable ink*) feature (section through one of four supports of Eiffel Tower); motif in colourless ink (Garabit Viaduct); see-through feature (Eiffel Tower); other features, idem 50 FRF.

Detail of offset printing on reverse, with motif from period photo.

500 FRF *by Roger Pfund* – 1994 – 153 x 80 mm (6.02 x 3.15 in.)
OBVERSE Portraits of scientists Pierre Curie (Paris, 1859–1906) and his wife Marie Sklodowska (Warsaw, 1867–Sancellemoz, 1934), Nobel Prize-winners (1903) for their work on radioactivity; coloured background representing radium salts in phial; extract from Marie's *Treatise on Radioactivity*; mobile X-ray unit.
REVERSE Chemistry laboratory, from photo by *service des mesures* of Radium Institute (created 1914), with symbolic reproduction of atomic structure.
WATERMARK Head of Marie Curie.
SECURITY FEATURES OVI (*optically variable ink*) feature (symbolic representation of subatomic particles); motif in colourless ink (chemical symbol for radium); see-through feature (beta ray, Greek letter beta); other features, idem 50 FRF.

Detail of line-intaglio printing (obverse). The truck is one of the 200 mobile radiography units nicknamed *les petites Curie* brought into service during the First World War on the initiative of Marie Curie.

EIRE IRELAND

5 IEP *by Robert Ballagh* – 1993 – 120 x 64 mm (4.72 x 2.52 in.)
OBVERSE Portrait of Sister Catherine McAuley (1778–1841) founder of Order of the Sisters of Mercy (Dublin, 1831) devoted to education and health of poor, after posthumous portrait; Dublin's Mater Misericordiae Hospital.
REVERSE Class with three children; blackboard with poem from *Songs Ascribed to Raftery*; on wall, Celtic motifs and map of a frontier-less Europe.
WATERMARK Female allegory of Ireland and denomination.
SECURITY FEATURES Intaglio printing; windowed, silver security thread with denomination; see-through feature (Celtic harp); microtext; latent image (letters IR).

On the classroom wall is a map of a 'frontier-less' Europe. It is rare to find a reference on a note to the construction of the European Union.

10 IEP *by Robert Ballagh* – 1993 – 128 x 68 mm (5.04 x 2.68 in.)
OBVERSE Portrait of Irish author James Joyce (Rathgar, 1882–Zurich, 1941), in whose works – largely autobiographical, such as *Dubliners* and *Ulysses* – Ireland plays major role; panoramic view of Dublin and counties of Dublin and Wicklow, after nineteenth-century drawing by T.R. Harvey.
REVERSE Reproduction of eighteenth-century head, sculpted by Edward Smyth for Customs House in Dublin, personifying River Liffey; city map of Dublin; Joyce's signature and extract from *Finnegan's Wake*.
WATERMARK Female allegory of Ireland and denomination.
SECURITY FEATURES Idem 5 IEP.

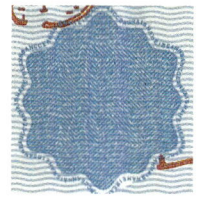

On all Eire notes there is a 'latent' image, i.e. visible only in low-angled light: the letters IR for Irish republic. Further, this motif is surrounded by microprint lettering: *Banc Ceannais na hEireann*: Central Bank of Ireland (Gaelic).

20 IEP *by Robert Ballagh* – 1992 – 136 x 72 mm (5.35 x 2.83 in.)
OBVERSE Portrait of Irish politician Daniel O'Connell (Carhen House, Kerry, 1775–Genoa, 1847), who led popular Catholic emancipation movement and whose parliamentary career was distinguished by fight for Irish freedom, after print by John Gubbins; view of Derrynan Abbey, Kerry, after original in National Library.
REVERSE Text of commitment made by O'Connell in 1845; building known as the 'Four Courts', after original in the National Library.
WATERMARK Female allegory of Ireland and denomination.
SECURITY FEATURES Idem 5 IEP.

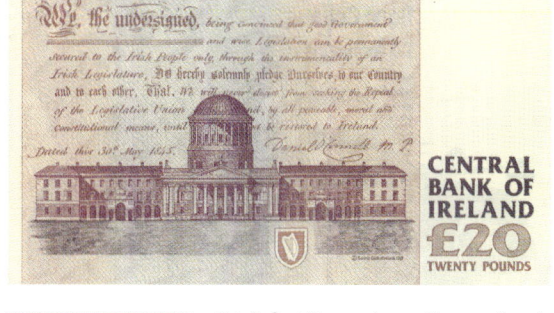

Detail of printing on obverse. The use of precise detail is a weapon in the fight against counterfeiting. The task of designers consists, for the most part, of adaptation and layout, as all elements selected for use on a note are based on existing work.

50 IEP *by Robert Ballagh* – 1995 – 144 x 76 mm (5.67 x 2.99 in.)
OBVERSE Portrait of politician, historian and poet Douglas Hyde (Roscommon, 1860–Dublin, 1949), first president of independent Eire; building known as Àras an Uachtaráin; drawing of foot of Ardagh chalice.
REVERSE Bagpipe player; crest of Conradh an Gaelige from sixteenth-century manuscript.
WATERMARK Female allegory of Ireland and denomination.
SECURITY FEATURES Idem 5 IEP + OVI (*optically variable ink*) feature.

The text on the obverse of Eire notes is in Gaelic, that on the reverse in English. Until 1977, the two languages appeared side by side on both faces.

100 IEP *by Robert Ballagh* – 1996 – 152 x 80 mm (5.98 x 3.15 in.)
OBVERSE Portrait of politician Charles Stewart Parnell (Avondale, 1846–Brighton, 1891), leader of Irish Nationalist movement; his home, Avondale House in Rathdrum, Wicklow county; a dog.
REVERSE Fragment of Parnell Monument, Dublin; extract from Parnell's 1886 declaration in response to introduction of Home Rule Bill.
WATERMARK Female allegory of Ireland and denomination.
SECURITY FEATURES Idem 50 IEP + motif visible under UV (celtic harp and denomination).

A Celtic harp, emblem of Ireland, figures on every denomination. If you look at the note against the light, the emblem appears complete.

ITALY ITALIA

1,000 ITL *by Giovanni Pino* – 1990 – 112 x 61 mm (4.41 x 2.40 in.)
OBVERSE Portrait of educationist Maria Montessori (Chiaravalle, 1870–Noordwijck, 1952), first Italian woman doctor and promoter of new teaching methods based on children's creativity; stylised figure of child; pieces of puzzle.
REVERSE *Children at Study*, after painting by A. Spadini; pieces of puzzle.
WATERMARK Head of Maria Montessori; monogram BI.
SECURITY FEATURES Intaglio printing; security thread.

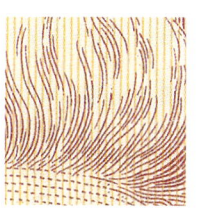

Anatomical details (here, of the hair) are exceptionally well drawn on Italian notes.

2,000 ITL *by G. Savini* – 1990 – 118 x 61 mm (4.65 x 2.40 in.)
OBVERSE Portrait of physicist Guglielmo Marconi (Bologna, 1874–Rome, 1937), Nobel Prize (1909) for contribution to study of Hertzian waves; geometric design symbolising radio communication by Hertzian waves.
REVERSE Radio apparatus invented by Marconi, with transmitting aerials; the vessel *Elettra*; background: suggestive of Hertzian waves.
WATERMARK Head of Marconi and monogram BI.
SECURITY FEATURES Idem 1,000 ITL + see-through feature (rosette).

Detail of wireless telegraphy apparatus developed by Marconi. The technical details on a large number of European notes are designed to inform the public – but also to complicate the task of counterfeiters.

5,000 ITL *by G. Savini* – 1985 – 126 x 70 mm (4.96 x 2.76 in.)
OBVERSE Portrait of musician Vincenzo Bellini (Catania, 1801–Putteaux, Paris, 1835), prolific operatic composer; Massimo-Bellini Theatre, Catania.
REVERSE Allegory of lyrical art.
WATERMARK Head of Bellini and monogram BI.
SECURITY FEATURES Idem 1,000 ITL.

All Italian notes since 1893 have the state seal on the obverse. From 1971, this seal has featured a winged lion, emblem of Venice, and the arms of Genoa, Pisa and Amalfi.

10,000 ITL *by Giovanni Pino* – 1984 – 134 x 70 mm (5.28 x 2.76 in.)

OBVERSE Portrait of physicist Alessandro Volta (Como, 1745–1827), whose research into electricity led to prototype electric battery (1800); Volta battery.
REVERSE The *Tempio Voltiano* at Como.
WATERMARK Head of Volta and monogram BI.
SECURITY FEATURES Idem 1,000 ITL.

For a considerable time, banknotes have depicted monuments and buildings associated with the famous. The *Tempio Voltiano*, at Como, was erected between 1925 and 1927 by the architect Frederico Frigerio in neo-classical style in recognition of the cult status enjoyed by Volta.

50,000 ITL *by Giovanni Pino* – 1992 – 149 x 70 mm (5.97 x 2.76 in.)

OBVERSE Portrait of architect, sculptor and painter Lorenzo Bernini, one of the greatest baroque masters (Naples, 1598–Rome, 1680); Triton Fountain, Rome.
REVERSE Equestrian statue; sketches for Bernini colonnade, St Peter's, Rome (1656–63).
WATERMARK Head of Bernini and monogram BI.
SECURITY FEATURES Intaglio printing; two incorporated security threads: first by watermark, with inscription 'Banca d'Italia', second in centre of note, consisting of simple plastic strip coated with opaque varnish; microtext; blind recognition features (tactile ink); OVI (*optically variable ink*) feature; see-through feature (stylised winged insect).

On this Bernini note, *guilloche* is used in abundance, forming motifs reflecting the baroque style of the artist.

100,000 ITL *by G. Savini* – 1994 – 156 x 70 mm (6.14 x 2.76 in.)
OBVERSE Portrait of baroque painter Michelangelo Merisio, called Caravaggio (Caravaggio, 1569–Porto d'Ercole, 1609); two figures from *The Fortuneteller*.
REVERSE Basket of fruit.
WATERMARK Head of Caravaggio and monogram BI.
SECURITY FEATURES See-through feature (branch); other features, idem 50,000 ITL.

Detail from Caravaggio's *The Fortuneteller*. From the nineteenth century, certain notes reproduced artistic masterpieces, presenting users with a gallery of Old Masters.

500,000 ITL *by G. Savini* – 1997 – 163 x 78 mm (6.42 x 3.07 in.)
OBVERSE Portrait of Italian Renaissance painter Raffaello Sanzio, called Raphael, (Urbino, 1483–Rome, 1520), after self-portrait in the Galleria degli Uffizi, Florence; left, detail from *The Triumph of Galatea*, fresco for the Palazzo Farnese, Rome.
REVERSE *The School of Athens*, fresco from the Stanza della Segnatura (Signature Room), Vatican Palace, Rome.
WATERMARK Head of Raphael and monogram BI.
SECURITY FEATURES See-through feature (swan with wings spread); other features, idem 50,000 ITL + fibres/motifs visible under UV.

The theme of Raphael's famous fresco (Palazzo Farnese, Rome) was borrowed from the writings of Philostratus. Galatea was a sea-nymph who refused the advances of the Cyclops Polyphemus, being already in love with Acis, a shepherd. She dived into the sea to escape Polyphemus' anger and rejoined the other Nereids.

LUXEMBOURG

100 LUF – 1986 – 142 x 76 mm (6.77 x 2.99 in.)
OBVERSE Portrait of John (Berg, 1921), Grand Duke of Luxembourg 1964–2000; Grand-Ducal Palace.
REVERSE View of city of Luxembourg, after Weyer.
WATERMARK Head of Grand Duke John.
SECURITY FEATURES Intaglio printing; security thread.

The copyright notice of banks of issue appears on an increasing number of notes, with establishments claiming rights of authorship over their designs. This means that banks can oppose the reproduction of their notes, for example for commercial purposes.

1,000 LUF – 1985 – 154 x 76 mm (6.06 x 2.99 in.)
OBVERSE Portrait of John (Berg, 1921), Grand Duke of Luxembourg 1964–2000; château of Vianden.
REVERSE Historic buildings of Echternach; illumination; extract from liturgical manuscript.
WATERMARK Head of Grand Duke John.
SECURITY FEATURES Idem 100 LUF + alatent image; OVI (*optically variable ink*) feature; see-through feature (decorative pattern); blind recognition features (tactile ink); microtext.

When choosing banknote designs, banks frequently opt for fonts with small characters, which not only lend the notes character but make them hard to photocopy.

5,000 LUF – 1993 – 160 x 76 mm (6.30 x 2.99 in.)
OBVERSE Portrait of John (Berg, 1921), Grand Duke of Luxembourg 1964–2000; château of Clervaux.
REVERSE Centre Européen de Luxembourg-Kirchberg; map of Luxembourg fortifications.
WATERMARK Head of Grand Duke John.
SECURITY FEATURES See-through feature (bartizan); other features, idem 1,000 LUF.

The serial number on a note is principally to identify its legitimate owner. Here, the Institut Monétaire Luxembourgeois, in a playful allusion to ever-lengthening figures, presents the figures pictorially.

NETHERLANDS NEDERLAND

10 NLG *by R.D.E. Oxenaar* – 1968 – 142 x 76 mm (5.84 x 2.99 in.)
OBVERSE Stylised portrait of Baroque painter Frans Hals (Antwerp, c. 1581 or 1585–Haarlem, 1666), portraitist of the Dutch bourgeoisie, after self-portrait in Indianapolis Museum, USA.
REVERSE Linear design suggesting colour-grinder, and ruff or 'fraise'.
WATERMARK Cornucopia.
SECURITY FEATURES Microtext; blind recognition features (tactile ink); fibres visible under UV.

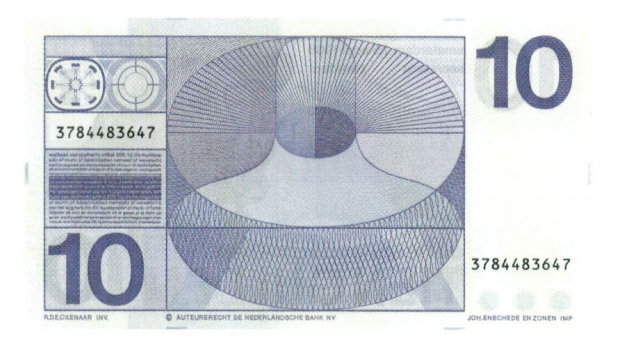

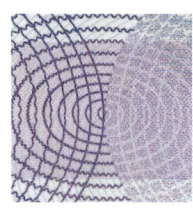

Networks of guilloche work are a graphical element in the battle for security. Designers, however, have adapted the technique to lend their notes individual aesthetic qualities.

10 NLG *by Jaap T.G. Drupsteen* – 1997 – 136 x 76 mm (5.35 x 2.99 in.)
OBVERSE Geometric motifs.
REVERSE Geometric motifs.
WATERMARK Kingfisher (*Alcedo atthis ispida*).
SECURITY FEATURES Intaglio printing; fibres incorporated into paper pulp and visible under UV; microtext, obverse: 0.2 mm (0.008 in.); reverse: 0.3 mm (0.012 in.); blind recognition features (tactile ink); see-through feature (stickleback); colour details altering on reproduction.

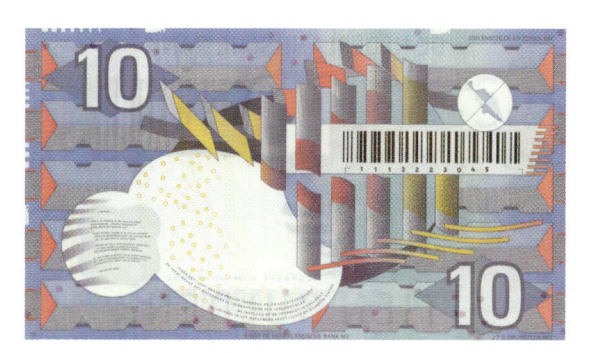

Several Dutch notes employ bar codes, which allow automated sorting and identification.

25 NLG *by Jaap T.G. Drupsteen* – 1989 – 142 x 76 mm (5.59 x 2.99 in.)
OBVERSE Geometric motifs.
REVERSE Geometric motifs.
WATERMARK Robin.
SECURITY FEATURES Idem 10 NLG + see-through feature (poppy and tulip); metameric ink, revealing image of fish (reverse) when viewed through red filter.

The Nederlandsche Bank has recently issued three notes with abstract designs. The only figurative elements employed on these notes are the see-through feature (here, a tulip) and the watermark.

50 NLG *by R.D.E. Oxenaar* – 1982 – 148 x 76 mm (5.83 x 2.99 in.)
OBVERSE Sunflower bloom with bee.
REVERSE Map of IJsselmeere polders; field of sunflowers and sky with clouds.
WATERMARK Bee.
SECURITY FEATURES Intaglio printing; fibres incorporated into paper pulp and visible under UV; blind recognition features (tactile ink); see-through feature (geometrical shape).

For two centuries, the bee has featured on notes more than any other creature. It is known for its industry, and lives in a hierarchical society.

100 NLG *by R.D.E. Oxenaar* – 1977 – 154 x 76 mm (6.06 x 2.99 in.)
OBVERSE Common snipe (*Gallinago gallinago*); landscape of dunes.
REVERSE Head of great snipe (*Gallinago media*); rainbow and flower.
WATERMARK Head of great snipe.
SECURITY FEATURES Microtext; blind recognition features (tactile ink).

Until the 1980s, the Nederlandsche Bank employed portraits of famous historical figures like other European nations. In search of a change, it began to commission innovative designs inspired by Nature.

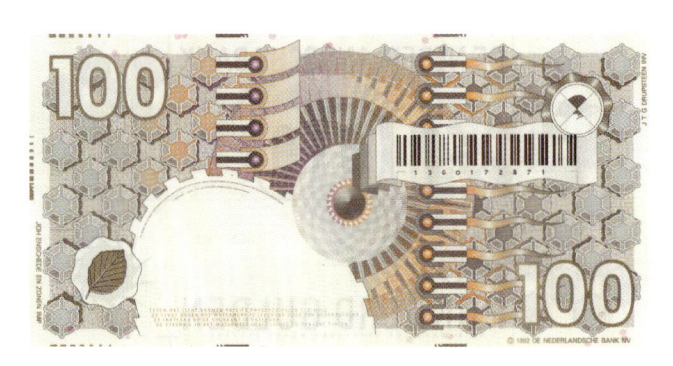

100 NLG *by Jaap T.G. Drupsteen* – 1992 – 154 x 76 mm (6.06 x 2.99 in.)
OBVERSE Geometric designs.
REVERSE Geometric designs.
WATERMARK Little owl.
SECURITY FEATURES Idem 50 NLG + see-through feature (mouse); colour details altering on reproduction.

Based on the same principle as the 'strap' found on French notes, this feature appears black when photocopied. It has been developed through co-operation between issuing banks and manufacturers of photocopying machines.

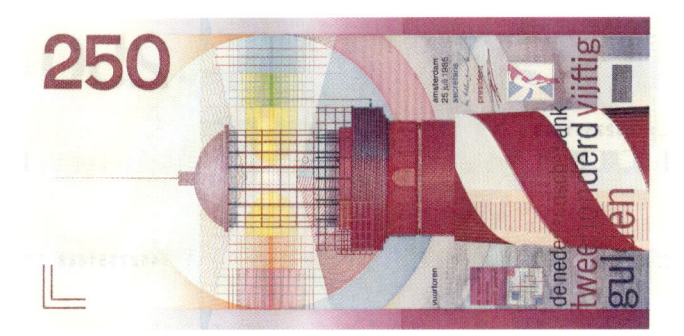

250 NLG *by R.D.E. Oxenaar and J.J. Kruit* – 1985 – 160 x 76 mm (6.30 x 2.99 in.)
OBVERSE Lighthouse.
REVERSE Map of Netherlands coast with sites of beacons; clouds; dune landscape; Ameland Light.
WATERMARK Rabbit with letters VHP.
SECURITY FEATURES Idem 50 NLG + see-through feature (oystercatcher); colour details altering on reproduction; metameric ink revealing image of rabbit (reverse) when viewed through red filter.

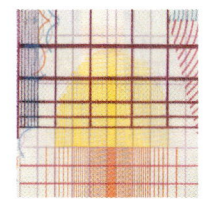

The beam of this Dutch lighthouse includes all the colours of the rainbow; but since the invention of the colour photocopier, these variations have lost most of their effectiveness against counterfeiting.

1,000 NLG *by R.D.E. Oxenaar* – 1972 – 160 x 76 mm (6.30 x 2.99 in.)
OBVERSE Stylised portrait of Benedict de Spinoza (Amsterdam, 1632–The Hague, 1677), philosopher of Jewish descent, considered as a precursor of modern philosophy, after portrait in Haags Gemeentemuseum in The Hague; geometric shapes.
REVERSE Stylised representation of mathematical approximation of infinity, after theories of Spinoza.
WATERMARK Geometric solids (pyramid, bowl and rectangular parallelepiped).
SECURITY FEATURES Idem 10 NLG of 1968.

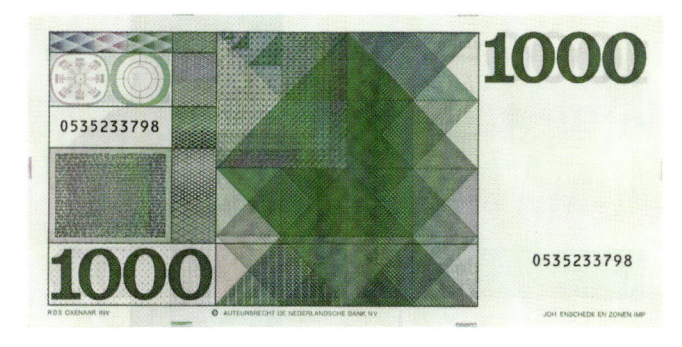

On Dutch notes, the designer's name appears, as well as that of the printers.

1,000 NLG *by Jaap T.G. Drupsteen* – 1994 – 166 x 76 mm (6.54 x 2.99 in.)
OBVERSE Geometric designs.
REVERSE Geometric designs.
WATERMARK Lapwing.
SECURITY FEATURES See-through feature (lapwing egg); other features, idem 100 NLG of 1992.

On the most recent Dutch notes, brief poems composed for the purpose feature in microprint.

AUSTRIA ÖSTERREICH

20 ATS – 1988 – 123 x 62 mm (4.84 x 2.44 in.)
OBVERSE Portrait of wartercolourists Moritz Michael Daffinger (Vienna, 1790–1849), one of most famous Biedermeier artists, specialising in portraits, miniatures and flowers; palette and brushes.
REVERSE The Albertina, gallery housing some of Daffinger's works.
WATERMARK Stylised arms of Austria.
SECURITY FEATURES Intaglio printing; blind recognition features (tactile ink); OVI (*optically variable ink*) feature; see-through feature (floral pattern); security thread.

The arms of Austria, appearing on all the country's notes, consist of a heraldic eagle holding a hammer and sickle in its claws.

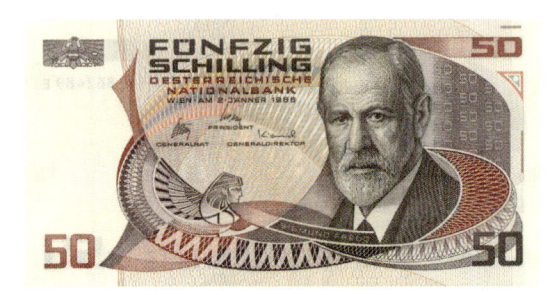

50 ATS – 1986 – 130 x 65 mm (5.12 x 2.56 in.)
OBVERSE Portrait of psychiatrist Sigmund Freud (Freiberg, Moravia, 1856–London, 1939), founder of psychoanalysis and author of studies devoted mainly to human unconscious, sexuality and interpretation of dreams; Sphinx's head.
REVERSE Josephinum, Vienna.
WATERMARK Stylised arms of Austria.
SECURITY FEATURES See-through feature (ornamental detail); other features, idem 20 ATS.

The façade of the Josephinum, Vienna. Now the seat of the Institute of the History of Medicine, it contains a unique collection of medical instruments dating back to the 1700s and archives relating to the practice of medicine in the capital.

100 ATS – 1984 – 137 x 68 mm (5.39 x 2.68 in.)
OBVERSE Portrait of economist Eugen Böhm von Bawerk (Brno, 1856–Vienna, 1914), professor at Innsbrück and Vienna and Minister of Finance (1900–4). From 1884 to 1889 published *Kapital und Kapitalzins*, celebrated for theory of interest and championship of capitalism; caduceus.
REVERSE Façade of the Academy of Sciences, Vienna.
WATERMARK Stylised arms of Austria.
SECURITY FEATURES See-through feature (guilloche); other features, idem 20 ATS.

Detail of guilloche work. This form of ornamentation is first found on Austrian notes of 1816.

500 ATS – 1997 – 148 x 72 mm (5.83 x 2.83 in.)

OBVERSE Portrait of Rosa Mayreder, née Obermayer (Vienna, 1858–1938), known initially as painter; won further acclaim for work with feminist movements and writings on women's problems and sociology of sexes.
REVERSE Group of women and portrait of Rosa and Karl Mayreder.
WATERMARK Portrait of Rosa Mayreder.
SECURITY FEATURES Intaglio printing; security thread with denomination; see-through feature (A for *Austria*); microtext; OVI (*optically variable ink*) feature; fibres/motifs visible under UV; Kinegram (arms of Austria); iridescent band, 2 cm (0.79 in.) wide; motif absorbing infrared; number on reverse in brown magnetic pigment; denomination in tactile ink.

The date seen on bank notes is generally not the date of issue, but indicates when the decision to issue was taken.

1,000 ATS – 1997 – 154 x 72 mm (6.06 x 2.83 in.)

OBVERSE Portrait of Karl Landsteiner (Vienna, 1868–New York, 1943), Austrian biologist, discoverer of blood groups and Rhesus factor, Nobel Prize for medicine, 1930.
REVERSE Karl Landsteiner in his laboratory.
WATERMARK Portrait of Karl Landsteiner.
SECURITY FEATURES Idem 500 ATS + latent image (denomination).

This very recent, high-denomination note sports an impressive number of security features. Some represent older methods, such as the watermark and security strip; others, like Kinegram, are cutting-edge technology. This portion of the note masks a latent image (the number 1,000), visible only when the note is tilted.

5,000 ATS – 1988 – 154 x 72 mm (6.06 x 2.83 in.)

OBVERSE Portrait of Wolfgang Amadeus Mozart (Salzburg, 1756–Vienna, 1791), musician and composer, one of greatest masters of opera and melodic forms, composer of symphonies, sonatas and piano concertos, religious and chamber music.
REVERSE National Opera House; statue.
WATERMARK Arms of Austria.
SECURITY FEATURES See-through feature (mask); Kinegram with head of Mozart facing two directions; other features, idem 20 ATS.

The see-through feature or register gauge: the theatrical mask (upper right-hand corner, obverse; upper left, reverse) appears complete when viewed against the light.

PORTUGAL

500 PTE – 1997 – 125 x 68 mm (4.92 x 2.68 in.)
OBVERSE Portrait and signature of João de Barros (Viseu, 1496–Ribeira, 1570), historian, humanist, high-ranking official responsible for colonies and chronicler of Portuguese conquests; map of Africa and Europe; two musical angels.
REVERSE Allegory of Portuguese discoveries in Asia; extract from Barros's *Decadas da Asia*.
WATERMARK Head of João de Barros.
SECURITY FEATURES Intaglio printing; see-through feature (armillary sphere); microtext; security thread, appears red under UV; fibres/motifs visible under UV (compass roses); latent image (denomination).

The watermark shows the head of João de Barros. Known as the 'Livy of Portugal', he is considered one of the founders of Portuguese historiography.

1,000 PTE – 1996 – 132 x 68 mm (5.30 x 2.68 in.)
OBVERSE Portrait of explorer Pedro Alvares Cabral (Belmonte, c. 1460–Santarem, c. 1526), discoverer of Brazil (1500); Cross of the Order of Christ.
REVERSE Caravel; tropical flora and fauna; extract from *Pero Val de Gamini*.
WATERMARK Head of Pedro Alvares Cabral.
SECURITY FEATURES See-through feature (Cross of the Order of Christ); other features, idem 500 PTE.

Most modern European notes have security motifs visible only under ultra-violet light; on this Portuguese example, the design consists of three compasses.

2,000 PTE – 1995 – 139 x 68 mm (5.47 x 2.68 in.)
OBVERSE Portrait of explorer Bartolomeu Dias (Algarve, c. 1450–Cape of Good Hope, 1500) who sailed round Africa and Cape of Good Hope in 1487; compass, compass rose; seal of Portugal.
REVERSE Caravel rounding Cape of Good Hope; compass; old map of Africa; quotation from *Lusiads*, epic poem by Luís de Camões.
WATERMARK Head of Bartolomeu Dias.
SECURITY FEATURES Idem 1,000 PTE.

On four Portuguese notes a cross of the Order of Christ appears when they are held against the light.

5,000 PTE – 1995 – 146 x 75 mm (5.75 x 2.95 in.)

OBVERSE Portrait and signature of Vasco da Gama (Sines, 1469–1524), discoverer of route to Indies via Cape of Good Hope (1497), founded settlements in Mozambique and was Viceroy of Portuguese Indies; armillary sphere; Cross of the Order of Christ.
REVERSE Caravel; arms of Portugal; background of luxuriant vegetation; lower left, fragment from *Lusiads* by Portuguese poet Luis Camöes; embarkation of Vasco da Gama.
WATERMARK Head of Vasco da Gama.
SECURITY FEATURES Idem 1,000 PTE.

Detail of the embarkation of Vasco da Gama. To the Portuguese, the fifteenth and sixteenth centuries were a golden age, and over the last hundred years notes of the Banco de Portugal have frequently featured heroic figures of the period.

10,000 PTE – 1996 – 153 x 75 mm (6.02 x 2.95 in.)

OBVERSE Portrait and signature of the Infante Dom Henrique (Oporto, 1394–Sagres, 1460), known as Henry the Navigator, sponsor of Portuguese voyages of discovery to African coasts; compass; seal of Henry the Navigator; hour-glass; background of fleur-de-lys and Cross of the Order of Christ.
REVERSE Caravel with lateen sails; left, Henry's motto: 'I strive to do well'; quotation from *Mensagem* of E. Pessoa.
WATERMARK Head of Henry the Navigator.
SECURITY FEATURES Idem 1,000 PTE + OVI (*optically variable ink*) feature; iridescent band.

This motif (heraldic lion holding a banner) changes colour depending on the angle from which it is viewed.

FINLAND SUOMI

20 FIM *by Torsten Ekström, Erik Bruun and Pentti Rahikainen* – 1997 – 142 x 69 mm (5.59 x 2.72 in.)
OBVERSE Portrait of writer Väinö Linna (Urjala, 1920–Tampere, 1992), best known for his epic war novel *The Unknown Soldier* (1955), after photograph by Studio KukaSiskot.
REVERSE Industrial building on River Tammerkoski, Tampere.
WATERMARK Head of writer Väinö Linna.
SECURITY FEATURES Intaglio printing; windowed, silver security thread; microtext; motifs visible under UV; latent image; see-through feature (geometrical pattern); hologram (bird in flight against background of smaller birds, with final words of Linna's novel *The Unknown Soldier*.)

This very recent Finnish note has a hologram featuring birds. The holograms found on bank and credit cards work on a similar principle.

50 FIM *by Torsten Ekström, Erik Bruun and Pentti Rahikainen* – 1991 – 142 x 69 mm (5.59 x 2.72 in.)
OBVERSE Portrait of architect and designer Alvar Aalto (Kuortane, 1898–Helsinki, 1976), after photograph by Trond Hedström; curving lines inspired by Aalto's designs.
REVERSE Celebrated work by Aalto: Finlandia Hall, Helsinki.
WATERMARK Head of Alvar Aalto.
SECURITY FEATURES Intaglio printing; windowed, silver security thread; microtext; motifs visible under UV; latent image.

Microprint varies in size. Some types can be read with the naked eye, others are very hard to decipher. Such is the case with this Finnish note, where the text is contained within the zero of the denomination; in fact, it repeats the name of the issuing bank.

100 FIM *by Torsten Ekström, Erik Bruun and Pentti Rahikainen* – 1991 – 142 x 69 mm (5.59 x 2.72 in.)
OBVERSE Portrait of composer Johan (Jean) Sibelius (Hämeenlinna, 1865–Jarvenpää, 1957), doyen of Finnish classical music, after period photograph; undulating lines symbolising waves of music.
REVERSE Four white swans in flight, reflecting Sibelius's love of nature; northern lake and forest.
WATERMARK Head of Johan (Jean) Sibelius.
SECURITY FEATURES Idem 50 FIM.

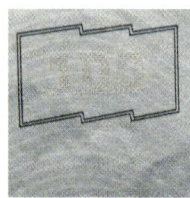

If the note is examined in a skimming light, the 100-mark denomination will appear in the upper right-hand corner.

500 FIM *by Torsten Ekström, Erik Bruun and Pentti Rahikainen* – 1991 – 142 x 69 mm (5.59 x 2.72 in.)
OBVERSE Portrait of poet, linguist and physician Elias Lönnrot (Karjalohja, 1802–1884), after 1841 lithograph by Johan Knutson; Lönnrot edited version of Finnish national epic *Kalevala*; *kantele*, Finnish national instrument.
REVERSE Finnish landscape based on Punkuuharju in eastern Finland: Lönnrot drew his inspiration from beauty of nature.
WATERMARK Head of Elias Lönnrot.
SECURITY FEATURES Windowed, plastic security thread; other feautures, idem 50 FIM + Kinegram (denomination and emblem of Bank of Finland against background of snowflakes).

The emblem of Finland, which has figured on all notes since the mid-1800s: a lion standing upright and holding a sword, with its hind legs trampling the blade and guard of a Russian sabre.

1,000 FIM *by Torsten Ekström, Erik Bruun and Pentti Rahikainen* – 1991 – 142 x 69 mm (5.59 x 2.72 in.)
OBVERSE Portrait of economist and statesman Anders Chydenius (Sotkamo, 1729–1803), after a painting by Pehr Fjellström (1760s); merchant vessel, alluding to Chydenius's free-trade theories.
REVERSE Principal entrance of Sveaborg fortress, near Helsinki; seagulls in flight.
WATERMARK Head of Anders Chydenius.
SECURITY FEATURES Idem 500 FIM.

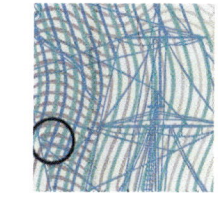

The security strip, like the watermark, can be seen against the light, and can only be partly reproduced by photocopying.

SWEDEN SVERIGE

20 SEK – 1997 – 120 x 67 mm (4.72 x 2.64 in.)
OBVERSE Portrait of writer Selma Lagerlöf (Mårbacka, 1858–1940), winner of Nobel Prize for literature 1909, after photo by Studio Jaeger; first line of her novella *Gösta Berlings Saga*; forested landscape (Värmland).
REVERSE Flight of wild geese, with reference to *The Wonderful Adventures of Nils Holgersson*.
WATERMARK Head of Selma Lagerlöf.
SECURITY FEATURES Intaglio printing; blind recognition features (tactile ink); security thread; motifs visible under UV; microtext.

The Wonderful Adventures of Nils (Holgersson) tells how Nils, reduced to the size of an elf, flies off on the back of a farm goose searching for its wild brethren. The fields and meadows in the background are traced using a chequering machine and printed by offset.

50 SEK – 1996 – 120 x 72 mm (4.72 x 2.83 in.)
OBVERSE Portrait of soprano Jenny Lind (Stockholm, 1820–Malvern, 1887) after lithograph of 1845; musical score; sectional view of the old Stockholm Opera, designed by architect Carl Fredrik Adelcrantz.
REVERSE Silver harp, with representation of tonal range; extract from musical score of Sven-David Sandström.
WATERMARK Head of Jenny Lind.
SECURITY FEATURES Intaglio printing; security thread; blind recognition features (tactile ink); microtext.

The score seen on the obverse is genuine – from Bellini's opera *Norma*.

100 SEK – 1986 – 140 x 72 mm (5.51 x 2.83 in.)
OBVERSE Portrait of botanist Carl Linnaeus (Råshult, 1707–Uppsala, 1778), the father of modern plant and animal classification, after a painting by Swedish artist Alexander Roslin; botanic gardens at Uppsala; reproductive organs of plants (drawings from the *Praeludia of Linnaeus' Sponsalia Plantarum*)
REVERSE Drawings illustrating fertilisation of flowers; bee, pollen grains, stigma and pistil, germ.
WATERMARK Head of Carl Linnaeus; from October 2001, also denomination.
SECURITY FEATURES Idem 50 SEK + from October 2001, holographic band (arms of Sweden – three crowns – plus denomination); iridescent band; see-through feature; fibres/motifs fluorescent under UV.

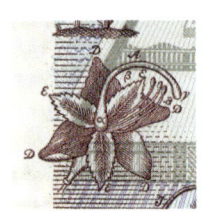

Issuing banks have commemorated several botanists and naturalists, including Mutis (Spain), Linnaeus (Sweden), Darwin (Great Britain) and Anna Maria Sibylla Merian (Germany). Their scientific drawings are both aesthetic and highly detailed.

500 SEK – 1989 – 150 x 82 mm (5.91 x 3.23 in.)
OBVERSE Portrait of King Carl XI (Stockholm, 1655–97), after painting by Daniel Klöcker von Ehrenstrahl (1682); façade of head offices of Sveriges Riksbank, Stockholm (founded under Carl XI).
REVERSE Portrait of mechanical, mining and hydraulic engineer Christopher Polhem (Visby, 1661–Stockholm, 1751), leading figure in Swedish industrial revolution; copper mine at Falun and pumping machinery; toothed wheel; Polhem's mathematical jottings.
WATERMARK Head of Carl XI; from 2001, also denomination.
SECURITY FEATURES Idem 100 SEK.

Detail of extraction machinery developed by Polhem for the copper mines at Falun. The same engineer began a canal to link the Baltic with the North Sea, and invented new methods for the construction of blast furnaces.

1,000 SEK – 1989 – 160 x 82 mm (6.30 x 3.23 in.)
OBVERSE Portrait of King Gustav Vasa (Lindholm, 1496–Stockholm, 1560), founder of Swedish nation, after painting attributed to Cornelius Arentz; view of Stockholm, after painting on wood attributed to Urban Malare.
REVERSE Reproduction of wood engraving featuring agricultural activities, from work by Olaus Magnus (1555).
WATERMARK Head of King Gustav Vasa.
SECURITY FEATURES Idem 50 SEK.

The microprint on this note is incorporated within one of the circles close to the head of Vasa: *Scripturam in propria habeant lingua*, or 'They shall read the Scriptures in their own tongue': a reference to the fact that in the reign of Gustav Vasa, Sweden adopted the reformed religion.

UNITED KINGDOM: ENGLAND

5 GBP *by Roger Withington – 1993 – 135 x 70 mm (5.31 x 2.76 in.)*
OBVERSE Portrait of Elizabeth II (London, 1926), Queen of the United Kingdom and Head of the Commonwealth since 1952; Britannia; royal monogram.
REVERSE Portrait of engineer George Stephenson (Wylam, 1781–Tapton, 1848), acclaimed as inventor of steam locomotion; locomotives by Stephenson; his signature.
WATERMARK Head of Queen Elizabeth II.
SECURITY FEATURES Intaglio printing; blind recognition features (tactile ink); windowed, silver security thread.

In 1829, a locomotive built by George Stephenson (the *Rocket*) was the winner in a speed trial, thereby definitively establishing the inventor's reputation. Stephenson's design was based on the principle of tubular heating.

10 GBP *by Roger Withington – 1993 – 142 x 75 mm (5.60 x 2.95 in.)*
OBVERSE Portrait of Queen Elizabeth II; Britannia; royal monogram.
REVERSE Portrait of Charles John Huffam Dickens (Landport, 1812–Gad's Hill, 1870), Victorian novelist and social critic, whose works include *Pickwick Papers*, *Oliver Twist*, *David Copperfield*; books; pens; cricket match, after episode in *Pickwick Papers*; Dickens's signature.
WATERMARK Head of Queen Elizabeth II.
SECURITY FEATURES Idem 5 GBP.

Humour is a rarity on banknotes; this is an exception, with a cricket match scene inspired by an episode in The Pickwick Papers.

10 GBP *by Andrew Ward – 2000 – 142 x 75 mm (5.60 x 2.95 in.)*
OBVERSE Queen Elizabeth II; cephalopod fossils; royal monogram.
REVERSE Portrait of naturalist and biologist Charles Robert Darwin (Shrewsbury, 1809–Downe, 1882), founder of the theory of evolution by natural selection, author of *On the Origin of Species by Means of Natural Selection* (1859); hummingbird (Galapagos Islands) sipping nectar from flower; Darwin's magnifying glass; his compass; vessel *Beagle* on the horizon; trilobite and ammonite fossils; Darwin's signature.
WATERMARK Head of Queen Elizabeth II.
SECURITY FEATURES Idem 5 GBP + microtext; hologram (image of Britannia and denomination); motifs visible under UV.

Though notes are no longer convertible into gold, those of the Bank of England still carry the three-centuries-old message 'I promise to pay the bearer on demand the sum of …'

UNITED KINGDOM: ENGLAND

20 GBP *by Roger Withington and Andrew Ward* – 1999 – 150 x 80 mm (5.91 x 3.15 in.)
OBVERSE Queen Elizabeth II; musical notes and bass clefs; royal monogram.
REVERSE Portrait of Sir Edward Elgar (Lower Broadheath, 1857–Worcester, 1934), self-taught musician and composer; musical angel copied from decoration of Worcester Cathedral; St Cecilia, patron saint of musicians; west front of Worcester Cathedral; Elgar's signature.
WATERMARK Head of Queen Elizabeth II.
SECURITY FEATURES Idem 10 GBP of 2000.

Britannia has appeared on all notes of the Bank of England since its foundation. The version on the present £20 note is that drawn in 1855 by Daniel Maclise, who used his eighteen-year-old daughter as his model.

50 GBP *by Roger Withington* – 1994 – 156 x 85 mm (6.14 x 3.35 in.)
OBVERSE Head of Queen Elizabeth II; Britannia; royal monogram.
REVERSE Portrait of Sir John Houblon, first Governor of Bank of England (1632–1711); his house in Threadneedle Street, later headquarters of Bank of England; commissionaire of Bank of England; Houblon's signature.
WATERMARK Head of Queen Elizabeth II.
SECURITY FEATURES Idem 5 GBP + rose and silver-foil medallion to right of Queen's portrait.

The portrait and monogram or cipher of Queen Elizabeth II appears on all present Bank of England notes.

The Euro Zone

From 1 January 2002, euro notes and coins will replace the national issues currently in use in twelve of the EU countries:

AUSTRIA

BELGIUM

FINLAND

FRANCE

GERMANY

GREECE

ITALY

LUXEMBOURG

NETHERLANDS

PORTUGAL

REPUBLIC OF IRELAND (EIRE)

SPAIN

EURO ZONE

5 EUR *by Robert Kalina* – 120 x 62 mm (4.72 x 2.44 in.)
OBVERSE Greco-Roman style façade, including arch flanked by pairs of columns with Ionic capitals; stars of European flag; flag of European Union.
REVERSE Three-level aqueduct, with arches smaller at successive levels; satellite map of Europe.
WATERMARK As obverse; denomination.
SECURITY FEATURES Intaglio printing; paper tinted during manufacture; security thread; holographic band (denomination and euro symbol), colour-variable, irridescent strip; see-through feature (denomination).

The French overseas *départements*, an integral part of the EU, figure on all current euro notes.

10 EUR *by Robert Kalina* – 127 x 67 mm (5.00 x 2.64 in.)
OBVERSE Romanesque church portal with three staggered arches: capitals of supporting columns have ornamental sculptures; stars of European flag; flag of European Union.
REVERSE Romanesque stone bridge with semicircular arches, massive pillars and buttresses (or false piers); satellite map of Europe.
WATERMARK As obverse; denomination.
SECURITY FEATURES Idem 5 EUR.

The denomination of each note appears in the upper left-hand corner (obverse) when held against the light.

20 EUR *by Robert Kalina* – 133 x 72 mm (5.24 x 2.83 in.)
OBVERSE Two Gothic stained-glass rose windows; stars of European flag; flag of European Union.
REVERSE Fortified Gothic bridge with rib vaulting; satellite map of Europe.
WATERMARK As obverse; denomination.
SECURITY FEATURES Idem 5 EUR.

The Gothic-style window as seen in the watermark.

50 EUR *by Robert Kalina* – 140 x 77 mm (5.51 x 3.03 in.)

OBVERSE Renaissance-style window above diamonded bossage and flanked by two Ionic columns supporting triangular neo-classical pediment; stars of European flag; flag of European Union.
REVERSE Renaissance bridge with barrel vaulting, projecting keystone, emergent piers; satellite map of Europe.
WATERMARK As obverse; denomination.
SECURITY FEATURES Intaglio printing; paper tinted during manufacture; security thread; OVI (*optically variable ink*) feature (denomination); holographic patch (window as on obverse, plus key features of Renaissance style); see-through feature (denomination).

Denominations of 50 euros and above have a round hologram echoing the main theme on the obverse, here forms found in neo-classical architecture.

100 EUR *by Robert Kalina* – 147 x 82 mm (5.79 x 3.23 in.)

OBVERSE Baroque porch flanked by two *atlantes* bearing capitals; frieze with superimposed pediment decorated with scrolls and *pots à feu* (form of urn); stars of European flag; flag of European Union.
REVERSE Typical eighteenth-century bridge with wide basket arches and slender emergent piers; satellite map of Europe.
WATERMARK As obverse; denomination.
SECURITY FEATURES Holographic 'patch' (porch as on obverse; plus key features of baroque style); other features, idem 50 EUR.

On higher values, the denomination (reverse, lower right) changes colour depending on the angle at which the note is held.

200 EUR *by Robert Kalina* – 153 x 82 mm (6.28 x 3.23 in.)

OBVERSE Façade of plant house, illustrating growing use of iron and glass in nineteenth-century architecture; stars of European flag; flag of European Union.
REVERSE Single-span all-metal viaduct with parabolic vault; satellite map of Europe.
WATERMARK As obverse; denomination.
SECURITY FEATURES Holographic patch (façade as on obverse, plus key features of 'iron-and-glass' style); other features, idem 50 EUR.

The five groups of initials on the obverse are variations of the name of the European Central Bank in the eleven official EU languages.

500 EUR *by Robert Kalina* – 160 x 82 mm (6.43 x 3.23 in.)

OBVERSE Façade in glass, steel and concrete with reference to rationalist architecture of twentieth century and curtain-wall invented by Bauhaus school; stars of European flag; flag of European Union.
REVERSE Twentieth-century cable-stayed bridge, near-horizontal, with roadway suspended from two monumental pillars by steel cables under tension; satellite map of Europe.
WATERMARK As obverse; denomination.
SECURITY FEATURES Holographic patch (façade as on obverse, plus key features of Bauhaus style); other features, idem 50 EUR.

The EU flag appears on all euro notes, even though, for the moment, only twelve nations have adopted the single currency.

Bibliography

1. General publications

A. DE BOER, *Papiergeld*, Haarlem, 1980.
Les couleurs de l'argent, exh. cat., Paris, Musée français de la Poste, 1991.
DEUTSCHE BUNDESBANK, *Frühzeit des Papiergeldes. Beispiele aus der Geldscheinsammlung der Deutschen Bundesbank*, Frankfurt, 1970.
V.H. HEWITT éd., *The Banker's Art. Studies in Paper Money*, 1995.
W. KRANISTER, *The Moneymakers International*, 1989.
J. MARCHAL and M. PIQUET-MARCHAL, 'Essai sur la nature et l'évolution du billet de banque', *Revue internationale d'histoire de la banque*, no. 14, 1977, p. 1–87.
M. MONESTIER, *L'art du papier-monnaie*, Paris, 1982.
A. PICK, *Papiergeld*, Brunswick, 1967.
A. PICK, *Papiergeldkatalog Europa seit 1900*, Munich, 1970.
A. PICK, *Papiergeld Lexikon*, Munich, 1978.
A. PICK, *Standard Catalog of World Paper Money*, Munich-United States, 6th edition, 1990.
WALZ, *Falschgeld: Spannendes und Kriminalistisches, Ernstes und Amüsantes aus der Welt der Geldfälscher*, Regenstauf, 1999.

2. Belgium

BANQUE NATIONALE DE BELGIQUE, *Le franc belge. Monnaies et billets belges depuis 1830*, Brussels, 1994.
BANQUE NATIONALE DE BELGIQUE, *Le règne de Guillaume Ier. Monnaies et billets de 1815 à 1830*, Brussels, 1997.
M. DANNEEL et Y. RANDAXHE, *Nos billets ont 149 ans*, Brussels, Banque nationale de Belgique, 2000.
A. SCHWARZENBACH, *Portraits of the Nation. Stamps, Coins and Banknotes in Belgium and Switzerland 1880–1945*, Bern, 1999.

3. Denmark

DANMARKS NATIONALBANK, *The Coins and Banknotes of Denmark*, Copenhagen, 1999.
L. HANSEN, *Danmarks officielle Pengesedler, Official Paper Money of the Kingdom of Denmark, 1713–1983*, Copenhagen, 1983.

4. Germany

DEUTSCHE BUNDESBANK, *Deutsches Papiergeld 1772–1870*, Frankfurt, 1963.
DEUTSCHE BUNDESBANK, *Die Noten der Deutschen Bundesbank*, Frankfurt, 1964.
DEUTSCHE BUNDESBANK, *Das Papiergeld im Deutschen Reich 1871–1948*, Frankfurt, 1965.
DEUTSCHE BUNDESBANK, *Von der Baumwolle zum Geldschein. Eine neue Banknotenserie entsteht*, Frankfurt, 1996.
H.O. EGLAU, *Mehr Schein als Sein. Als die Mark Kapriolen schlug. Deutsches Notgeld 1914–1923*, Düsseldorf, 1998.
D. HOFFMANN, *Das Notenbuch*, Regenstauf, 1989.
K. JAEGER and U. HAEVECKER, *Die deutschen Banknoten seit 1871*, Basle, 1972.
A. KELLER, *Das Papiergeld des Deutschen Reiches von 1874 bis 1945*, Berlin, 1952.
A. KELLER, *Deutsche Kleingeldscheine 1916–1922*, Berlin, 1952–1955.
A. KELLER, *Das Papiergeld der altdeutschen Staaten vom 17. Jahrhundert bis zum Jahre 1914*, Berlin, 1953.
A. KELLER, *Das Notgeld von 1914*, Berlin, 1956.
A. KELLER, *Das Notgeld der deutschen Inflation 1923*, Berlin, 1959–1961.
A. KELLER, *Das Papiergeld der Deutschen Kolonien*, Münster, 1967.
A. PICK, *Deutsche Länder- und Privatnotenbanken, Geldscheine des Landesregierungen, Provinzialverwaltungen und Bezirksregierungen 1872–1948*, Berlin, 1975.
A. PICK and U. RIXEN, *Papiergeld-Spezialkatalog Deutschland 1874–1980 (Bundes Republik und DDR)*, Munich, 1998.
H. ROSENBERG, *Die Banknoten des Deutschen Reiches ab 1871*, Hamburg, 1997.

5. Greece

D. NIKOETOPOULOS, *The Bank Notes of Greece*, The Credit Bank, 1979.

6. SPAIN

J.M. ALEDON CUESTA, *La peseta: catalogo basico: la moneda española desde 1868 y los billetes desde 1783*, 1997.
BANCO DE ESPAÑA, *Los billetes del Banco de España, 1782–1979*, 1979.
BANCO DE ESPAÑA, *Exposicion de papel moneda español*, 1979.
El billetario español (1783–1978): exposicion de monedas y billetes de España, exh. cat., Mexico, Fabrica nacional de moneda y timbre and Banco de España, 1978.
C. CASTAN RAMIREZ and J.R. CAYON, *Catalogo de los billetes españoles: 1782–1979*, 1978.
J.A. VICENTI, *Billetes españoles, 1783–1977*, 1978.

7. France

L'art du billet. Billets de la Banque de France 1800–2000, exh. cat., Paris, Musée Carnavalet, 2000.
BANQUE DE FRANCE, *Les billets de la Banque de France*, Paris, 1993.

M. Daspre, *Trois siècles de billets français*, Paris, 1990.
C. Fayette, *Les billets français du dix-neuvième siècle*, Jard-sur-Mer, 1990.
C. Fayette, *Les billets français du vingtième siècle*, Jard-sur-Mer, 1997.
G. Jacoud, *Le billet de banque en France (1796–1803)*, Paris, 1996.
M. Kolsky, *Les billets des DOM-TOM*, Paris, 1987.
M. Kolsky and M. Muszynski, *Les billets de la Banque de l'Indochine*, Monaco, 1997.
J. Lafaurie, *Les assignats et les papiers-monnaies émis par l'Etat au XVIIIe siècle*, Paris, 1981.
A. Mercier, *L'argent des révolutionnaires*, cat. exp., Paris, CNAM, Musée national des Techniques, Paris, 1989.
M. Muszynski, *Les assignats de la Révolution française*, Courson-Monteloup, 1981.
S. Peyret, *Les billets de la Banque de France. Deux siècles de confiance*, Paris, Banque de France, 1995.

8. Eire

D. Young, *Guide to the Currency of Ireland. Legal Tender Notes 1928–1972*, Dublin, 1972.
D. Young, *Guide to the Currency of Ireland. Consolidated Bank Notes 1929–1941*, Dublin, 1977.
M. McDevitt, *Irish Banknotes 1928–1998*, Dublin, 2000.

9. Italy

G. Crapanzano, *Soldi d'Italia. Un secolo di cartamoneta*, cat. exp., Parma, Fondazione Cassa di Risparmio di Parma, 1995.
F. Gavello and C. Bugani, *Lir-Euro. Biglietti della Banca d'Italia*, Bologna, 1998.
S. Gullino éd., *Catalogo unificato delle monete italiane*, 1983.
A. Mini, *La carta moneta italiana 1746–1960*, Palermo, 1967.
R. Mori, *Il biglietto di banca*, 1984.

10. Luxembourg

P. Margue and M.-P. Jungblut, *Le Luxembourg et sa monnaie*, Luxembourg, 1990.
R. Probst, *Catalogue illustré du papier-monnaie luxembourgeois*, 1984.
R. Weiller, *Cent vingt-cinq ans de papier-monnaie luxembourgeois*, Luxembourg, Banque internationale à Luxembourg, 1981.

11. The Netherlands

J. Bolten, *Het Nederlandse bankbiljet en zijn vormgeving; met een catalogus door P.J. Soetens*, Amsterdam - Leyde, 1987.
J. Bolten, *Het Nederlandse bankbiljet 1814–2002. Vormgeving en ontwikkeling*, Leyde, De Nederlandsche Bank, 1999.
J.J. Grolle, *Geschiedenis van het Nederlandse bankbiljet*, Bussum, 1991.
J. Mevius and F.G. Lelivelt, *Speciale catalogus van de Nederlandse bankbiljetten van 1814 tot heden*, 2 vol., Vriezenveen, 1981.
M.M.G. Fase, J.R. Steinhauser and J. de Vries, *Het Nederlandse bankbiljet in zijn verscheidenheid*, Amsterdam - Deventer, 1986.

12. Austria

W. Kranister, *Die Geldmacher. Vom Gulden zu Schilling*, Vienna, 1985.

13. Portugal

Banco de Portugal, *Arte e imagem nas notas do Banco de Lisboa*, Lisbon, 1996.
Banco de Portugal, *O papel-moeda em Portugal*, edited by M. Rui de Sousa e Silva and A. Ramos Pereira, Lisbon, 1997.

14. Finland

T. Talvio, *The Coins and Banknotes of Finland*, Helsinki, Bank of Finland, 1987.

15. Sweden

L.O. Lagerqvist and E. Nathorst-Böös, *Sedlar*, Stockholm, 1971.
A. Platbarzdis, *Sveriges forsta Banksedlar*, Stockholm, 1960.
A. Platbarzdis, *Sveriges Sedlar*, vol. I, Lund, 1963.
L. Wallén, *Sveriges Sedlar*, vol. I–II, Stockholm, 1984.

16. United Kingdom

V.H. Hewitt and J.M. Keyworth, *As Good as Gold: 300 Years of British Bank Note Design*, London, 1987.

Index

NAMES OF PERSONS

Aalto, Alvar, 150
Adelcrantz, Carl Fredrik, 152
Adler, Hans, 79
Albert II (Belgium), 125
Albrecht VII of Rudolstadt, 47
Albuquerque, Alfonso of, 38, 47
Alexander II (Russia), 37
Allard, Josse, 38, 41
Alfonso XIII (Spain), 41
Alvarez Cabral, Pedro, 148
Amadeus-Dier, Erhard, 93
Ampère, André Marie, 49
Ancher, Anna, 127
Ancher, Michael, 127
Andrieu, Bertrand, 101, 103
Antonello di Messina, 51
St Antônio of Lisbon, 49
Arentz, Cornelius, 153
Armellini, Carlo, 59
Arnim, Bettina von, 128

Ballagh, Robert, 137, 138
Barbetti, Rinaldo, 46
Barre, Jean-Jacques, 101, 103, 107
Barros, João de, 148
Baschet, Marcel, 135
Baudry, Paul, 111
Bayard, Chevalier, 38, 40
Bayeu, Francisco, 51
Bellini, Vincenzo, 139, 152
Benhamou, Emile, 82
Bernini, Gian Lorenzo, 140
Berthelot, Marcelin, 96
Bismarck, Otto von, 78
Bittrof, Max, 104, 118
Blixen, Karen, 126
Böhm von Bawerk, Eugen, 51, 146
Bohr, Niels, 127
Bojarski, Czeslaw, 82
Boland, Véronique, 125
Bolten, Jacob, 110, 111
Borja Freire, Francisco de, 101
Bossoli, Carlo, 12
Boumboulina, Laskarina, 53
Bradbury, William, 94
Braemt, Joseph Pierre, 101
Brentano, Elisabeth (see Arnim, Bettina von)
Brisset, P., 97
Broling, Carl-Abraham, 101
Bruun, Erik, 105, 150, 151
Brusenbauch, Artur, 110
Bruyn the Elder, Barthel, 51

Cabarrus, Francisco, 49
Cabasson, H., 97
Cabral, Pedro Alvarez (see Alvarez Cabral)
Camões, Luis de, 47, 148, 149
Caravaggio, Michelangelo Merisi, 51, 141
Carrier-Belleuse, Albert Ernest, 28
Carte, Anto, 44, 105
Cavour, Camillo Benso, count of 47
Cézanne, Paul, 135
Cham, 10
Charbonne, J. Louis, 76
Charles III (Spain), 6
Charles X (France), 77
Charles X (Sweden), 3
Charles XI (Sweden), 53, 153
Chateaubriand, François René de, 51
Chazal, Camille, 20, 108
Chydenius, Anders, 151
Cicero, 82
Cionini, T., 98
Cloquemin, Gabriel, 78
Columbus, Christopher, 47, 49, 51, 112, 134
Contamin, Victor, 136
Corneille, Pierre, 51
Cornouailles, 7
Cortés, Hernán, 133
Cranach the Elder, Lucas, 104
Curie, Marie, 136
Curie, Pierre, 136

Daffinger, Jacques, 96
Daffinger, Moritz Michael, 146
D'Annunzio, Gabriele, 68
Dante Alighieri, 47, 49
Darwin, Charles, 152, 154
Debussy, Claude, 135
Degen, Jakob, 77
Delacroix, Eugène, 55, 58
Der Kinderen, Antonie, 111
De Valera, Eamon, 60
Devrient, Alphonse, 94
Diaz, Bartolomeu, 148
Dickens, Charles, 128, 154
Döpler, Emil, 108
Doré, Gustave, 101
Droste-Hülshoff, Annette von, 128
Drupsteen, Jaap T.G., 143, 144, 145
Duisenberg, Wim, 120
Dürer, Albrecht, 51
Dutert, Ferdinand, 136
Duval, Georges, 40

Eccleston, Harry, 106
Echegeray y Eyzaguirre, José, 49
Edler von Schönfeld, Johann Ferdinand, 88
Ehrenstrahl, David Klöcker von (see Klöcker von Ehrenstrahl)
Ehrlich, Paul, 129
Eiffel, Gustave, 136
Eisenmenger, August, 103
Ekström, Torsten, 54, 150, 151
Elgar, Edward, 155
Elisabeth II (United Kingdom), 154, 155
Emma (Netherlands), 41
Engels, Friedrich, 51
Ensor, James, 51, 124
Eschle, Max, 63
Esteve, Rafael, 51, 101

Falké, Pierre, 21
Farini, Carlo Luigi, 12
Fayette, Claude, 121
Fendi, Peter Franz, 30, 103, 108
Ferdinand I (Austria), 78
Ferdinand of Aragon (Spain), 49, 134
Fernández, Antonio, 48
Fernández de Córdoba, Gonzalo, 47
Fjellström, Pehr, 151
Flameng, François, 96, 108, 111, 115
Fontaine, Pierre, 103
Franco Bahamonde, Francisco, 48, 134
St Francis of Assisi, 49
Franz Joseph I (Austria-Hungary), 37, 78
Frederick II (Prussia), 64
Freud, Sigmund, 51, 146
Freund, Jean-François, 35
Frigerio, Federico, 140
Fristrup, 108
Führich, Jozef von, 103

Galileo, 47
Galle, André, 101
Gallén-Kallela, Akseli, 69, 105
Gama, Vasco da, 47, 81, 83, 149
Garibaldi, Giuseppe, 59
Gatteaux, Nicolas Marie, 88
Gaulle, Charles de, 44, 55, 73
Gauss, Carl Friedrich, 128
Geiger, Carl Joseph, 103
Geiger, Peter Johann, 103
Gérard, Auguste Fernand, 106
Giesecke, Hermann, 94
Goethe, Johan Wolfgang von, 17, 64, 129
Golaire, Monique, 124, 125
González Sepúlveda, Mariano, 101
Goya y Lucientes, Francisco de, 51, 101
Grimm, Jacob, 130
Grimm, Wilhelm, 130
Gubbins, John, 137
Gustaaf I Wasa (Sweden), 153
Gutenberg, Johannes, 47, 49
Gyzis, Nikolaos, 131

Hahn, Albert, 33
Hals, Frans, 143
Hammarsten-Jansson, Signe, 105
Harrison, John, 41
Harvey, T.R., 137
Hedström, Trond, 150
Heiberg, Johanne Luise, 126
Heilmann, Gerhard, 46
Hendrickx, Henri, 29, 102, 103
Henry the Navigator, 47, 149
Hergé (Georges Remi), 81
Hickleep, Patrick, 50
Himmler, Heinrich, 82
Hitler, Adolf, 15
Holbein the Younger, Hans, 51
Horta, Victor, 125
Houblon, John, 155
Hugo, Victor, 51
Huguenin, André, 62
Huguet, Jean-François, 5
Hyde, Douglas, 138

Isabel II (Spain), 87
Isabella of Castile (Spain), 49, 134
St Isabel of Portugal, 49
St Isidore of Seville, 48, 49

Jacoud, Gilles, 10, 11
James, Saint, 48
Jean of Luxembourg, 142
Jonas, Lucien, 52
Jongert, Jacob, 106, 110
Jourdain, 19
Joyce, James, 137
Juan Carlos I (Spain), 134
Juan y Santacilia, Jorge, 134
Juel, Jens, 51
Julius Caesar, 49

Kalina, Robert, 119, 121, 157
Kampf, Arthur, 41, 102
Kapodistrias, Joannis, 57, 131
Kaulbach, Wilhelm von, 103, 111
Keynes, John Maynard, 117
Khnopff, Fernand, 112
Klenze, Leo von, 103
Klimsch, Ferdinand, 43
Klimt, Gustav, 112, 113
Klöcker von Ehrenstrahl, David, 153
Knutson, Johan, 151
Kohl, Helmut, 25
Kolokotronis, Theodoros, 132
Koraes, Adamantios, 131
Kossuth, Lajos, 57
Krøyer, Peder Severin, 127
Krüger, Bernhard, 82
Kruit, J.J., 145
Kun, Bela, 79

Lagerlöf, Selma, 152
Landsteiner, Karl, 51, 147
Laufberger, Ferdinand, 103
Lavery, Hazel, 41
Law, John, 5, 6, 87
Lefeuvre, Jean, 50
Leipold, Joseph, 106
Leonardo da Vinci, 47, 49, 51
Leopold II (Belgium), 101
Leopold III (Belgium), 53
Liebig, Justus von, 49
Lind, Jenny, 152
Linna, Väinö, 150
Linnaeus, Carl, 49, 152
Lion Cachet, Carel Adolph, 105
Löffler, Berthold, 105, 108, 110
Lönnrot, Elias, 151
Louis XIV (France), 4, 5
Louis XVI (France), 88
Louis II of Bavaria, 103
Luis I (Portugal), 34, 35
Lumière, Auguste and Louis, 53
Lynen, Amédée, 105

McAuley, Catherine, 137
Mac Caskie, George Tell, 106
Machiavelli, Niccolò, 98
Maclise, Daniel, 155
Magnus, Olaus, 153
Magritte, René, 51, 55, 124
Malare, Urban, 153
Malou, Jules, 19
Manna, Giovanni, 47
Marconi, Guglielmo, 139
Mariën, Marcel, 55
Martin, Saint 49
Martínez, 106
Marx, Karl, 51
Masino-Bessi, Florenzo, 106
Maura, Bartolomé, 101, 106
Mayreder, Karl, 147
Mayreder, Rosa, 147
Mazzini, Giuseppe, 56, 59
Mees, Willem Cornelis, 34, 49
Merian, Maria Sibylla, 130, 152
Merson, Luc Olivier, 106, 111, 112, 113
Meruvia, Roque, 48
Metschnikov, Elie, 129
Meunier, Constantin, 51
Michelangelo Buonarroti, 51
Minguet, Guillaume, 35
Moctezuma II, 133
Modigliani, Amedeo, 55
Molière, 50, 51
Mollien, Nicolas François, 17
Montald, Constant, 29, 111, 112
Montesquieu, Charles Louis de, 51
Montessori, Maria, 139
Morriën, Johannes Hendericus, 34, 108

Moser, Koloman, 105, 109, 110
Mouchon, Louis Eugène, 47, 103, 106, 112
Mozart, Wolfgang Amadeus, 147
Müller, Heinz, 83
Murillo, Bartolomé Esteban, 51
Mussolini, Benito, 82
Mutis, José Celestino, 133, 152
Myron, 132

Napoleon Bonaparte (France), 7, 49, 57, 77, 103
Napoleon III (France), 103
Naujocks, Alfred, 82
Neuer, Heinrich, 101
Neumann, Johann Balthazar, 129
Nicholas II (Russia), 37
Nielsen, Carl August, 126
Niépce, Nicéphore, 96
Normand, Charles, 103
Nurmi, Paavo, 54
Nüsser, Heinrich, 36, 105
Nyblin, Daniel, 37

O'Connell, O'Connell, Daniel, 137
Oxenaar, R.D.E., 111, 143, 144, 145

Palmstruch, Johan, 3, 4, 153
Pannemaker, Adolphe François, 101
Paola (Belgium), 125
Papanicolaou, George, 132
Paquot, Nathalie, 125
Parnell, Charles Stewart, 138
Pasteur, Louis, 49, 55
Peglow, Karl, 82
Peiret, Sylvie, 28
Percier, Charles, 27, 103, 108
Perkins, Jacob, 88
Permeke, Constant, 51, 125
Pessõa, Fernando, 149
Pfund, Roger, 106, 114, 135, 136
Phidias, 132
Philip of Macedon, 131, 132
Philostratus, 141
Pick, Albert, 121
Pius IX, 58
Pino, Giovanni, 139, 140
Pinzón, Martín Alonso, 134
Pitt, William, 9, 22, 77
Pizarro, Francisco, 133
Polhem, Christopher, 153
Ponsaers, Kenneth, 124, 125
Poortman, Maurice, 105
Poughéon, Robert, 42

Quaden, Guy, 120

Racine, Jean, 51
Rahikainen, Pentti, 150, 151
Raphael [Raffaello Sanzio], 51, 141
Reim, Otto, 106

Rembrandt van Rijn, Harmensz., 49
Reventlow, Christian Ditlev, 46
Reynders, Didier, 120
Ribeiro, J.B., 8, 106
Ribera, 106
Richelieu, cardinal, 55
Richir, Herman, 105
Rigas Velestinlis-Ferraios, 131
Rimbaud, Arthur, 55
Ritter von Bohr, Peter, 78
Rochussen, Charles, 90
Romagnoli, known as Romagnol, 106
Roozendaal, Jan, 52
Roslin, Alexander, 152
Rosnero, 51
Rottmann, Carl, 132
Rubens, Peter Paul, 51
Runeberg, Walter, 37
Rusiñol, Santiago, 51
Rüssler, Rudolf, 39, 103

Saarinen, Eliel, 43, 89, 103, 105, 108, 112, 114
Sack, Stephen, 74
Saffi, Aurelio, 59
Saint-Aubin, Augustin de, 88
Saint-Exupéry, Antoine de, 51, 135
Salazar, António de Oliveira, 54
Solomon, 49
Salzmann, Franz von, 36, 88, 112
Sandström, Sven-David, 152
Santillan, Ramon de, 49
Savini, G., 139, 141
Sax, Adolphe, 124
Schacht, Hjalmar, 14, 15
Scheyring, J., 104
Schiestl, Heinz, 64
Schinkel, Karl Friedrich, 103
Schoelcher, Victor, 52
Schönfeld, Johann Ferdinand Edler von (see Edler von Schönfeld)
Schrödinger, Erwin, 51
Schuman, Robert, 119
Schumann, Clara, 129
Schumann, Robert, 129
Seger, J., 42
Senefelder, Aloys, 90
Sepkovich, Boris, 81
Sequeira, Domingos Antonio de, 34, 103
Serveau, Clément, 103
Sibelius, Jean, 150
Siemens, Werner von, 49
Skorzeny, Otto, 82
Sleper, Jan, 49
Smith, Adam, 18
Smolianoff, Salomon, 81, 82
Smyth, Edward, 137
Sorolla y Bastida, Joaquín, 51
Sousa, Antonio Sergio, 54
Spaak, Paul Henri, 117

Spadini, Armando, 139
Spinoza, Baruch, 145
Staeck, Klaus, 118
Stallaert, Joseph, 105
Stavrou, George, 47
Stein, Karl vom, 49
Stephenson, George, 154
Stieber, Wilhelm, 78
Stüler, Friedrich August, 103
Sully, Duc de 49

Talbot, William Henry Fox, 96
Talvio, Tuukka, 53
Tardieu, Pierre Alexandre, 88
Tasso, Torquato, 12
Thumann, Paul, 19, 102
Tirpitz, Alfred von, 40
Titian, 51
Titz, Louis, 97, 105
Tsokos, Dionysios, 131

Ulloa de la Torre-Guiral, Antonio de, 134

Van der Waay, Nicolaas, 36, 102, 103
Van Geetruyen, 19
Van Orley, Barend, 51
Vaquer, Enrique, 95, 101, 106
Velasquez, 51
Victor-Emmanuel II (Italy), 34
Victoria (Great-Britain-Ireland), 34
Villegas, José, 33
Vloors, Emile, 37, 38, 111
Volta, Alessandro, 140
Voltaire, 51

Wagner, F.G., 108
Wanderer, Friedrich, 40, 108
Ward, Andrew, 154, 155
Welsbach, Auer von, 51
Werner, Anton von, 13
Weyer, 142
Wiener, Léopold, 101, 107
Wilcox, Russ, 93
Wilhelm I (Germany), 112
Wilhelm II (Germany), 34
Wilhelmine (Netherlands), 103
Wilkinson, Robert, 94
Wirkkala, Tapio, 105
Withington, Roger, 154, 155

Zaranski, 81
Zola, Emile, 60
Zuolaga, Ignacio, 51

BANKS, ASSOCIATIONS AND COMPANIES

Abel Smith & Co., 27
American Bank Note Company, 47, 94, 95, 102, 106
Association of Austrian Banks and Bankers, 79

Badische Bank, 14
Banca dello Stato Pontificio (later Banca Romana), 12
Banca d'Italia, 14, 16, 20, 34, 44, 46, 71, 98, 106
Banca Nazionale negli Stati Sardi, 12
Banca Nazionale nel Regno d'Italia (later Banca d'Italia), 12, 18, 36, 47, 94
Banca Nazionale Toscana, 12, 47
Banca Romana, 12, 14, 44, 59, 94
Banca Toscana di Credito, 12
Banco Comercial do Porto, 8, 106
Banco de Bilbao, 31
Banco de Cadiz, 28
Banco de España, 8, 20, 24, 31, 33, 36, 47, 48, 49, 51, 69, 90, 93, 94, 95, 101
Banco de Isabel, 87, 90
Banco de Lisboa (later Banco de Portugal), 8, 22, 34, 38, 86, 88, 101, 103, 106
Banco de Portugal, 8, 34, 35, 47, 54, 81, 83, 86, 94, 106, 112
Banco di Napoli, 12, 14, 34, 47, 94
Banco di Santo Spirito di Roma, 6
Banco di Sicilia, 12, 14
Banco Español de San Fernando (later Banco de España), 8, 78, 90, 101
Banco Italo-Germanica, 36
Banco Nacional de San Carlos, 8, 9, 17, 49, 88
Bank of Amsterdam, 3
Bank Deutscher Länder, 118
Bank für Süddeutschland, 94
Bank of Crete, 94
Bank of England, 4, 6, 8, 9, 10, 16, 18, 22, 25, 27, 30, 34, 46, 77, 79, 82, 84, 86, 87, 92, 93, 98, 106, 112, 114
Bank of Greece, 16, 53, 94
Bank of Scotland, 4, 6
Banque de Belgique, 8
Banque de Flandres, 89
Banque de France, 7, 8, 10, 11, 18, 23, 25, 27, 28, 29, 40, 42, 50, 60, 73, 79, 83, 85, 87, 88, 90, 91, 93, 96, 97, 101, 103, 106, 107, 108, 113, 114, 115
Banque Nationale de Belgique 11, 15, 16, 18, 19, 24, 29, 31, 35, 38, 44, 55, 60, 70, 77, 84, 85, 87, 88, 90, 94, 96, 97, 101, 102, 105, 106, 107, 112, 114, 120
Banque Nationale du Luxembourg, 94
Banque territoriale, 18
Bayer, 67
Bayerische Hypotheken- und Wechsel-Bank, 94, 102-103
Bayerische Notenbank, 16
Bradbury, Wilkinson & Co., 69, 94, 102, 106

Caisse centrale de la France d'outremer, (later Institut d'émissions des départements d'outremer), 52
Caisse de Crédit industriel, 60
Caisse (française) des comptes courants, 28
Cassa Mediterranea di Credito per la Grecia, 70, 71
Central Bank of Ireland, 10, 50
Commission internationale de police criminelle pour la répression du faux monnayage, 79
Compagnie d'Occident, 5
Compagnie française des Indes, 5
Currency Commission Ireland, 10
Currency Commission of the Irish Free State, 11, 41

Danmarks Nationalbank, 53, 121
Danziger Privat-Actien-Bank, 112
Delvaux, 17
Deutsche Bundesbank, 25, 51, 92, 106
Deutsche Rentenbank, 49
Dondorf & Naumann, 94

Enschedé, Joh., 89, 111
European Monetary Institute (EMI), 118
European Payments Union, 25, 117
European Central Bank (ECB), 117, 118, 119, 120
European Savings Banks Group, 117
Europol, 121
Exclusive Issuing Bank of Epirothessalia, 102

Federal Reserve Bank, 106
Fenian Brotherhood, 60
Financieel Archief, 79
Fox, Fowler and Co., 10

Geraer Bank, 31, 78
Giesecke & Devrient, 69, 90, 93, 94
Giro- und Lehn-Banco, 6, 14
Goebel company, 90
Great Yarmouth Bank, 27
Guyot (paper mill), 85

Hannoversche Bank, 34, 78, 94

Imprimerie filigranique G. Richard et Cie, 102
Institut d'émissions des départements d'outremer (see Caisse centrale de la France d'outremer)
Institut monétaire luxembourgeois, 142
Internationale Bank in Luxemburg, 22, 31
Interpol, 79, 83
Ionian Bank, 94

Koening & Bauer, 90
Königliche Preussische Kassen-Anweisung, 98
Kurhessische Leih- & Commerzbank, 90

Leipziger Bank, 94

Masure et Perrigot (paper mill), 86
Mines domaniales de la Sarre, 69

National Bank of Greece, 43, 47, 94, 102
Naumann, C. (later Dondorf & Nauman), 89, 94
Nederlandsche Bank, 16, 18, 22, 32, 34, 36, 43, 49, 51, 52, 53, 88, 90, 96, 102, 105, 106, 108, 110, 111
Norrköpings Enskilda Bank, 31

Oesterreichische Nationalbank, 67, 92, 93, 108, 119
Österreichisch-Ungarische Bank (later Österreichische Nationalbank), 34, 38, 39, 68, 79, 103, 109, 113
Office de répression du faux monnayage (Office for the Repression of Counterfeiting), 82

Papeterie d'Arches, 86, 93
Papeterie Blanchet Frères & Kléber, 86
Papeterie du Marais, 85, 86
Papeterie Portals, 85, 86, 93
Papeterie de Sainte-Marie 86
Pommersche Ritterschaftliche Privat-Bank, 78
Preussische Bank (later Reichsbank), 14, 23
Privilegirte Österreichische National-Bank (later Österreichisch-Ungarische Bank), 6, 11, 30, 34, 36, 38, 78, 96, 102, 108, 112

Reichsbank, 13, 14, 15, 16, 19, 22, 23, 31, 34, 36, 40, 41, 42, 49, 51, 60, 63, 64, 65, 67, 70, 85, 94, 98, 102, 105
Riksens Ständers Bank (later Sveriges Riksbank), 4, 7, 8, 30, 34, 84, 86, 101
Royal Bank of Scotland, 96

Sächsische Bank, 94
Schneberg, 96
Schwartz, 64
Scotland Yard, 81
Shepton Mallet and Somersetshire Bank, 27
Smalands Bank, 49
Société des Nations, 65, 67, 68, 81
Société Générale de Belgique, 8
Société générale des Pays-Bas (later Société générale de Belgique), 22
Society for the Encouragement of Arts, Manufactures and Commerce, 77
Southampton Commercial Bank, 27
Spechthausen (paper mill), 85
Staatsbank der DDR, 51
Stockholms Banco, 3, 4, 87

Suomen Pankki (Bank of Finland), 33, 37, 43, 54, 89, 94, 103, 105, 106, 108, 114
Suomen Yhdyspankki Bank, 43, 44
Sveriges Riksbank, 8, 16, 53, 90, 115, 153
Sveriges Rikes Ständers Bank (see Riksens Ständers Bank)

Tervakoski (paper mill), 84
Thomas De La Rue & Co., 69, 94
Thrissell Co., 90

Vaasan Osale Pankki, 69
Van Houtum & Palm (paper mill), 84

Waterlow & Sons, 81, 83, 94
Wiener-Stadt-Banco, 6, 77, 88, 96

Photographic credits

ABBREVIATIONS IN THE CAPTIONS

BE: BANK OF ENGLAND
BEsp: BANCO DE ESPAÑA
BF: BANQUE DE FRANCE
BG: BANK OF GREECE
BI: BANCA D'ITALIA
BIL: BANQUE INTERNATIONALE À LUXEMBOURG
BNB: BANQUE NATIONALE DE BELGIQUE
BP: BANCO DE PORTUGAL
CBI: CENTRAL BANK OF IRELAND
DBB: DEUTSCHE BUNDESBANK
DNB: DE NEDERLANDSCHE BANK
ONB: ÖSTERREICHISCHE NATIONALBANK
SP: SUOMEN PANKKI (BANK OF FINLAND)
SRB: SVERIGES RIKSBANK

Photographs are to be credited to the owners of the works of art cited in the captions, except as indicated below. Every effort has been made to contact copyright-holders of illustrations. Any copyright-holders whom we have been unable to reach or to whom inaccurate acknowledgement has been made are invited to contact the publisher.

Antwerp, Felix Tirry: pp. 3, 12 (below), 16, 21, 23, 29, 36 (Belgium), 38, 44, 63, 64, 68, 69, 73 (top), 76, 89 (middle), 89 (below), 101
Bordeaux, MBA/Lysiane Gauthier: p. 58
Bruges, Hugo Maertens: pp. 31, 32, 34, 36 (The Netherlands), 49, 55, 88, 100, 110, 119, 121, 127 (detail 500 DKK), 132 (detail 5,000 GRD), 143 (detail 25 NLG), 148 (details 500 and 1,000 PTE)
Brussels, Belga: pp. 120 (top), 120 (below)
Brussels, Musées royaux des Beaux-Arts de Belgique/Cussac: p. 104
Hamburg, Carstensen: p. 13
London, Bridgeman-Visual Arts Library: p. 7 (top)
Paris, Keystone: p. 73 (middle)
Paris, Photothèque des Musées de la Ville/Ph. Joffre: p. 78
Paris, Réunion des Musées nationaux/Arnaudet: p. 111
Paris, Roger-Viollet: pp. 10, 45, 65, 66, 67, 80
Stockholm, Jan-Eve Olsson: pp. 36 (Sweden), 86 (top), 114
© Hergé/Moulinsart 2001: p. 81

Acknowledgements

It would be unthinkable to conclude a work devoted to banknotes without repaying the debt we owe all who have played a role in its production. Especially, we would like to mention Victor Nieto Alcaide and Brice Le Blévennec, who conceived the original idea of a book on the paper money of Europe; Dr Jean J.M. Moreau, that very fine linguist; the various issuing banks who very kindly placed a huge amount of picture material at our disposal, as did the European Saving Banks Group; Mme Danneel and her staff at the cultural department of the Banque Nationale de Belgique, into whose inexhaustible resources we delved time and again; and Professors Michel Dumoulin and Eric Bussière, who agreed to conduct a thorough review of the text.

A book like this is the fruit of a collaboration between numerous contributors. At Fonds Mercator, we are indebted to Jan Martens, Ann Mestdag and Dirk Vandemeulebroecke, who oversaw the co-ordination of the translations, while the layout is the result of Joël Van Audenhaege's talent – and much midnight oil.

Last but not least, we must pay tribute to the editorial team: Natascha Langerman, who developed the original concept and oversaw its completion; Geneviève Defrance, who led the hunt for the illustrations; and proof-reader Denis Laurent – relentless in his war upon errors – with whom, in particular, we enjoyed some passionate debates on the artistic value of the banknote.

To all the above, our deepest gratitude.